D1520010

Reagan on War

Number Ten: Foreign Relations and the Presidency

Reagan on War

A Reappraisal of the

Weinberger Doctrine,

1980–1984

Gail E. S. Yoshitani

Texas A&M University Press
College Station

This paper meets the requirements of ANSI/NISO Z39.48-1992
(Permanence of Paper).
Binding materials have been chosen for durability.

Library of Congress Cataloging-in-Publication Data

Yoshitani, Gail E. S., 1968–
Reagan on war : a reappraisal of the Weinberger doctrine, 1980–1984 / Gail E. S.
Yoshitani. — 1st ed.
p. cm. — (Foreign relations and the presidency ; no. 10)
Includes bibliographical references and index.
ISBN-13: 978-1-60344-259-6 (cloth : alk. paper)
ISBN-10: 1-60344-259-6 (cloth : alk. paper)
ISBN-13: 978-1-60344-577-1 (e-book)
ISBN-10: 1-60344-577-3 (e-book)
1. United States — Military policy. 2. United States — Foreign relations — 1977–1981.
3. United States — Foreign relations — 1981–1989. 4. United States — Foreign
relations — Philosophy. 5. Intervention (International law) 6. National security —
United States — Decision making. 7. Civil-military relations — United States.
8. Weinberger, Caspar W. 9. Reagan, Ronald. I. Title. II. Series: Foreign relations
and the presidency ; no. 10.
UA23.Y678 2011
355'.03357309048 — dc23
2011018933

This work expresses the opinions of the author and
does not represent the views of the US Department of Defense,
the Department of Army, or the US Military Academy.

For my husband, Shaw,
and our sons,
Evan and Davis

CONTENTS

Illustrations / ix
Preface / xi
Acknowledgments / xv

1. Defining and Challenging the Vietnam Syndrome / 1
2. A Short Primer on Domestic Political Realities / 19
3. The Casey Doctrine. Using Proxy Forces in
Central America / 33
4. The Pentagon Doctrine: Using American Military Power
Decisively in Lebanon / 60
5. The Shultz Doctrine: Using American Military Power
to Support Diplomacy / 84
6. The Weinberger Doctrine: A New Pattern for
Civil-Military Relations / 113

Notes / 143
Bibliography / 215
Index / 241

ILLUSTRATIONS

Ronald Reagan delivers his first inaugural speech / 2

The Reagans during the inaugural parade / 6

The Reagan Administration's first National Security
Council meeting / 39

Reagan meets with Rep. Silvio O. Conte about El Salvador / 45

William Casey and Gen. David Jones / 57

Reagan meets with Sen. Charles Percy
and Rep. Clement Zablocki / 73

Reagan and key advisors discuss Lebanon / 87

Reagan and Pres. Amin Gemayel of Lebanon / 96

Reagan, George Shultz, and Robert McFarlane discuss Grenada / 115

Reagan, Shultz, and McFarlane discuss Grenada with
Prime Minister Eugenia Charles of Dominica / 117

Gen. John W. Vessey Jr. briefs congressional leaders
on Grenada / 121

PREFACE

WHILE WAITING FOR A PLANE in Kansas City in 2006, my reading was interrupted by an adjacent gentleman who observed aloud, "Your eyes need to be balanced." I was immediately intrigued by this observation because my eyesight indeed had been giving me problems during my research. When I mentioned that I was studying the Weinberger Doctrine, the man smiled broadly and proclaimed that he had always appreciated Secretary of Defense Caspar Weinberger because he understood the difference between *power* and *force*. At that time I nodded knowingly in agreement, but many months would pass before I fully appreciated the distinction between these words and how central it is to unraveling the Weinberger Doctrine. The Reagan administration's pattern of civil-military relations, as announced in this policy, was a perfect paradox— seemingly inconsistent with the known facts, but when understood correctly not problematic at all.

At the time of my flight, like most observers of history, I believed that the Weinberger Doctrine epitomized the "Vietnam syndrome," a term coined by Pres. Ronald Reagan in 1980 to describe the reluctance of American statesmen not only to use military force but also to carry out policies that sought to defend and foster freedom and liberty abroad.[1] I was trying to resolve why of all people Ronald Reagan, after a landslide reelection in 1984, would have his secretary of defense take the podium in front of the National Press Club and announce what appeared to be such a renunciatory doctrine. If ever there was a president willing to use US power to bring about positive change on the world stage, it was Reagan. Had his experiences during his first term in office left him suffering from his own case of Vietnam syndrome?

At the heart of Weinberger's speech, entitled "The Uses of Military

Power," were six tests for American leaders to consider when using military force in pursuit of national interests:

>   (1) *First,* the United States should not commit forces to
>   *combat* overseas unless the particular engagement or occasion
>   is deemed vital to our national interest or that of our allies. . . .
>
>   (2) *Second,* if we decide it *is* necessary to put *combat* troops
>   into a given situation, we should do so wholeheartedly, and
>   with the clear intention of winning. . . .
>
>   (3) *Third,* if we *do* decide to commit forces to combat over-
>   seas, we should have clearly defined political and military ob-
>   jectives. . . .
>
>   (4) *Fourth,* the relationship between our objectives and
>   the forces we have committed—their size, composition[,] and
>   disposition—must be continually reassessed and adjusted if
>   necessary. . . .
>
>   (5) *Fifth,* before the U.S. commits combat forces abroad,
>   there must be some reasonable assurance we will have the sup-
>   port of the American people and their elected representatives
>   in Congress. . . .
>
>   (6) *Finally,* the commitment of U.S. forces to combat
>   should be a last resort.[2]

Reporting on the speech, one contemporary journalist wrote, "The
speech appeared to be the clearest enunciation of military policy since
President Reagan was elected in 1980."[3] Others quickly coined the six
tests as the "Weinberger Doctrine," and the name immediately spread
through the press.[4]

Given the record of candidate and then President Reagan, the doctrine appeared to be very restrictive and to mark a significant departure
for his administration. In the 1980 presidential campaign, Reagan had
vowed to scrap the Strategic Arms Limitation Treaty (SALT II) negotiated by the Carter administration, rebuild American military power,
confront and roll back Soviet expansionism, and contain Cuban proxy

activity in the Third World. In his first term, Reagan stayed true to those promises by not returning to SALT and by spending billions to rebuild the nation's strategic and conventional military forces. Additionally, the administration dispatched military advisors to help the government of El Salvador overcome an insurgency supported by Cuba and the Soviet bloc and spent millions building a proxy force to fight the Communist-led government in Nicaragua. Marines were dispatched to Lebanon on two separate occasions to maintain order and check Soviet influence in the region. Finally, the administration sent military forces to Grenada to remove Marxist dictator Maurice Bishop and approved two large show-of-force exercises focused on Nicaragua.

This study presents an explanation for the evident contradiction between the rhetoric of Reagan, the actions of his administration, and Weinberger's six tests. The Weinberger Doctrine emerges from a combination of historical lessons, hard experience, intense ideological and political struggle within the administration, and a need to describe a way for America to respond to gray-area challenges, such as irregular warfare and state-sponsored terrorism. Reagan surely did not intend for the Weinberger Doctrine to serve as a barrier against US efforts to defend and foster freedom and liberty abroad. Rather, the doctrine codified principles he and his administration had followed throughout their first term in deciding when and how to use military force.

In the United States, any approach taken to build and employ military power is not simply a product of beliefs regarding the threat and America's position in the world, it also intrinsically involves the nation's political system and laws. Scholars explore these concepts under the purview of civil-military relations. In a theoretical construct, civil-military relations bridge the gap between the military security needs of a nation and its social norms governing the use of violence. The Weinberger Doctrine was a pattern of civil-military relations that synthesized concerns about potential threats and requirements of world involvement with domestic political realities and social norms that had previously led to both extremes of dangerous isolationism and overzealous involvement.

Such synthesis hinged not only upon leaders like Reagan and Weinberger but also upon average Americans, such as the gentleman at the
airport, who understood that there is a difference between *power* and
force. Weinberger noted in his speech: "National power has many components, some tangible—like economic wealth, technical pre-eminence.
Other components are intangible—such as moral force, or strong national will. Military forces, when they are strong and ready and modern,
are a credible—and tangible—addition to the nation's power. When
both the intangible national will and those forces are forged into one
instrument, national power becomes effective."[5] In other words, when
the will and means of the American people are coupled to a military
unit, it represents *power* and as such can accomplish challenging military and political objectives. Yet without that coupling, a military unit is
merely a *force* with an effectiveness limited to the reach of its weapons.
Weinberger's six tests sought to maximize the will and means coupled to
a military force by capitalizing on the strengths of American ideals and
accounting for the peculiarities of US domestic political realities.

Henry Kissinger has written, "A great president must be an educa-
tor, bridging the gap between his people's future and its experience."[6]
The Weinberger Doctrine is symbolic of one plank in the bridge that
Reagan and his cabinet leaders built for Americans to carry the nation
from its past experiences to its future. The Weinberger Doctrine is also
indicative of the president's "higher realism."[7] Reagan understood that
national power becomes effective when the tools of statecraft are used
in a legitimate way, hence the higher purpose. He was also grounded
in realism and understood how important it was for national security
that military power always be used decisively. Just as the gentleman at
the airport observed about human eyes, a nation's ability to use power
legitimately and decisively can fall out of balance. The former human
condition is resolved with corrective lenses; the latter national dilemma
with correct principles. With the United States at war against terrorism
since 2001, Reagan's "higher realism" and the story of how his administration sought to correct the imbalance they found in the nation's pattern of civil-military relations is instructive.

ACKNOWLEDGMENTS

I WOULD LIKE TO START by thanking the Lord for bringing all the people acknowledged here into my life. It is humbling to reflect upon how many hands and minds were brought together over distant time and space to create this book. I will do my best to properly acknowledge and thank those involved, knowing full well that there is no way to adequately do so and in full recognition that despite such good help, errors remain for which I must accept full responsibility.

I would be remiss if I did not thank all the sources of help I received during my research. First, Gen. (Ret.) John William Vessey Jr. honored me with the privilege of being the first researcher into his archive and kindly replied to my email queries, while Caspar Weinberger Jr. graciously allowed me access to his father's materials, and K. T. McFarland and Adm. (Ret.) John Poindexter volunteered to share their experiences serving in the Reagan administration. Second, many dedicated librarians and archivists helped me along the way: Michael J. Browne and Sheri Lewis at the Combined Arms Research Library, Susan Lemke and Scott Gower in the Special Collections at the National Defense University Library, and Lisa Jones at the Ronald Reagan Library. Each of them provided both invaluable assistance and good cheer. I also owe a great debt to the dedicated professionals at the Library of Congress. Third, I would like to make note of the research monies granted to me from The Omar N. Bradley Historical Research Fellowship as well as the West Point Faculty Development and Research Fund, made available from endowments managed by the Association of Graduates.

My colleagues in the Department of History at West Point past and present have served brilliantly as role models, mentors, friends, and master motivators and helped me see this project through to completion. Special thanks are owed also to Profs. Joseph Glatthaar and Robert Citino, who served as visiting professors in the department. I cannot adequately express how much I appreciate the time and excitement they showed toward my early work. Professor Glatthaar was integral in helping me complete my dissertation, while Professor Citino helped make sure my book manuscript made it into the hands of my wonderful editor at Texas A&M University Press, Mary Lenn Dixon, who has deftly guided me through the publication process. I am also very grateful for my doctoral advisor and toughest critic, Prof. Alex Roland, who stuck with me when others did not, as well as Profs. Tami Davis Biddle, Dirk Bonker, and John Thompson, who not only served as doctoral advisors but also provided encouragement to write this book. Special thanks are due to Van Mobley and Christopher Maynard, who served as readers for the manuscript and offered intelligent advice for improvement. Finally, I want to thank Kevin Brock, who edited this work and provided numerous helpful comments.

Growing up, I was very fortunate to attend a small high school in Michigan where teachers poured their hearts and souls into their students. Margret Handren, Vibeke Eggen, Janet Maxim, Richard Welty, and Randall Knight each in their own special way excited me about what they liked to call "life, living, and the universe." While a cadet at West Point, my history instructor, Col. (Ret.) James Johnson, planted in my mind the prospect of becoming a historian and years later played an integral role in my joining the Department of History.

I was also very fortunate over the past decade to have the officers in small group 7B, Col. (Ret.) Donald Lunday and his wife, Pat; Col. (Ret) Michael Matheny; and Lt. Col. (Ret) Donald Jones, give me the confidence to express ideas I did not dare share with others. I thank the wonderful prayer warriors from Fort Leavenworth, Kansas, and West Point, New York, for their witness: members of the Grierson Street Bible Study and Tuesday Morning Fellowship Breakfast, Kaye and Syvette Davis, Tom and Jean Schmidt, Barry and Carol Bazemore, Ray and Lori Amparan, Ms. Bobby Cason, Marci Miller, Linda Lewis, Jennifer Munro, Loretta Woody, Barbara Jean Rider, and Terri Geffert.

To my parents, Stan and Nancy Sanders, who I have not called as often as I should have these past five years, I thank you for your unconditional love, patience, and special assistance with this book. To my in-laws, Ken and Izumi Yoshitani, I thank you for generously helping our family time and again so that we can continue to serve. Finally, to my husband, Shaw, and sons, Evan and Davis, you are all so special to me and make my life so much fun. Shaw, without you there would be no book. Evan and Davis, thank you for all the assistance you lent both in making this voyage possible and very enjoyable. Davis, you provided me with many quiet hours to work by waking me at odd hours in the night and ensured that I had plenty of fun along the way by taking me outside to play football. Evan, my baby bird, you ensured I was awake early on weekend mornings and kept me company while I typed away. You also provided me a great laugh when you told a friend, "My Mom talks about Caspar Weinberger all the time, but he is not a relative."

Lastly, I would like to tip my hat to an institution very dear to me: the United States Army. The army, which values education for all its soldiers, funded all my schooling. I cannot express how grateful I am for the intellectual liberation that has come from that education.

Reagan on War

1

DEFINING *and* CHALLENGING

the VIETNAM SYNDROME

O<small>N 20 JANUARY 1981</small>, Ronald Wilson Reagan was sworn in as the fortieth president of the United States. While every orderly transfer of power is a testament to the American democratic system, this inauguration possessed its own dramatic script. Mere minutes after Reagan delivered his inaugural address, having just promised his fellow Americans an "era of national renewal," a plane carrying fifty-two American hostages departed from Tehran after 444 days of captivity in the hands of the new revolutionary government of Iran. The drama was not lost on contemporaries. *Time* magazine captured the emotions of the country: "[W]ithin 41 minutes, a presidency began, an ordeal ended, and the nation was swept by a sense of shared emotion and exuberance not felt in years. Even Ronald Reagan, at ease with the implausibilities of fictive film, would have rejected the script as beyond belief. . . . Watching on television, getting the word from a neighbor or a passer-by on the street, . . . Americans learned of the hostages' release and felt a surge of national relief, a rebirth of confidence and hope, however transitory, that rivaled the first landing on the moon."[1]

Looking back at the news stories on that day, one cannot help but

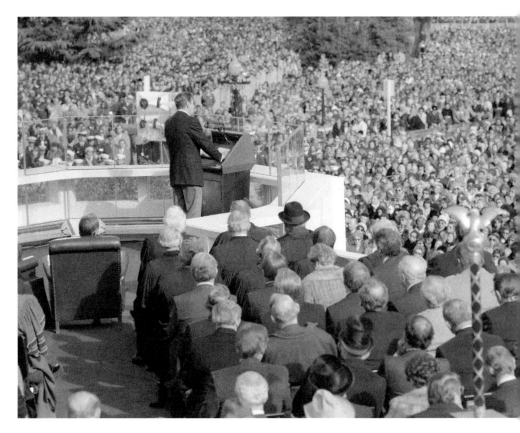

President Reagan delivers his inaugural speech. Courtesy Ronald Reagan Library.

be struck by a number of contrasts. Pictures from the inauguration show Pres. Jimmy Carter ashen and depleted, while President-elect Reagan appeared remarkably well rested and ruddy cheeked. Carter had stayed up for two days straight, only taking an occasional catnap on a couch in the small study adjacent to the Oval Office, working desperately to get the hostages released on his watch. Michael Deaver, Reagan's deputy White House chief of staff, assumed that the president-elect would be practicing the most important speech of his life to that point. Instead he found Reagan on the morning of the inauguration still sleeping comfortably at eight o'clock.[2]

Even the weather seemed to respond to each man's spirit. Caspar Weinberger, who was confirmed later in the day as secretary of defense, recounted in his memoirs: "[W]hen President-elect Reagan took the inaugural oath, his voice infused the air with his characteristic confidence and sparkling vigor, lifting the pall and almost literally parting the clouds. As I had witnessed many times before, Reagan effortlessly summoned brightness; a golden stream of sunlight broke through the dark sky, first shining only on him, then showering everyone present."[3] There is an almost-religious connotation to the Weinberger description—dark forces gripping the nation were counteracted by light showering forth from a new, vibrant leader. A polar opposite, the exhausted Carter left after the ceremony and with his entourage flew to a dark, rain soaked Plains, Georgia.[4]

The most critical contrast between the old and new administrations came in the words that Americans heard from their new leader. In his inaugural address, Reagan told his listeners that there were no limits to what the United States could achieve. "It is time for us to realize that we are too great a nation to limit ourselves to small dreams. We are not, as some would have us believe, doomed to an inevitable decline. I do not believe in a fate that will fall on us no matter what we do." He called for his countrymen to believe in themselves and to believe in their individual and collective capacity "to perform great deeds, to believe that together, with God's help," they could "resolve the problems" facing the country. Reagan urged, "So, with all the creative energy at our command, let us begin an era of national renewal."[5] It was a message that contrasted sharply with the one Americans had received from President Carter eighteen months earlier.[6]

In 1979, in a Sunday evening televised address about energy and national goals, Carter had informed his audience that the true problems of the nation were much deeper than gasoline lines, energy shortages, inflation, or recession.[7] Instead, he warned the more worrisome problem was that Americans were suffering from "a crisis of confidence" that posed a "fundamental threat to American democracy." The president informed Americans that over the last generation, their confidence in the future and their faith in the ability of "citizens to serve as the ultimate rulers and shapers" had declined. "For the first time in the history of the country," he declared, "a majority of our people believe the next five years will be worse than the past five years. Two-thirds of our people do not even vote. The productivity of American workers is actually dropping, and the willingness of Americans to save for the future has fallen below that of all other people in the Western world." Finally, he added, there was evidence of a growing disrespect for government, churches, schools, and media.

The roots of these problems, according to Carter, lay in Vietnam, Watergate, inflation, the country's dependence on foreign oil, and the assassinations of John F. Kennedy, Robert Kennedy, and Martin Luther King Jr. These events had served to undermine many of the country's core beliefs: "ballots not bullets," invincible armies, just wars, honorable leadership, and limitless resources.[8] The nation was at a historic turning point: Americans could decide to continue down the path of self-indulgence and consumption, which Carter described as a path fraught with conflict, chaos, and certainty of failure, or Americans could solve their energy problems through sacrifice. The president urged the path of sacrifice because not only would it resolve the energy crisis but also allow Americans to resolve their crisis of confidence by rekindling a "sense of unity" and "confidence in the future," giving the nation and each individual "a new sense of purpose." He concluded, "There is simply no way to avoid sacrifice."[9]

While Carter offered six steps for solving the energy problem, those points were largely subordinated to his broader argument that Americans were suffering a "crisis of spirit" and needed to be prepared to face limits and make sacrifices.[10] At a press conference afterward, one of Carter's aides spoke of a "malaise" having "descended on American society."[11] Although the president had not used the term, his address was soon dubbed the "malaise" speech by the media.

Carter seemed to have struck a chord with his fellow Americans.

One poll found 77 percent agreed with the statement "there is a moral and spiritual crisis, that is, a crisis of confidence, in the country today." Additionally, his approval rating jumped from 26 percent to 37 percent following the speech.[12] Although Carter did not officially announce that he was running for reelection until 4 December 1979, his "malaise" speech and subsequent request for the resignations of five cabinet members were largely seen as the start of his reelection campaign.[13]

When Ronald Reagan announced his intent to run for president on 13 November 1979, his message was decidedly different. In his declaration of candidacy, Reagan repudiated Carter's calls for Americans to learn to live with limits and argued that the nation's crisis of confidence was not caused by a failure of spirit but by a failure of leadership.[14]

> Our leaders attempt to blame their failures on circumstances beyond their control, on false estimates by unknown, unidentifiable experts who rewrite modern history in an attempt to convince us our high standard of living, the result of thrift and hard work, is somehow selfish extravagance which we must renounce as we join in sharing scarcity. I don't agree that our nation must resign itself to inevitable decline, yielding its proud position to other hands. I am totally unwilling to see this country fail in its obligation to itself and to the other free peoples of the world. The crisis we face is not the result of any failure of the American spirit; it is failure of our leaders to establish rational goals and give our people something to order their lives by. If I am elected, I shall regard my election as proof that the people of the United States have decided to set a new agenda and have recognized that the human spirit thrives best when goals are set and progress can be measured in their achievement.[15]

Reagan asserted that America's problems could be solved with sound leadership and policies rather than by placing limits and shouldering large sacrifices.[16]

Ronald and Nancy Reagan wave during the inaugural parade.
Courtesy Ronald Reagan Library.

On 4 November 1980, Americans elected Ronald Reagan as their new president in an unprecedented landslide. Reagan won 50.8 percent of the popular vote, 489 electoral votes, and forty-four states, while Carter received 41.0 percent of the popular vote, 49 electoral votes, and six states and the District of Columbia. To that point in the twentieth century, only two elected incumbent presidents had failed to win a second term—William Howard Taft, whose party had split in 1912, and Herbert Hoover in 1932 during the Great Depression. Furthermore, Carter received the lowest percentage of the popular vote of any incumbent Democratic president in US history.[17] Reagan asserted that he was a leader who could remove the roadblocks of government and help overcome the three issues he identified as undermining national confidence: a poor economy, an energy crisis, and a perceived weakness in defense.[18] The election results appeared to validate Reagan and his roadmap for the future.

A "Referendum of Unhappiness" or a "Mandate to Rendezvous with Destiny"?

DESPITE THE CONVINCING VICTORY, some post-election survey results suggested caution on the part of the new administration in interpreting its landslide victory as clear support for its conservative agenda.[19] One conducted in January 1981 indicated that the election results were best construed as an overwhelming rejection of Carter and his administration, with 63 percent of respondents indicating the Reagan victory was mostly a rejection of the Carter administration, while only 24 percent answered that it was a mandate for Reagan's conservative policies.[20] Carter's own polltaker characterized the election as "a referendum of unhappiness" on the president.[21] Another pollster for Democratic candidates said that the 1980 results were indicative of "a call for order and stability" by Americans in the areas of foreign policy, world prestige, and the economy. "It [stability] was that side of the equation that people were buying into, not necessarily the change side."[22]

Sources more generous toward the Reagan administration's agenda suggested that the dominant political ideology for the country had shifted to support conservative principles in solving the nation's urgent problems.[23] Others went so far as to suggest that Reagan had received a mandate for his campaign pledge to "make America great again" in the world and for "dramatic economic innovation."[24] In the end, the 1980 election was clear on what Americans disapproved—President Carter's leadership—but less clear on what it wanted or expected the Reagan administration to do differently.

Such an ambiguous outcome is not uncommon in American politics. V. O. Key and Milton C. Cummings, who studied the US electorate over a twenty-four-year period, posited that the electorate's role is best understood as an appraiser of past events. According to them, voters provide leadership direction only in so far as it is possible to see what actions citizens approved or disapproved in the past.[25] Thus like its predecessors, the Reagan administration would have to figure out on its own what the electorate would allow.

Regardless, Reagan and his closest advisors entered office in January 1981 believing that the election had provided a mandate from voters to follow the domestic and foreign-policy agenda they had articulated during the campaign. In his first press conference, the president-elect was asked if he felt "totally wedded to the Republican Party platform" on which he had run, given the fact that he had received millions of independent votes. Reagan replied: "I am—I ran on the platform; the people voted for me on the platform; I do believe in that platform, and I think it would be very cynical and callous of me now to suggest that I'm going to turn away from it. Evidently, those people who voted for me—of the other party or independents—must have agreed with the platform also."[26]

The Reagan Administration's Platform

AT THE HEART OF Reagan's platform was a promise to renew the nation's confidence to pursue its interests and to lead on the international stage.[27] He identified America's poor economic outlook, strategic vulnerability, and weakness and vacillation under President Carter's indecisive leadership as the primary sources of the nation's faltering confidence. Reagan's promise of renewal would come through decisive leadership and the rebuilding and reasserting of US strength—economically and militarily.

Nevertheless, Reagan did not believe rebuilding economic and military power on its own was enough; in addition, a renewal of the American spirit and sense of purpose must also occur. An important component in that process of renewal was to rebuild confidence in the nation's ability to legitimately and decisively use the tools of statecraft—diplomatic, economic, and military—in pursuit of national interests.[28]

Alongside Reagan's political rhetoric regarding the nation's security problems, one must also understand his interpretation of the nation's economic problems and his proposals to resolve them. As the administration made decisions regarding when and how it could pursue its policy objectives on the international stage, other agenda items, such as the economy, would play interrelated and influential roles.

Edwin Meese III, Reagan's counselor, recounted that on the administration's first day, everyone working in the cabinet knew what the president wanted to accomplish and understood the program he wanted to use. Meese explained that all knew the expectations because the ideas Reagan "spelled out in the campaign—and in all the years preceding it[—]were, essentially, the program. There wasn't the usual disparity between election rhetoric and governing agenda; what you heard was what you got."[29] In an interview after leaving office, Reagan said, "I had an agenda I wanted to get done. I came with a script."[30] That script was proclaimed by Reagan while on the campaign trail in 1980 to describe the economic and security problems facing the nation and how he proposed to resolve them if elected.

The Economy: The Problem and Reagan's Proposed Solution

In his speech at the Republican national convention in July 1979, Reagan metaphorically described the nation's economic problems: "First, we must overcome something the present administration has cooked up: a new and altogether indigestible economic stew, one part inflation, one part high unemployment, one part recession, one part runaway taxes, one part deficit spending and seasoned by an energy crisis. It's an economic stew that has turned the national stomach."[31]

Many analysts agreed with his overall assessment, if not his specific diagnosis. The US economy was a mess in the 1970s, as was much of the world economy.[32] Prices more than doubled in that decade, while output had only increased by two-thirds the rate of the 1960s. Unemployment kept creeping higher and was over 7 percent by 1980.[33]

Throughout the presidential campaign, Reagan spoke about the nation's economic problems and offered a solution that rested upon two policies: cutting taxes and reducing government spending.[34] Specifically, he called for a 30-percent reduction in income-tax rates over a period of three years and a hiring freeze and review of all federal programs. He told one audience in July 1980: "I believe it is clear our federal government is overgrown and overweight. Indeed, it is time for our government to go on a diet. Therefore, my first act as chief executive will be to impose an immediate and thorough freeze on federal hiring."[35]

Justifying this governmental diet, Reagan invoked the Tenth Amendment, which he noted, "is explicit in pointing out that the federal government should do only those things specifically called for in the Constitution. All others shall remain with the states or the people."[36] Reagan vowed to conduct a thorough review of the federal government and transfer unnecessary functions, and the sources of taxation to pay for them, to the state and local governments. He also promised to stop waste, extravagance, and outright fraud in federal agencies and programs and to place prudent limits on the regulation of business.[37]

These proposals for cutting taxes and the size of the federal government were key components in what became known as "Reaganomics" or the "Reagan Revolution."[38] Reaganomics rested on supply-side economic theory, which argues that tax cuts and deregulation afford businesses more capital that can be reinvested and turned into greater profits. Ultimately the increased profits increase tax revenues despite having lower tax rates.[39] Supply-siders believe that taxation negatively affects the economy by lowering people's incentive to want to work, save, invest, and take risks. Craig Roberts, who served as Reagan's assistant secretary of the Treasury for economic policy and played a significant role in managing the administration's economic policy during its first two years, described the power in Reagan's supply-side platform: "It gave him an employment policy that did not rely on inflation and government programs. It gave him an anti-inflation policy that did not rely on the pain and suffering of rising unemployment. And it gave him a budget policy that eliminated the deficit through economic growth instead of balancing the budget on the backs of taxpayers." Reagan's optimism and belief in the capabilities of both the American people and the US economy contrasted greatly with the rest of the Republican establishment, prompting his primary opponent in the 1980 presidential campaign, George H. W. Bush, to call his policy "voodoo economics."[40]

Reagan saw big government as the cause of problems rather than the solution and repeatedly emphasized to his audiences the "proper" relationship between a government and its people. He believed that the United States had prospered like no other nation in the world because the original American system of government had allowed the "energy and individual genius of man" to be unleashed to a greater extent than ever known before in the history of mankind.[41] But over time, he argued, individuals began to abandon the belief that they could solve their own problems and had begun to rely on an "intellectual elite" in a "far-distant capital."[42] Thus, Reagan concluded, "[i]t is no coincidence that our present troubles parallel and are proportionate to the intervention and intrusion in our lives that result from unnecessary and excessive growth of government."[43] He pledged to restore to Washington the capacity to do its job without dominating people's lives.[44]

Administration leaders wanted the Reagan Revolution to take hold before Congress took its traditional recess in early August. Meese explained that they calculated approximately 180 days from the inauguration until the recess in which "to make a determined effort to accomplish our objectives."[45] Therefore, the first few months were seen as a critical time for those charged with moving the major agenda items forward.

National Security: The Problem and Reagan's Proposed Solution

In addition to addressing the nation's economic problems, Reagan also sought solutions for the nation's security problems, emphasizing three themes: America's role in the world, the will or spirit to fulfill that role, and the capability to fulfill that role. In his acceptance speech at the Republican national convention, Reagan expressed all three themes. "Let our friends and those who may wish us ill take note: the United States has an obligation to its citizens and to the people of the world never to let those who would destroy freedom dictate the future course of human life on this planet. I would regard my election as proof that we have renewed our resolve to preserve world peace and freedom. This nation will once again be strong enough to do that."[46]

Reagan spoke tirelessly of the responsibility of the United States to establish lasting world peace; "Divine Providence" had left America an "island of freedom" that could serve as a refuge for everyone yearning "to breathe freely."[47] America was to serve as a model for "a troubled and afflicted mankind . . . , [a] shining city on a hill."[48] Yet he expected Americans to do more than simply sit and passively reflect their freedom for the world to see. Instead, Reagan wanted them to be involved in defending and spreading freedom, and specifically he wanted the nation to win the Cold War without any accommodation of the Soviet Union.

While campaigning on behalf of Sen. Barry Goldwater in 1964, Reagan called the US policy of accommodation with communism "a utopian solution of peace without victory." Reagan found it morally repugnant to ensure American security and freedom from the threat of atomic destruction by saying to the millions in slavery behind the Iron Curtain, "Give up your dreams of freedom because we have to save our own skin, we are willing to make a deal with your slave masters."[49] The United States should support countries opposed to communism, even those led by authoritarian regimes whose human-rights records were poor.[50] Reagan also desired to put freedom on the offensive in the Third World and roll back the gains communists had made during the 1970s in places like Angola, Ethiopia, Nicaragua, El Salvador, North and South Yemen, and Cambodia.[51]

According to Reagan, the nation's weakened economic and defensive capabilities, as well as a series of setbacks on the international stage during the 1970s, had shaken its confidence to serve as a leader on the international stage. Many disagreed, stating that the national consensus regarding America's role in the world, which had formed at the beginning of the Cold War, had been destroyed by the war in Vietnam. These critics questioned if the American people still were willing to make sacrifices for the cause of freedom.[52]

The "Vietnam syndrome" was the broad label put on the US hesitancy to exert military power to influence events abroad.[53] Reagan's conceptualization of this problem included hesitancy on the part of Americans to pursue national interests using other measures as well, such as proxy forces, covert operations, or even support for a large buildup of nuclear and conventional forces. Yet for him, the idea of such a syndrome should be set aside. In his speeches, Reagan contended that Americans in 1980 were no less willing than their forefathers to use their power or to make sacrifices to keep what he called their "rendez-vous with destiny" so long as their leaders explained what actions were required and why.[54] Regarding the home front, he described that destiny as one in which Americans upheld "the principles of self-reliance, self-discipline, morality, and . . . responsible liberty."[55] Regarding the larger world, Reagan described that destiny as one in which Americans carried out a foreign policy that was "firm and principled" and sought change by "leadership and example."[56]

In his speech to the Republican nominating convention, rather than attribute the nation's hesitancy to a lack of consensus or will, Reagan blamed poor leadership at the national level. The "weakness" and "vacillation" from indecisive leaders had resulted in the series of recent setbacks the nation had endured.[57] For Reagan, the American spirit was constant; what was changeable was leadership.[58]

Thus, he asked his listeners to consider whether or not the nation was stronger and more respected in July 1980 as it had been three and a half years ago before Carter became president. Prior to posing that question, though, Reagan identified a series of troubling events of significant importance during this time: the recent revelation of a Soviet combat brigade in Cuba, the seizure of the American hostages in Iran, and the Soviet invasion of Afghanistan.[59]

The first event occurred at the end of August 1979, when it was publicly revealed that a brigade of between 2,000 and 3,000 Soviet troops was stationed in Cuba.[60] Although the unit posed no military threat to the United States, Reagan and other opponents of the Carter administration profited from its existence to support several items on their political agenda. For instance, senators who were eager to stall the ratification process of the second Strategic Arms Limitation Treaty (SALT II) had one more excuse to do so. The first SALT had been signed by Pres. Richard Nixon and ratified by Congress in 1972. SALT II was an attempt by the Carter administration to further limit the nuclear arsenals of the two superpowers.

Much of the effectiveness of that treaty would lay in the trustworthiness of the Soviets and the ability of the United States to verify Russian compliance. The fact that a Soviet combat brigade had operated for so many years only ninety miles from Florida without an accurate determination of its purpose left many senators questioning whether the US intelligence community could truly verify Russian adherence to the treaty. Additionally, the disclosure seemed to provide evidence that the Soviet Union was behaving in provocative and challenging ways. The troops in Cuba reportedly not only trained Cuban soldiers but also enabled them to leave and serve as proxies in the communist revolutions occurring in Africa and Central America.[61] One Democratic senator from Florida used the event to shine a spotlight on American resolve, viewing the situation as a "test of U.S. firmness or lack of it" in dealing with the Soviet Union.[62] If the nation lacked resolve on this issue, then it might not be able to ensure Soviet compliance with SALT II. In contrast, during his campaign, Reagan used the brigade issue as evidence of the nation's eroded capabilities for action.

In an early brief to reporters on the Cuban situation, Carter had stated, "We consider the presence of a Soviet combat brigade in Cuba to be a very serious matter and that this *status quo is not acceptable* [emphasis added]."[63] The president explained:

> This Soviet brigade in Cuba is a serious matter. It contributes to tension in the Caribbean and the Central American region. The delivery of modern arms to Cuba and the presence of Soviet naval forces in Cuban waters have strengthened the Soviet-Cuban military relationship. They've added to the fears of some countries that they may come under Soviet or Cuban pressure. During the last few years, the Soviets have been increasing the delivery of military supplies to Cuba. The result is that Cuba now has one of the largest, best equipped armed forces in this region. These military forces are used to intrude into other countries in Africa and the Middle East.[64]

But since no treaty or law had been broken, there was not any pressure exerted from the larger international community upon the Soviet Union when it refused to budge. Thus, Carter and his administration were forced to defuse the situation by moderating American concern in a subsequent address to the nation. The president explained that the nation did not "face any immediate, concrete threat that could escalate into war or a major confrontation." Instead, the United States faced a "challenge" to find a way to "give a measured and effective response to Soviet competition and to Cuban military activities around the world."[65]

Over the next few months, that challenge became even more pronounced and spread beyond concerns regarding the Soviets and their Cuban proxies. In November the US embassy in Tehran was overrun by a group of militants in support of Iran's revolution, and fifty-two American diplomats were taken hostage. At the end of December, the Soviet Union invaded Afghanistan in an effort to preserve the communist regime in that nation. That move also put Soviet forces one step closer to oil supplies in the Middle East. Concerns escalated even further in April 1980, when an attempted rescue of the hostages ended in a fiery disaster. Could the United States still protect its own security interests and those of its allies, or was it a "superpower" in name only?

Reagan turned these events into evidence to support his call for rebuilding the nation's military might. Throughout his campaign, Reagan claimed that the Soviet Union took advantage of the period of détente in the 1970s to build up its military capabilities and create an arsenal larger than anything required for a strong defense. In addition to increasing its conventional forces along the Chinese border, modernizing the forces of the Warsaw Pact, and increasing its theater and strategic nuclear capabilities, the Soviet Union had begun to transform itself from a land power to a maritime power by improving its navy. The Russians' increasing global reach was evident, Reagan contended, in its aid to proxy forces that promoted Marxist-Leninist governments in areas of strategic importance.[66] Finally, he warned that the Soviet preponderance of nuclear power was such that, if they were not properly deterred, they might be emboldened to launch an attack on the United States and its European allies.

These concerns were certainly not new for Reagan. Between his time as governor of California and his inauguration as president, Reagan delivered hundreds of radio addresses in which he expressed those same concerns regarding the nation's defenses and foreign policies.[67] Reagan also served as a member of the board of directors for the Committee on the Present Danger (CPD), a group formed shortly after Carter's election with the expressed purpose of advocating stronger defense and foreign policies for the nation. In its policy statement, "Common Sense and the Common Danger," the group warned that the United States, world peace, and the cause of human freedom were severely threatened by the Soviet Union, and unless the nation took "decisive steps . . . to change the course of its policy," its economic and military capacity would soon "become inadequate to assure peace and security."[68] The group was particularly troubled by détente and SALT II.

In the mind of at least one observer, the CPD succeeded in turning the debate over SALT II into a larger national debate over the nation's security in general.[69] In his memoir, Cyrus Vance, Carter's secretary of state, did not specify the impetus for the national debate, but he did provide an accurate description of it: "The hearings [on SALT II] launched a great national debate that focused not only on the terms of the treaty, but on a much broader range of issues: the nature of the U.S.-Soviet relationship; the role of nuclear arms control in U.S. foreign policy; trends in the military balance; the adequacy of our defense capabilities, programs, and spending; the will of the West to protect its interests; and finally, the nature and scope of U.S. national interests."[70] Reagan addressed these same issues in his 1980 campaign.

Convincing the public that there was a need to spend more on defense was not a difficult matter in 1980, amid the backdrop of the Iranian hostage crisis and the Soviet invasion of Afghanistan. Public-opinion polling indicated a significant spike in January in the number of Americans who favored spending more on defense. While an NBC poll from September 1979 showed that 38 percent of respondents believed the nation was spending too little for defense, four months later, in January 1980, that poll showed a sharp increase to 69 percent. Additionally, polling data showed that Americans were beginning to express a greater willingness to consider the use of military force to defend other countries, particularly if the threat was coming from the Soviet Union.[71] Some argued that the Iranian hostage affair had caused the nation to move beyond the Vietnam syndrome.

Writing in early December 1979, prior to the Soviet invasion of Afghanistan, one journalist reported that the Iranian crisis had served to mark the close of the post-Vietnam era. He quoted a senior official, who had served in several administrations, as declaring, "[i]n terms of domestic politics, this [the seizure of American hostages] has put the end to the Vietnam syndrome." Republicans and Democrats on Capitol Hill echoed a statement made by John C. White, the Democratic national chairman: "We may have reached a turning point in our attitude toward ourselves and that is a feeling that we have a right to protect legitimate American interests anywhere in the world." Nevertheless, while leaders were expressing a greater willingness to consider intervention, they also were expressing caveats drawn from lessons in Vietnam. One senator explained that US foreign involvement should only be undertaken very selectively: "Other countries have to show the will and the capability to help themselves. We should help those who really want us and where there is pro-American support."[72]

Although some observers argued that Americans seemed willing to rattle the nation's saber again, candidate Reagan warned that the United States would require more than better military capabilities in order to check the Soviet Union's imperialist ambitions. The nation's success in achieving those ends also depended on fulfilling its role as an international leader. If elected, Reagan vowed to fulfill that leadership role by following a strategy he called "peace through strength."[73]

In the "peace through strength" strategy, peace was not simply the absence of war.[74] Instead, it was conceived as a world hospitable to American society and its liberal-democratic ideals in which the United States and its allies were free from the threat of nuclear war and had access to vital resources, such as oil, and vital transportation and communications routes.[75] Reagan believed that such a peace was dependent upon US strength, which would come from rebuilding the nation's economic and military might, pursuing reductions in nuclear arms with the Soviet Union, and actively working to roll back communism and to spread freedom and democracy.[76]

The Republican platform for 1980 specified eight general principles and goals of the "peace through strength" strategy:

> To inspire, focus, and unite the national will and determination to achieve peace and freedom; To achieve overall military and technological superiority over the Soviet Union; To create a strategic and civil defense which would protect the American people against nuclear war at least as well as the Soviet population is protected; To accept no arms control agreement which in any way jeopardizes the security of the United States or its allies, or which locks the United States into a position of military inferiority; To reestablish effective security and intelligence capabilities; To pursue positive non-military means to roll back the growth of communism; To help our allies and other non-Communist countries defend themselves against Communist aggression; and To maintain a strong economy and protect our overseas sources of energy and other vital raw materials.[77]

Clearly, these were extremely ambitious policy objectives, and accomplishing them would require a president to use *all* the tools of statecraft. Yet remarkably, Reagan entered office in 1981 with no clearly enunciated doctrine on when and how to use military power as a tool of statecraft. This fact is even more notable when one considers that throughout his campaign, Reagan had attributed the nation's hesitancy for action to poor leadership at the national level. Could he and his administration be prepared to provide better leadership without a clear policy on when and how to use military power?

2

A SHORT PRIMER *on* DOMESTIC
POLITICAL REALITIES

HILE RONALD REAGAN and the key leaders in his administration may not have entered office with a codified doctrine regarding when and how to use military power as a tool of statecraft, they did arrive with strong convictions. In addition, they were charged with leading a nation that had taken specific steps during the 1970s to codify an approach to the use of military power abroad. In the United States, any approach taken to building and employing military power is not simply a product of beliefs regarding the strategic threat and American power in the world, it intrinsically involves the nation's political system and laws. Scholars explore these concepts under the purview of civil-military relations. In a theoretical construct, civil-military relations connect the military-security needs of a nation with its social norms governing the use of violence. The country's values, beliefs, laws, and political system, as they influence when and how military power is used, constitute a nation's "domestic political realities."[1]

In his classic work on US civil-military relations, *Soldier and the State*, Samuel P. Huntington explained that prior to the start of the Cold War, the primary question Americans asked about civil-military relations was "what pattern . . . is most compatible with American liberal

democratic values?" Then with the start of the Cold War, that question
was revised to "what pattern . . . will best maintain the security of the
American nation?"[2] After the experiences of "limited war" in Korea and
Vietnam, Americans added two additional questions: "What pattern
will ensure that American power is used legitimately?" and "What pattern will ensure that American power is used decisively?"

Each question is representative of political realities influencing the
approach an administration may adopt for using military power. For
instance, case studies of events in Central America and the Middle
East (discussed in later chapters) show that the approaches adopted by
the Reagan administration were influenced greatly by contemporary
domestic political realities. Ultimately, the Weinberger Doctrine codified the pattern of civil-military relations Reagan used throughout his
first term, one that sought to ensure that US power was not only used in
a way compatible with American liberal-democratic values and providing the best security but also used military power in both a legitimate
and decisive way.

A more-detailed investigation of American domestic political realities reveals a change over time from the end of World War II to Reagan's
inauguration. As political realities changed during the late 1960s and
1970s, born from the nation's experience with the Vietnam War and
Watergate, legislation passed in response would challenge the Reagan
administration as it sought to assert its leadership on the world stage.
In addition, the lessons the military took away from its experiences of
fighting limited wars in Korea and Vietnam proved influential on policy
doctrine in the 1980s.

The "Age of Consensus": Domestic Political
Realities Following World War II

MOST SCHOLARS classify the period from the 1940s until the
mid-1960s as one of foreign-policy consensus in the United States. That
harmony was largely based upon common perceptions of the threat,

common opinions regarding the purposes for US power in the world, and common beliefs regarding the efficacy of military power. During that time, Americans subscribed to six fundamental propositions regarding the international system, as identified by Richard Melanson:

(1) Alone among the nations of the Free World the United States has both the material power and the moral responsibility to create a just and stable international order. . . . (2) In light of the interdependent nature of the world, U.S. security interest must be necessarily global. . . . (3) Soviet and Soviet-inspired aggression and subversion constitutes the primary threat to world peace. . . . (4) The policy of containment represents the best way to stop further Soviet and Soviet-sponsored expansion. . . . (5) The United States must possess nuclear weapons in order to help deter a Soviet attack on it and its allies. . . . (6) A stable, open world economy required American leadership.[3]

John Ehrman has classified these themes as being part of the "vital center ideology" that emerged in the late 1940s and served as the standard for mainstream liberal thinking and official foreign-policy rhetoric until the mid-1960s, when they were disrupted by revisionist thinking and the Vietnam War.[4]

During the twenty years of vital-center consensus, American foreign policy was largely constructed and directed by a para-institutional group known as the foreign-policy "establishment." As described by one scholar, this establishment was "a relatively homogeneous group of bankers, lawyers, and Foreign Service officers, largely from the northeastern part of the United States, largely pragmatic and centrist in beliefs."[5] The group held common beliefs on both the ends and means of US foreign policy, that international communism was a mortal threat to Western values, and that the nation's responsibility was to provide the international leadership and resources to fight this threat.[6]

To that end the establishment believed that the president should lead foreign policy without interference from Congress, finding support for this position from both congressional leaders and the "attentive public." The attentive public, classified as such because they paid close attention to foreign-policy matters, was inclined to follow the leadership of the president and was typically described as well educated, internationalist minded, and receptive to the nation's involvement overseas.[7]

During the age of consensus, congressional-executive cooperation over the conduct of foreign policy was wide ranging, with congressional leaders giving deference to the president and his policies, which often called for American involvement overseas and the use of military power.[8] The support that Harry S. Truman, Dwight D. Eisenhower, and John F. Kennedy received stemmed from the belief of both Congress and the attentive public that the Soviet/communist threat was significant and that the best course of action was to support the nation's overall strategy of containing the spread of communism.[9] The growth of this threat perception occurred in the late 1940s and was aided by both international and domestic events.

Abroad, the Soviet test of a nuclear weapon, the "loss" of China, and the war in Korea led many to conclude that the communists were indeed a significant threat that needed to be confronted. Domestically, the principal conclusions of National Security Council Report 68 (NSC-68), a top-secret study conducted for Truman in an effort to systematize the strategy of containment, were widely publicized. John Lewis Gaddis explained: "The whole point of the document had been to shake the bureaucracy, Congress, and the general public into supporting more vigorous action [against the Soviets.]"[10] Specifically, NSC-68 called for much-greater defense spending. Americans' concern was heightened further by Sen. Joseph R. McCarthy's claims that large numbers of communists and Soviet spies and sympathizers worked inside the federal government.[11]

Gallup-poll results demonstrate the dramatic change in public opinion about the Soviet Union in the late 1940s. At the end of World War II, close to 50 percent of surveyed Americans responded that the Soviets could be trusted to cooperate when the war was over. In 1947 the percentage holding that view was lower, but still 43 percent held that the Soviets would work with the United States. But by June 1949, only 20 percent still felt that way.[12]

To demonstrate their support of policies meant to contain communism, congressional leaders passed joint resolutions authorizing the president to take necessary measures, even to use military power, in order to prevent its further spread. Truman's decision to dispatch US forces to Korea in 1950 was covered under such a resolution. In 1955 congressional leaders passed a resolution providing Eisenhower authorization to use military force to counter the communist threat against Formosa. Lastly, in 1962 Kennedy received support to use force to resist communism in the Western Hemisphere when Congress passed a resolution on Cuba.[13]

The one social group that remained unsupportive of US involvement overseas was the mass public. Unlike the attentive public, these Americans generally were poorly educated and uninterested in foreign policy. As a group they were against involvement in the affairs of other countries unless vital national interests were at stake, and even then they wanted swift, decisive action, not long-term commitments.[14] But the mass public was largely inert and only became active in the foreign-policy process during elections, when they essentially passed judgment on the performance of leaders.[15]

This pattern remained stable until the mid-1960s, when the beliefs shared by the establishment, congressional leaders, and the attentive public were challenged by revisionist thinking and the Vietnam War experience.[16] An anti-establishment movement arose within the mass public, and congressional leaders cast aside their deference to the president and sought greater oversight and participation in foreign policy.[17]

A New Pattern: Political Realities in the Mid-1960s and 1970s

REVISIONIST THINKING challenged the establishment's most fundamental propositions on three accounts. First, the communist threat was less than that typically argued by the vital center. Second, many people in the Third World genuinely wanted to follow communism and should not be prevented from doing so. Third, the United States was more to blame for the Cold War than the Soviet Union. Despite knowing the weakness of the Soviet Union following World War II, US policymakers had insisted on forcing the Soviets to conform to American expectations and indoctrinated the American people to view them as an enemy.[18]

Although William Appleman Williams captured these themes in his 1959 work, *The Tragedy of American Diplomacy*, Americans did not subscribe to his view until the mid-1960s as the Vietnam War escalated. Many questioned the contention that the Soviets and communism were at the base of all world problems and began to think that perhaps America itself was culpable.[19] William Schneider described the ideological polarization that occurred within American leadership at that time: "Counter-elites emerged on both the right and the left to challenge the supremacy of the old foreign policy establishment," which in turn split the attentive public and shattered the consensus that had been shared since the 1940s.[20]

From this embroilment three groups emerged: neo-isolationists, Cold War internationalists, and post–Cold War internationalists.[21] Neo-isolationists perceived the problems facing the United States as stemming from internal issues, such as inflation, unemployment, and environmental damage, and were against any international involvement. In contrast, both the Cold War internationalists and post–Cold War internationalists emphasized addressing the problems facing the world at large. Although both groups perceived the Soviet Union as the major threat to the nation and world peace, they differed on the degree of culpability. Cold War internationalists tended to blame the Russians for all ills in the world, whereas the post–Cold War internationalists believed that other issues needed to be considered, such as poverty, pollution, and the scarcity of natural resources, all of which impeded better relations between developed and developing nations. As such, Cold War internationalists wanted to rebuild US military power to challenge the Soviets, while post–Cold War internationalists wanted to work with the Soviets to address problems common to all of humanity.[22]

In addition to the ideological splits within the establishment and attentive public, there was a change in the mass public. As it became more active in foreign policy during the later stages of Vietnam, the mass public was not driven so much by ideology, as within the establishment and attentive public, but instead by a rejection of those in power. These Americans lost confidence in the president and the nation's foreign-policy leaders, who came to be seen as corrupt, incompetent, and ineffective. This mood of hostility toward leadership was sustained by the mass media, whose themes were anti-establishment as well.[23]

No longer inert, the mass public had to be considered by American leaders when charting the nation's foreign policy. The importance of public opinion lies not in compelling leaders to avoid certain course of actions but in generating the support that is necessary for the pursuit of a course of action. As Schneider explains: "The question is sometimes asked whether, and how, public opinion constrains foreign policy. Does public opinion compel foreign-policy-makers to take certain actions or not take others? Putting the question this way reverses the actual direction of causality. Public opinion is reactive, not prescriptive; the operative relationship is one of support, not constraint. Policymakers do not look to the public for specific policy direction. But they must mobilize public support for the policies they want to pursue, or at least preempt opposition to them."[24] Yet the mass public is well known for its unpredictable swings of support. One reason for this contradictory behavior is its preference for both strength and peace.[25] Thus, mass-public support is sometimes gathered into an alliance with the Right when it plays to the need for a strong defense. At other times, it is just as easily allied with the Left when it plays to the public's strong desire for peace. As an example (discussed in the next chapter), the public supported Reagan's call for a large military buildup but not his call for more involvement in El Salvador.

As the mass public's influence increased, there was a corresponding change in the role of Congress in foreign policy. Vietnam and Watergate contributed significantly to congressional leaders abandoning their deference to the president, and they now sought a greater oversight role and more participation in policymaking.[26] In 1966 the chairman of the

Senate Foreign Relations Committee, J. William Fulbright (D-Ark.), chaired nationally televised hearings on Vietnam in which congressmen questioned Pres. Lyndon B. Johnson's policies in order to try to reduce his range of action without their consent.[27] The quagmire of Vietnam was not the only event that drove congressional leaders to forego their earlier deference. As Cynthia Arnson has explained, "Watergate, with its revelations of presidential corruption and even criminality, served to further weaken the executive and undermine its prestige, paving the way for a congressional foreign policy challenge."[28]

To that end, Congress passed legislation in the 1970s that afforded its leaders greater participation and oversight in how the nation conducted foreign relations. In an essay on the topic, Sen. John Tower (R-Tex.) wrote: "The 1970s were marked by a rash of Congressionally initiated foreign policy legislation that limited the President's range of options on a number of foreign policy issues. The thrust of the legislation was to restrict the President's ability to dispatch troops abroad in a crisis, and to proscribe his authority in arms sales, trade, human rights, foreign assistance and intelligence operations. During this period, over 150 separate prohibitions and restrictions were enacted on Executive Branch authority to formulate and implement foreign policy."[29] While there were many pieces of legislation, three in particular—the War Powers Resolution of 1973, the Hughes-Ryan Amendment of 1974, and the Clark Amendment of 1976—played key roles in the Reagan administration's decision making regarding support toward Central America, Lebanon, and Grenada.

As already discussed, in the "age of consensus," the joint resolution became a commonly used policy device to carry out the nation's strategy of containment. These congressional declarations were meant to deter would-be adversaries by demonstrating the commitment of the public to the president and his policy.[30] In 1964, Congress passed the Gulf of Tonkin Resolution, which allowed the "President, as Commander in Chief, to take all necessary measures to repel any armed attack against the forces of the United States and to prevent further aggression."[31] As the Vietnam War subsequently unfolded, many congressional leaders felt that President Johnson had abused the measure's open language. Thus, in 1970 Congress repealed the resolution and later, determined to ensure that such a situation did not occur again, passed the War Powers Resolution in 1973.

The War Powers Resolution had the stated purpose to fulfill the intent of the framers of the Constitution by ensuring "that the collective judgment of both the Congress and the President will apply to the introduction of United States Armed Forces into hostilities, or into situations where imminent involvement in hostilities is clearly indicated by the circumstances." It directed that the president, as commander in chief, could send armed forces into areas of hostilities or imminent hostilities only under any of three conditions: "(1) a declaration of war, (2) specific statutory authorization, or (3) a national emergency created by attack upon the United States, its territories or possessions, or its armed forces." Additionally, the president must terminate military action after sixty days "unless the Congress (1) has declared war or has enacted a specific authorization for such use of United States Armed Forces, (2) has extended by law such sixty-day period, or (3) is physically unable to meet as a result of an armed attack upon the United States."[32] Clearly, the resolution if followed could greatly restrict a president's actions by congressional consultation, setting time limits on his actions, and allowing Congress to directly remove armed forces at any time.

A second piece of restrictive legislation was the Hughes-Ryan Amendment to the Foreign Assistance Act. This amendment, named after its sponsors, Sen. Harold Hughes (D-Iowa) and Rep. Leo Ryan (D-Calf.), was adopted in 1974. It called for congressional oversight of intelligence activities, specifically prohibiting the CIA from engaging in any actions other than intelligence gathering unless the president issued an official "finding" that an operation was important to national security. The president was required to submit his finding to no less than six congressional committees having access to intelligence information. Though the law was meant to provide Congress with intelligence oversight, it was also seen as a means to limit covert operations. Like the War Powers Resolution, the principal thrust of Hughes-Ryan was anti-interventionist.[33]

Passed in 1976, a third piece of legislation was the Clark Amendment to the US Arms Export Control Act, named for its sponsor, Sen. Dick Clark (D-Iowa). It barred US aid from going to anti-communist forces in Angola. Pres. Gerald Ford wanted to restrain Soviet-Cuban activities in that African country, but this legislation prevented his efforts to counter them "covertly," sending a clear message that Congress not only wanted to be involved in oversight activities but also would be involved in the actual practice of foreign affairs. The days of congressional and public deference to the president were clearly over.

Congressional leaders and the mass public were not the only Americans to express unease about US military power. Following the war in Korea and again after Vietnam, military leaders enunciated their own concerns regarding the legitimate and decisive use of armed strength, sharing three strong convictions: first, the use of military power should have the support of the American people and their congressional leaders; second, military forces in action ought to be given clear objectives; and third, military forces ought to be given the means and freedom of action required to conclude matters quickly and decisively.

Where military leaders diverged was over their conceptualization of the role the armed forces should play as a tool of statecraft. Some believed that military power ought to be reserved as a last resort, after other means for achieving a particular vital interest had failed or were unlikely to work. Those with such sentiments see a great distinction between the military and diplomacy and believe that force should be used only after all peaceful, nonmilitary measures have failed to achieve the state's objectives. In contrast, other leaders view the use of armed force very similarly to Carl von Clausewitz, who argued that military power is a legitimate tool of statecraft that may be used to help leverage one's diplomacy.[34]

For the first group, control of the military power is to be placed in the hands of military leaders and the objectives they are assigned should be total subjugation of an enemy or nothing less than total "victory." The second group is much more tolerant of political leaders controlling the use of military power because military power is conceptualized as a tool of statecraft. As such it is best used in conjunction with other tools such as diplomacy and ought to be controlled by civilian political leaders.[35]

Samuel P. Huntington has observed that the "military man tends to see himself as the perennial victim of civilian warmongering" and that "the military mind . . . urges the limitation of state action to the direct interests of the state, the restriction of extensive commitments, and the undesirability of bellicose or adventurous policies."[36] As further illustration of military leaders' relative restraint, he wrote:

> The military man normally opposes reckless, aggressive, belligerent action. If war with a particular power is inevitable at a later date with decreased chances of success, the military man may favor "preventative war" in order to safeguard national security. Normally, however, he recognizes the impossibility of predicting the future with certainty. War at any time is an intensification of the threats to the military security of the state, and generally war should not be resorted to except as a final recourse, and only when the outcome is a virtual certainty. This latter condition is seldom met except in the case of a powerful state fighting an isolated minor or backward nation. Thus, the military man rarely favors war. He will always argue that the danger of war requires increased armaments; he will seldom argue that increased armaments make war practical or desirable. He always favors preparedness, but he never feels prepared. Accordingly, the professional military man contributes a cautious, conservative, restraining voice to the formulation of state policy. . . . He is afraid of war. He wants to prepare for war. But he is never ready to fight a war.[37]

In 1977 Richard Betts published a study that updated Huntington by investigating whether or not military leaders were still hesitant to recommend the use of military power. Betts studied the advice military leaders gave to the president when considering commitment of US forces to combat, beginning with the Berlin blockade of 1948 and ending with the 1972 Christmas bombing of Hanoi, a period during which he identified a total of 101 incidents. He found that the military was not as passive as Huntington had argued, but that it also was not "the stereotype of a belligerent chorus of generals and admirals intimidating a pacific civilian establishment" so often portrayed. "In most of the cases where some soldiers were vocally ahead of the civilians in urging the use of force," he concluded, "there were other soldiers giving advice similar to or more cautious than that of principal civilians. This balanced the leverage that the aggressive officers could invoke on grounds of expertise. This picture changes, however, in decisions on the degree of force to use once a decision to commit conventional military units has been made. Generals prefer using force quickly, massively, and decisively to destroy enemy capabilities rather than rationing it gradually to coax the enemy to change his intentions."[38] Betts's findings indicate that the military viewpoint regarding *when* to use force was relatively mixed. Yet there was a consensus on *how* to use it once called upon—overwhelmingly and decisively. Victory was the goal and best achieved by using decisive force.

In turn, Betts's work was updated by David Petraeus in his 1987 dissertation, "The American Military and the Lessons of Vietnam." Petraeus wrote this study as a young major on his way to lieutenant general and a widespread reputation for a pragmatic approach to the use of force in Iraq.[39] Extending Betts's study by looking at the post-Vietnam period, Petraeus argued in his introduction:

I had expected findings similar to those of Betts—that in any one case some military leaders would offer more activist advice, while others would offer less activist advice, in comparison to that of the principal civilians. I found, however, that in no cases were the military as activist in their advice as the civilians most prone to take action—such as Kissinger in the Nixon/Ford years, Brzezinski during the Carter administration, and several different officials in the Reagan administration. In short, the military since 1973 had conformed much more closely to the

Huntington view (originally presented in 1957) than they had during the period of Betts' analysis.[40]

Specifically, Petraeus found that military leaders did not want troops committed to combat unless specific conditions were obtained. These were that "public support is assured, military objectives are clear and reasonably attainable, and commanders are provided sufficient forces and the freedom necessary to accomplish their missions." Additionally, he discovered that "once the decision to use force" was made, "the military . . . frequently, and understandably, sought to employ as much force as they . . . felt necessary to bring the commitment to a speedy and victorious conclusion."[41]

While Petraeus explained that the difference between his findings and those of Betts ought to be understood as the influence of the Vietnam War, his work provides valuable insight by demonstrating that the difference regarding when and how to use military power among many of these views was "not quite as distinct as it may appear," rather it was "more of nuance than of unprecedented change." His research indicated similar views existent coming out of the Korean War during the 1954 deliberations over intervention in Indochina and the 1960s debates over commitment of US troops in Laos and Vietnam. He illustrates the views of senior officers said to be members of the "Never Again" club.[42] Those officers believed that the United States should not intervene in Asia unless "America was prepared to fight an all-out war, with the level of national commitment and mobilization necessary to accomplish the mission before public support eroded."[43]

Similar to congressional action in passing laws like the War Powers Resolution, in the 1970s military leaders did what they could to ensure that their concerns regarding legitimate and successful use of military power were met. First, they sought to guarantee that US military forces were kept from being sent off to fight without the support of the American people. An example of this effort came in the spring of 1973, when Army Chief of Staff Creighton Abrams and Secretary of Defense James Schlesinger met to develop a plan for the new structure of the army. The army was poised to expand from thirteen to sixteen divisions without changing its overall end strength of approximately 765,000 soldiers. This would be accomplished by filling out the combat units with reserve forces, which also would be responsible for many of the support functions for each division. The deal came to be known as the "Golden Handshake." The army would seemingly no longer be able to deploy without calling up reserve units. The significance of this was that the president would have to mobilize men and women from their jobs and families, which would naturally involve the American public and congressional leaders in the process. Abrams reportedly said to one of his subordinates, "They're *never* going to take us to war again without calling up the reserve."[44] Furthermore, this deal was seen as a way to limit civilian warmongering.

Military leaders also took measures to ensure that American military power would be reserved as a tool of last resort. The Pentagon understood that communist expansion in areas such as Central America could not go unchecked, but leaders there did not want to get dragged into another Vietnam-style quagmire or face a Korean stalemate. The way around this strategic dilemma was to support the concept of using proxy forces to do America's bidding in areas where matters easily could drag on for years. Proxy forces could provide the leverage political leaders desired and needed for their diplomatic efforts to work over time.

The overall plan was to support local and regional elites to keep order and provide a bulwark of anti-communism by providing them with arms, equipment, training, and even building bases from which to provide air and logistical support to proxy operations.[45] Such measures were to allow US military forces to stay on the sidelines until the situation evolved into one that called for complete subjugation or victory and had the complete support of the American people. The problem with this plan was that a presidential administration would have to gain support from Americans and their congressional leaders even to use such forces as a tool of statecraft. This problem came to a head in Central America.

3

❧

THE CASEY DOCTRINE

Using Proxy Forces in Central America

ONE OF THE REAGAN administration's first foreign-policy challenges arose in Central America, a situation inherited from the Carter years. As officials attempted to gain flexibility for action by reducing legal and political constraints on the use of military power, Secretary of State Alexander Haig proposed a controversial policy for the region, which involved pursuing a tough line against Cuba. After almost a year of consideration and deliberation, the administration finally arrived at its solution, an initial step in the evolution of its understanding of the relationship between national political objectives, the use of military power, and political realities.

Background on Central America

ON 17 JULY 1979 Anastasia Somoza Debacle resigned as Nicaragua's president. Somoza, whose family had ruled since 1936, was forced from office by a broad coalition of Marxists, capitalists, social reformers, and Christians, though most recognized that the key powerbrokers were members of the Sandinista National Liberation Front.[1] The

Sandinistas, funded through Cuba, publicly expressed their admiration for that nation and their hatred for the United States.[2] Before assuming power on 19 July, the new junta promised elections and the promotion of human rights while pledging to respect private property and to preserve a mixed economy. Such promises were designed in part to diminish the likelihood that the Carter administration might intervene militarily.[3] As it turned out, their concerns were unwarranted; Carter never seriously considered such an option.[4]

American policymakers were largely divided into two camps on how to respond to the Nicaraguan revolution.[5] One group viewed events as a positive step forward for that nation, arguing that the cause of the revolution was internal difficulties derived largely from social inequality and repressive leadership under the Somoza regime.[6] To ensure a stable future for Nicaragua, the best course for the United States would be to allow the Nicaraguan people to control their own destiny. They would not allow a radical revolution to take hold. Once in power, the Sandinistas would see the benefits of following a pragmatic course, which meant not jeopardizing the revolution by trying to export it to El Salvador, Guatemala, or Honduras. Such adventures would lead to Nicaragua's involvement in a superpower rivalry and its alienation from important democratic nations in Latin America. US strategists of this camp argued that the worst mistake Carter could make would be to confront the Sandinistas, a course the nation had taken with the Cuban revolution.[7] Instead, the United States ought to establish good relations with the new regime.

President Carter had approached Central America with this mindset when he entered office in 1976, and he took the same approach with the Sandinistas in 1979. In 1976 he believed that long-term US security interests would be best served by treating Latin American countries with respect and, through American power and influence, turning unpopular but survival-minded governments toward the promotion of human rights and the broadening of their political processes. To encourage traditional regimes, including Somoza's, to open up their political systems, Carter tied economic aid and security assistance to human-rights performance. While he believed it was unwise for the United States to support such repressive governments, he did not believe that the US role should be to overthrow established leadership.[8]

Communicating his willingness to respect the concerns and interests of small Latin American nations, Carter committed to new canal treaties with Panama with his first presidential-review memorandum (PRM 1).[9] He further emphasized human rights and democratic government by establishing the Interagency Group on Human Rights and Foreign Assistance, under the chairmanship of Deputy Secretary of State Warren Christopher, on 1 April 1977. This committee's function was to ensure that the amount of foreign aid received from the United States was directly tied to a government's human-rights performance. Somoza's government immediately came under scrutiny and was pressured to change.[10] The Nicaraguan dictator responded by ending martial law and censorship and making his cabinet more broadly representative, measures that provided the political space for the Sandinista-led revolution to begin. Finally, Carter demonstrated his commitment to established governments by not insisting that Somoza resign immediately, even though administration officials believed that the longer he stayed in office, the more likely it was that the radical Sandinistas would fill his place.[11]

Following the Sandinistas' seizure of power, Carter insisted that events in Nicaragua should not be viewed as a victory for Cuba and a loss for the United States: "It's a mistake for Americans to assume or to claim that every time an evolutionary change takes place or even an abrupt change takes place in this hemisphere, that somehow it's a result of secret, massive Cuban intervention."[12] Instead, the president encouraged Americans to trust the judgment of the Nicaraguan people. In an effort to avoid the path taken following the Cuban revolution, the administration sought to avoid confrontation and instead mold the new regime with provisions of emergency food and relief supplies.[13]

Carter's policy toward Central America in general and Nicaragua in particular was anathema to the second group of policymakers in Washington.[14] When the Sandinistas came to power, that camp believed that the administration had indeed "lost" Nicaragua to the communists. Somoza, who had been a longtime supporter of the United States in its fight against communism, should have been aided in his struggle against the Marxist Sandinistas. They thought of the Nicaraguan president as Pres. Franklin D. Roosevelt had of Somoza's father (and predecessor): "He [Somoza] may be a son of a bitch, but he's *our* son of a bitch."[15] They also agreed with Jeane Kirkpatrick's argument that authoritarian governments were more likely to reform than totalitarian governments.[16] The appropriate lesson from Cuba to these Americans was not that the United States had pushed Castro too hard but that it had pushed him too late, allowing his revolution time to consolidate its power.[17] Nicaragua was just another in a series of unsettling communist gains in the late 1970s, including the Vietnamese invasion of Cambodia in 1978 and the Soviet invasion of Afghanistan in 1979. Nicaragua might be the domino that would topple pro-Western governments in El Salvador, Guatemala, and Honduras, and a lack of action by the United States could signal weakness to geopolitical competitors. Finally, these policymakers were adamantly opposed to Carter's decision to sign away US "rights" to the Panama Canal, in which they presumed the nation had a vital strategic interest.

Such arguments anticipated the positions Ronald Reagan expressed during the presidential campaign in 1980 and during his first year in office. Well before the Sandinistas came to power, Reagan had denounced Carter's approach to Central America.[18] In radio addresses broadcast in the spring of 1979, he warned that "the Caribbean is rapidly becoming a Communist lake in what should be an American pond and the United States resembles a giant, afraid to move."[19] Reagan believed that the United States had lost control of its strategic backyard and needed to take action to regain its authority.

Taken on their own merits, the tiny republics of El Salvador and Nicaragua, the subjects of much debate during the Reagan administration's first term, hardly seemed critical to US foreign policy. They possessed neither raw materials nor significant economies and also lacked the military capability to threaten US territory or lines of communication. But in the context of the Cold War, the thought of "losing" another nation to communism in the Western Hemisphere was unacceptable. A paper prepared for the National Security Council (NSC), by Haig's State Department in February 1981 stated: "The fall of the government of El Salvador would represent a major reversal for the United States." It went on to explain: "We might have been able to maintain a posture of indifference toward the fate of that government [El Salvador] had it not been for the large scale and blatant external support for the insurgents. Given that support, it is essential that we not repeat a situation, particularly not in our own hemisphere, of permitting a government to fall because we have denied it legitimate means of self-help while the insurgents have received unlimited assistance from communist countries."[20] In addition to concerns about America's credibility should the communist insurgency in El Salvador succeed, the State Department highlighted US strategic concerns:

> Guerrilla success could be damaging to our strategic position in this hemisphere and elsewhere. For example, it could contribute to instability in other areas along the U.S. "southern flank," e.g., Mexico, Panama, Venezuela, etc. It could jeopardize critical oil and mineral resources, as well as key transportation and communication links. It could eventually force us to tie down forces and expend capital otherwise needed to cope with other threats. And a demonstration of U.S. ineffectuality in dealing with threats close [to] our own shores could make it even more difficult for us to increase cooperation and confidence among strategically placed countries many times more distant (for instance, in the Persian Gulf.)[21]

Even before Reagan was elected, William Casey, who would become his nominee for director of Central Intelligence, had "decided that El Salvador was, symbolically, the most important place in the world," surmising that "if the United States could not handle a threat in its backyard, Reagan's credibility would be at risk in the rest of the world."[22] One month before the election, Casey brought together a group of seventeen senior foreign-policy experts, including former president Gerald Ford, to serve as an interim advisory board.[23] The group identified the communist insurgency in El Salvador as "an immediate and important challenge to the incoming Administration."[24]

Contrary to the expectations of the noninterventionists, the Sandinistas did follow a radical path and became involved in the superpower rivalry. In the early 1980s, they began requesting arms from the Soviet Union, Algeria, Eastern Europe, and Vietnam and dispensing them to communist-inspired guerrillas in other nations, including El Salvador.[25] In January 1981, days before Reagan's inauguration, Sandinista-supported Marxist insurgents launched an attack to overthrow the Salvadoran government of Christian Democrat José Napoleon Duarte.[26] While heavily engaged in attempts to negotiate the freedom of US hostages in Iran, Carter suspended aid to Nicaragua and reinstated military and economic assistance to El Salvador on the nineteenth.[27] For the Reagan administration, which entered office the next day, the situation in El Salvador provided an opportunity to demonstrate to the world that it was ready to play a stronger role in Central America and unwilling to "lose" another small republic to Cuba and the Soviet Union.

Thus, at the administration's first NSC meeting on 6 February, the Caribbean Basin was at the top of the agenda. President Reagan told his cabinet leaders: "My own feeling—and one about which I have talked at length—is that we are way behind, perhaps decades, in establishing good relations with the two Americas. We must change the attitude of our diplomatic corps so that we don't bring down governments in the name of human rights. None of them is as guilty of human rights violations as are Cuba and the USSR. We don't throw out our friends just because they can't pass the 'saliva test' on human rights."[28] Secretary of State Haig noted: "This area is our third border. There is no question that it is in turmoil. . . . Yet these countries could manage if it were not for Cuba. Cuba exploits internal difficulties in these states by exporting arms and subversion." Furthermore, "Secretary Weinberger

The Reagan administration's first National Security Council meeting.
Courtesy Ronald Reagan Library.

and I have work underway on Caribbean contingencies. We will have
to deal with Nicaragua, El Salvador, and, most especially, with Cuba.
The worst thing would be to have the US dragged into another draining
experience like Vietnam." Secretary Weinberger responded: "There is
no doubt that we face a tough situation in El Salvador and Nicaragua.
The problem stems from Cuba. With some covert aid, we could disrupt
Cuban activities. I am not sure that most Americans understand the
situation there. The majority probably believes that these governments
are repressive and that we should not do anything provocative. We need
to explain to people that this is a dangerous situation for the U.S., and
that we may have to move strongly."[29]

Reporter Bernard Gwertzman and others have suggested that the administration selected El Salvador as an early test for its relations with both the Soviet Union and its allies, but that it was given more attention than it warranted because of its perceived significance as a symbol of American resolve.[30] In an interview on 13 March 1981 with Robert MacNeil and Jim Lehrer, Secretary of State Haig was asked if the administration had decided to highlight El Salvador and its ties to the Soviet bloc to further the case against international interventionism. Haig replied that El Salvador was experiencing a guerrilla movement fueled by Cuban armaments and Soviet-supplied equipment, and "it wasn't a contrived situation to draw the line on."[31] The minutes from the administration's first NSC meeting, and the ideas contained in the State Department paper of February 1981, are supportive of this contention. Nevertheless, years later Haig did note that Reagan "knew that his opportunity to act would not last long, that if [the president] was to have an effective policy in Central America and throughout the world, he must put its elements in place in the first months of his Administration."[32]

By early February, the administration had established five policy objectives:

(1) . . . halt the infiltration [of arms] to the insurgents [in El Salvador] from abroad;

(2) . . . help the Government of El Salvador . . . defeat the leftist insurgency;

(3) . . . minimize Soviet and Cuban influence both in El Salvador and in the region;

(4) . . . demonstrate U.S. resolve against international communist aggression;

(5) . . . restore Salvadoran stability by encouraging the Government to take measures to develop popular support including:

(a) ending security force abuses and curtailing extreme-right terrorism;

(b) proceeding with economic and agrarian reforms; and

(c) moving toward a peaceful political process and the promised 1982 elections.[33]

Three themes surface in the numerous memorandums and policy papers that key leaders in the administration exchanged regarding how to achieve those objectives. First, they recognized that there was a very good chance that US military power might have to be used. Nevertheless, they were determined to ensure that its use in any strategy would be both credible and sustainable. Credibility demanded that if military power was focused on Castro, it ought to be sufficient to cause him to back down; if he did not, then the nation should be prepared to respond with decisive force. At the same time, sustainability demanded that proposed military actions use resources conservatively. Any proposed action needed to take into account the nation's worldwide commitments and cost. Finally, they appreciated that being able to use military power in a credible manner and sustain its use ultimately rested upon whether or not the administration could gain and sustain public and congressional support.

Officials did not want to get into a similar position as the Carter administration regarding the Soviet combat brigade, when it declared the status quo would not stand and yet was unable to back those words with action. Rather the new administration wanted to avoid taking any rash action in the region until there was public and congressional support for its broad objectives. To that end Reagan officials immediately set out to address the political and legal constraints on the use of military power.

Shaping Political Reality to Gain Flexibility for Future Action

TO SEEK RELEASE FROM political constraints, the administration catered to public, congressional, and allied opinions regarding the promotion of progress in the Third World and the restraint of further incursions by the Soviets and their proxies. To that end officials presented briefings and published reports that described the Salvadoran junta as a moderate government, committed to human rights and political reform, fighting for survival against guerilla fighters supplied by Soviet-bloc nations.[34]

On 13 February, congressional leaders received a five-page State Department overview on El Salvador with a brief sketch of the three primary groups vying for power: Marxist guerrillas, right-wing extremists, and the moderate civilian-military government. The paper noted that over the past year, the US government had assisted the ruling junta because it was working to implement important social and political reforms, stop the violence of right-wing extremists, and defeat Marxist guerrillas. Further justification for the aid program lay in the fact that the regime faced guerrillas armed, trained, and supported with political and military advice from Cuba and other communist nations.[35] Five days later Secretary Haig followed up with a closed-door briefing to the Senate Foreign Relations Committee in which he again emphasized that the Salvadoran insurgents were receiving arms supplied by the Soviet Union, Cuba, Ethiopia, and Vietnam.[36]

The administration also sought to break down resistance from the American people. Another five days after Haig's session with the committee, the State Department published a "white paper" titled "Communist Interference in El Salvador." The purpose and motivation for the document was clear: "This special report presents definitive evidence of the clandestine military support given by the Soviet Union, Cuba, and their Communist allies to Marxist-Leninist guerrillas now fighting to overthrow the established Government of El Salvador. The evidence, drawn from captured guerrilla documents and war material and corroborated by intelligence reports, underscores the central role played by Cuba and other Communist countries beginning in 1979 in the political unification, military direction, and arming of insurgent forces in El Salvador."[37] The complete text, published in *The New York Times*, publicly revealed titillating details of Salvadoran guerrillas at the Hungarian embassy in Mexico City meeting with representatives from the German Democratic Republic (GDR), Bulgaria, Poland, Vietnam, Hungary, Cuba, and the Soviet Union; on other occasions they met directly with Castro in Cuba. Specific details emerged about trips by the leader of the Salvadoran Communist Party to the Soviet Union,

Vietnam, the GDR, Czechoslovakia, Bulgaria, Hungary, and Ethiopia to procure arms and gain support for the movement.[38]

Lastly, the administration sought to build support among its allies. In February Lawrence Eagleburger, assistant secretary of state for European and Canadian affairs, visited Bonn, Paris, Brussels, the Hague, and London to "share recent intelligence on outside support for the Salvadoran insurgency and provide background on the evolution of U.S. policy toward Central America."[39] Secretary of State Haig telegrammed those words to US embassies in Europe, Mexico, and El Salvador to describe the purpose behind Eagleburger's trip.

Between 14 and 19 February, Eagleburger briefed foreign ministers, NATO permanent representatives, and the European Community president on evidence to support the administration's claims that the Soviet bloc was arming rebels in El Salvador.[40] He reportedly used a slideshow of documents allegedly written by an El Salvadoran guerrilla leader tracking the military arms promised by Vietnam, Ethiopia, the Soviet Union, and Eastern European nations. He also showed photographic evidence of a tractor-trailer captured in Honduras that had a false bottom used to smuggle 150 M-16 assault rifles.[41] Two State Department–led interagency teams followed up Eagleburger's trip to continue the campaign and to provide an opportunity for exchanges with other key allied leaders.[42]

Despite this campaign to shore up support, the administration encountered resistance on 2 March when it formally announced its decision to send El Salvador $25 million in military aid and increase the number of military "trainers" there to fifty-four.[43] Each constituency—allies, the American public, and congressional leaders—voiced misgivings about the plan. Yet the policy objectives adopted for the region were unlikely to be achieved through rhetoric alone. Instead, they would require US leadership, resources, and the support of allies, the American public, and congressional leaders.

The European allies had registered their concerns during Eagleburger's trip. Though they were generally sympathetic, left-wing opposition at home made them unwilling to support the El Salvador proposal. West German chancellor Helmut Schmidt was in a particularly difficult position since leftists in his own Social Democratic Party were known supporters of the Salvadoran guerrillas. Therefore, the Europeans let Eagleburger and the other members of his delegation know that their support, in Haig's words, "could only, at best, be muted."[44]

In the United States, concerns over repeating the Vietnam experience were still prevalent, and the administration immediately began receiving clear signals from the public and congressional leaders to avoid greater military involvement in Central America. Americans registered their disapproval through polls, letters to political leaders, and protest marches. Reagan's presidential pollster, Robert Wirthlin, found in March 1981 that the president's popularity had suffered "a sharp and sudden drop," attributable to his decision to send military advisors to El Salvador. Despite the administration's efforts to emphasize that US military personnel would not accompany Salvadorans on missions or participate in combat operations, many saw the moves as first steps into a potential quagmire reminiscent of Vietnam.[45] Reagan had to use special executive authority to transfer $20 million of the $25 million he proposed as aid to El Salvador. The remaining $5 million had to be reprogrammed by the House appropriations subcommittee, a measure that was narrowly approved in late March.[46]

The New York Times reported that the vote was so close because congressional leaders found that their "constituents were overwhelmingly opposed to the military aid."[47] Rep. Silvio O. Conte (R-Mass.) received about 600 letters that were nearly 30-to-1 against sending military aid and advisers to El Salvador.[48] Sen. Charles H. Percy (R-Ill.), chairman of the Senate Foreign Relations Committee, reported 300 letters a week on the topic from constituents, three-quarters of them opposing military aid. Rep. Michael D. Barnes (D-Md.), chairman of the House Foreign Affairs Subcommittee on Latin America, said that 100 percent of the letters he received were against the administration's policy.[49] A Gallup poll conducted on 14 and 15 March found that two-thirds of the "informed" Americans surveyed believed the situation in El Salvador could develop

President Reagan meets with Republican congressman Silvio O. Conte about the situation in El Salvador. Courtesy Ronald Reagan Library.

into another Vietnam. The president's own mail showed that 96 percent of the letters expressed unhappiness with the direction the nation was taking in the region.[50]

In addition to writing letters, Americans staged protests across the nation. At Columbia University several hundred students held an outdoor rally; at Ohio State protestors conducted a fast at the state capitol; and at the University of Michigan, a group of 500 marched from the campus to the federal building in Ann Arbor. A march in Boston attracted more than 3,000 protestors, though other demonstrations were much smaller, such as the thirteen-person sit-in at the offices of Sen. Charles H. Percy (R-Ill.).[51]

Congress registered its concerns over Reagan's proposed actions by requesting that the administration heed the structural constraints imposed by the Arms Export Control Act (1976) and the War Powers Resolution. Congressional leaders followed this by writing legislation placing conditions on Salvadoran aid. Four days after the administration's announcement, Rep. Clement Zablocki Jr. (D-Wisc.), chairman of the House Foreign Affairs Committee, sent Secretary of State Haig a letter about growing congressional concern. He requested that his committee be provided with "a copy of the instructions and guidelines governing the activities of U.S. military personnel in El Salvador" and "a periodic report describing the internal security situation in El Salvador and the activities of U.S. military personnel there" in order to allow congressional oversight on the administration's compliance with these measures.[52]

Due to the overall threat present in El Salvador and the fact that the secretary of defense was considering awarding hostile-fire pay to the "trainers" sent to El Salvador, Sen. John Glenn (D-Ohio) felt very strongly that the administration ought to begin reporting under both laws: "How can we say that 12,000 people including four churchwomen killed, the Embassy shot up, American people in garrison with sidearms, hostile-fire pay, people getting killed all the time, isn't significant hostilities? That is just tortured logic to me. I can't see it. And I don't know why we don't declare it as such, report to us, then we have the confidence that we are going to get reports if there are future events like this in other countries."[53] In order to sidestep the reports to Congress under these laws, the administration revoked the hostile-fire-area designation for El Salvador.[54]

The second action came from both the House and the Senate, each body introducing legislation requiring the administration to end aid to El Salvador and withdraw military advisers unless the president was able to "certify" that human-rights conditions were improving.[55] While congressional leaders agreed with Reagan's decision to continue to support Duarte and his government, they could not agree upon how to deal with right-wing death squads and Marxist guerrillas. Each chamber heard extensive testimony, some of which argued that military aid would only feed more power to the extreme right and hinder Duarte's efforts at reform and a negotiated settlement. In the end, Congress compromised and decided that military assistance was required but that the El Salvador regime had to demonstrate progress in making reforms.[56]

The administration sought release from some of the legal constraints to its actions by requesting that the House Foreign Affairs Committee develop legislation allowing more flexibility in the conduct of security-assistance operations. Officials called for abolishing the Clark Amendment and requested exemption from reporting and funding restrictions. Several of Reagan's key cabinet leaders, such as Secretaries Haig and Weinberger, believed that the War Powers Resolution and the Arms Export Control Act, both passed by Congress in the 1970s in reaction to the Vietnam War and CIA covert activity, acted as legislative constraints on the president in his conduct of foreign policy.[57]

Despite their beliefs, Reagan, Haig, and Weinberger recognized that the War Powers was an issue that congressional leaders were not ready to tackle. Instead, the administration accepted that bitter pill for the moment and focused upon trying to get the Arms Export Control Act amended. In Secretary Haig's first formal appearance before the House Committee on Foreign Affairs, he urged Congress to abolish the Clark Amendment and to change the manner in which funds were appropriated for security assistance programs.[58] Regarding the amendment, he argued: "I am concerned and we are concerned about the provisions of the Clark Amendment, which is unique and unprecedented in American history. I am concerned about it . . . because it is a blatant restriction on executive authority . . . which presents an American President with a priori restriction on his ability to deal with any subject in that area with the kind of objectivity, flexibility, and, I hope clarity of thought that is necessary."[59] Haig also asked Congress to consider three measures to improve security-assistance response and eliminate the involvement of US forces: create a contingency fund for foreign crises; support a $350 million revolving weapons fund that would allow foreign buyers to receive arms faster; and reduce reporting requirements on arms shipments and overseas military advisors.[60]

The administration's policy toward El Salvador was just one piece of a larger strategy it was seeking to develop for the region as a whole. The importance of Central America to the nation's overall security was discussed in the very first NSC meeting, but Reagan's "National Security Decision Directive on Cuba and Central America" (NSDD-17), which established US policy toward the Americas, was not signed until 23 November 1981. The primary reason for the delay was that top administration officials could not agree on where to try to cut off the supplies going to the insurgents in El Salvador, either Cuba or Nicaragua.

At the same time Reagan was trying to convince congressional leaders, the public, and US allies that action was needed in Central America, Secretary Haig waged a similar campaign within the high councils of the administration, recommending interdiction of arms coming from Cuba. His policy solution was largely influenced by the lessons he had taken away from the Vietnam War.

The Haig Doctrine

ALEXANDER HAIG APPLIED TWO lessons from Vietnam to US policy in Central America. First, the nation needed to stop fighting proxies and start fighting the real enemy; second, the United States should not impose irrational limits on the use of power. The secretary believed that the United States had failed in Vietnam because it had focused too much on fighting the Vietcong, whom he viewed as proxies for the real enemies in the Soviet Union and North Vietnam, and because it had followed a doctrine of "incrementalism" that had prevented the nation from using its full power decisively.[61]

Regarding proxies, Haig wrote: "The United States . . . stubbornly refused to treat the Vietnam insurgency as anything other than a local problem. We knew . . . that if the war was, in important measure, an expression of North Vietnamese imperialism, that it nevertheless could not take place without the approval, the encouragement, and the massive support of the U.S.S.R. Yet we chose not to take the issue to the Soviet Union or even, in a meaningful way, to Hanoi. We chose, instead, to tangle ineffectively with the puppets, rather than the puppet masters."[62] To avoid this mistake in Central America, he advised the president to deal with the puppet masters, the Soviet Union and Cuba, rather than fight the puppets, the Salvadoran guerrillas and the Sandinistas.[63]

The secretary recommended that Reagan pursue this tough policy at the beginning of his administration, while he still possessed a large measure of discretion not only from his "honeymoon" in office but also from the forbearance of the Soviet Union.[64] Haig had learned through a series of conversations with Amb. Anatoly F. Dobrynin that the Soviets viewed Cuban activities in the Western Hemisphere as a matter strictly between the United States and Cuba. Thus, Haig reflected, "the way was open to solve the problem in Central America, and solve it quickly, through the unequivocal application of pressure. The question was, had we the will to do it promptly, while the President still enjoyed the freedom of action he had won at the polls?"[65]

Interestingly, the Soviet ambassador's message seemingly undermined the first of Haig's two lessons from Vietnam, that Russia was the puppet master in Central America. While the administration could point to military support sent to Salvadoran guerrillas from Nicaragua, the Soviet Union, Cuba, and other communist nations, Dobrynin's position belied Soviet instigation of insurgent activities in the region.[66] The secretary never appeared to have been troubled by that contradiction.

Haig fervently advocated taking quick and decisive action during crisis situations, such as that existing in Central America in 1981. "If not nipped in the bud," he declared, "a crisis not only blooms in its own right but pollinates new crises."[67] This conviction arose from his Korean War experience. As an aide in 1950 to Gen. Douglas MacArthur's chief of staff, Maj. Gen. Edward Almond, Haig was in the room or within earshot as MacArthur and the key members of his staff grappled with the political and military issues involved in fighting the nation's first limited war.[68] On 23 August, when the Joint Chiefs of Staff gathered to discuss MacArthur's proposed amphibious landing at Inchon, Gen. J. Lawton Collins, the army chief of staff, "strongly opposed . . . the landing," as Haig later recalled, "calling it a shoestring operation and pointing out that the consequences in case of failure would be calamitous." MacArthur listened to the points made by Collins and the others but ended the discussion by saying, "Gentlemen, we will land at Inchon on September 15 or you will have a new Supreme Commander in the Far East." Haig called MacArthur's decision to go forward with the operation despite the opposition "not vainglory but wisdom," for he had recognized that the fastest way to end the bloodshed and achieve a negotiated peace was to eliminate the fighting power of the enemy. The wisdom of the general's military strategy, Haig believed, lay in its decisiveness.[69]

In 1981 Haig wanted to pursue decisive action in Central America by cutting off the revolution's source of supply at Cuba, stopping the Cubans from spreading revolution to Central America and Africa, and striking a blow at what he still saw as Soviet adventurism. At the same time, he argued that the administration also needed to heed a second lesson he believed was born out of Vietnam: the nation's power should not be hamstrung by "incrementalism."[70] That doctrine, explained Haig,

> called for subtle escalation in the form of Western probes designed to show the U.S.S.R. our determination to stand firm against further Soviet challenges while avoiding countermeasures that would risk conflict. . . . Even in the gaming stage, it soon became clear that, in practice, incremental increases in force tended to intensify the risk rather than control it; as in a schoolyard scuffle, the possibility of either party backing away decreased with every shove and expletive, with the world press acting out the role of the crowd of taunting children. These ideas from the ivory tower contradicted the centuries of military wisdom embodied in Gen. Nathan Bedford Forrest's famous formula for victory, "Get there first with the most men." It seemed to me that any doctrine based on the notion of maximizing the enemy's strength while placing voluntary restraints on one's own freedom of action risked provoking the very outcome it sought to avoid.[71]

He argued that incrementalism was ineffective in persuading an adversary to alter his actions because the enemy would perceive that policy for what it was: "moral weakness and military folly."[72]

To avoid that pitfall, Haig called on the administration to combine its instruments of power—economic, diplomatic, and military—to pressure Cuba to modify its international behavior. He argued: "It was obvious that Cuba, an island nation of 11 million people lying 100 miles off the coast of the United States with a population of 230 million, simply could not stand up to the geostrategic assets available to the larger country."[73]

Although he subsequently claimed never to have contemplated direct military action against Cuba, Haig did advocate that the US apply its military strength "to the degree necessary." As he later stated his position: "I did envisage . . . an augmented U.S. military presence in the region. A carrier group, or two, maneuvering between Cuba and the Central American mainland would have been a useful reminder of the revival of keen U.S. interest in these waters and coasts and of our ability to blockade Cuba if that became necessary. Reinforcement of Army and Air Force units already in the region, and their advancement into a higher state of readiness, would have been desirable."[74] While Haig's solution appears counter to his second lesson, that contradiction disappears if his words are understood as a desire to follow a doctrine of flexible response or limited war.

"To the degree necessary" could be translated as "to the extent required to compel an adversary to do one's will." Haig was not opposed to limited war so long as the US forces involved possessed the means and were backed by the political determination required to destroy the enemy's will to resist. He was very critical of previous American presidents (such as Lyndon B. Johnson) who had applied US military strength only, in his view, to the extent that it did not detract from their political agenda.[75] Haig believed that the United States needed to be prepared to back its words with military power if necessary, even if that meant disrupting a president's domestic agenda by expending political capital on an action that did not have the wide support of the public or their leaders in Congress.

For Haig, it was not the strategies of limited war and flexible response that had precluded the United States from achieving decisive victory in Korea or Vietnam; instead, it was the ill-conceived notion that the nation could compel an adversary to respond by adopting progressively harsher methods. To start slow or show hesitation in Central America would lead to incrementalism and "Vietnamize" the situation. Such policies in the past had led the United States into a trap of committing ever more resources to a small objective, making it easier for an adversary to adapt to these small increases and thus compel another escalation.[76] Therefore Haig advised application of the military power and political will necessary to stop Cuba from continuing to export its communist revolution, but he did not believe that that objective would necessitate landing US forces in Central America.[77]

By the end of January 1981, Haig had instructed Robert McFarlane, counselor to the Department of State, to develop plans for rolling back Cuba's revolutionary activities in Central America and Africa. McFarlane convened a group of officials from the Pentagon, the CIA, and the State Department that unanimously decided that isolating Castro would require extensive military power and would jeopardize the nation's security interests in other regions. They recommended instead that the United States focus its efforts on isolating Nicaragua while working to improve the economic development of the surrounding countries.[78] Their presumption was that such efforts would moderate the revolutionary government in Nicaragua and prevent it from destabilizing other nations in the region.[79] Unhappy with the group's recommendations, Haig asked McFarlane to draw up plans for stationing American vessels to cut off supplies of oil going to Cuba or to intercept Soviet-bloc weapons leaving Cuba for Central America.[80]

Haig's plan to focus on Cuba reached the White House in May, but it was not new to some administration leaders. Secretary of Defense Weinberger recalled that, even before Reagan took office, Haig had made it "quite clear we would have to invade Cuba and, one way or another, put an end to the Castro regime."[81] He continued: "All agreed upon the nature of the Cuban regime and upon the basic risks it posed to us in view of Cuba's geographical position—its ability to interrupt our normal maritime trade, to interfere with any NATO reinforcement convoys that would have to pass close by Cuba, and to give the Soviets valuable intelligence capabilities."[82] Nevertheless, despite the threat to US interests, the more-aggressive military measures, including a blockade of Cuba or a quarantine of Central America, which Haig sought in order to make the administration's policy more credible, were never implemented.

The feasibility of Haig's plans rested on an assumption that the president could convince congressional leaders and the public to provide the support requisite for military success in a blockade or quarantine. Such operations would require the commitment of a significant number of air and naval resources over many months, and it might be very difficult to demonstrate tangible results.[83] Many senior leaders cautioned against the expenditure of the president's political capital for this, while others such as Weinberger believed that the domestic political realities (as described in chapter 2), would prevent him from gaining the will and means necessary to support such actions to a decisive end.[84]

Reagan's "troika"—Chief of Staff James Baker III, Counselor to the President Edwin Meese, and Deputy Chief of Staff Michael Deaver—decided early on that the problems with Cuba and Central America should not be elevated to the "presidential" level because of the political risk involved.[85] They wanted public focus to be on congressional passage of Reagan's economic program and worried that Haig's inflammatory rhetoric about the communist threat in Central America might disrupt this effort.[86] By public statements to the press in March 1981, the troika made clear to Haig that he should tone down his position.[87]

Additionally, Secretary of Defense Weinberger expressed concerns with Haig's plan and did not believe it heeded the lessons derived from Vietnam and other crises. Reagan's popularity aside, Weinberger was skeptical of any scheme that assumed that Congress and the American public would support the use of military power. He believed that assumption would hold only when military power was used to secure a vital national interest and did not think a blockade of Cuba met that requirement.[88] Weinberger later wrote: "I told the President that one of his predecessors had already tried that [invading Cuba] in a halfhearted way and that if we were to follow Al Haig's advice and if all went well, we *might* have a satisfactory result. But, I added, one of the principal lessons I had learned from the Vietnam experience was that we could not suddenly explode upon the American people a full-fledged war and expect to have their support. American public opinion would have to support such an action, and would therefore have to be convinced that our national interests required, indeed demanded, that we go to war."[89] Weinberger made a similar argument at his Senate confirmation hearing. When asked what lessons he had learned from the US experience in the Vietnam War, he replied: "It is not really possible, no matter what the skill, nor the size, nor the effectiveness of the American forces, to fight a war that does not have the understanding of the American people and the support of the American people. And I think another and perhaps subsidiary lesson from that would be that we cannot and should not enter a war that it is not vital for our national security to enter."[90]

When Weinberger arrived at the Pentagon, he found many who shared his sentiments. More importantly, he found that military leaders had internalized these lessons and developed strategies that would hopefully avoid having to relearn them. A 1977 Army War College study noted that "the continued presence of military missions [in Central America] is justified principally in terms of maintaining influence with a rather unique regional political elite who guide or control the destinies of many countries."[91] Therefore, military leaders favored covert operations run by the CIA and their associates to maintain influence in the region, support for security-assistance operations, and assistance for diplomacy with show-of-force operations.[92] In early 1980, Maj. Gen. Robert L. Schweitzer, director of strategy, plans, and policy in the Office of the Army Deputy Chief of Staff for Operations and Plans, visited Honduras and reportedly offered the ruling junta $5 million worth of equipment, $500,000 in training funds, and the lease of ten Huey helicopters at a nominal cost.[93] This was the kind of offer that US military leaders favored for Central American governments fighting communist insurgencies.[94]

In the end, the concerns of Weinberger and the troika carried the day. The administration determined that in Central America it would pursue the nation's interests and provide leadership on the international stage by providing the government of El Salvador with military assistance and by exerting pressure on Nicaragua rather than Cuba. Despite Haig's best efforts, Reagan had decided to cut the "umbilical cord" at the next level down from Cuba in regards to exporting communist revolution—Nicaragua.[95]

The Casey Doctrine

THE SPECIFICS OF THE administration's strategy were laid out in November 1981 in NSDD-17, which stated: "U.S. policy toward the Americas is characterized by strong support for those nations which embrace the principles of democracy and freedom for their people in a stable and peaceful environment. U.S. policy is therefore to assist in defeating the insurgency in El Salvador, and to oppose actions by Cuba, Nicaragua, or others to introduce into Central America heavy weapons, troops from outside the region, trained subversives, or arms and military supplies for insurgents."[96]

While NSDD-17 itself was classified "Top Secret," the majority of its points were immediately made public. The administration's appreciation for the importance of gaining and maintaining public and congressional support for its strategy is demonstrated in the first decision spawned by the directive: "Create a public information task force to inform the public and Congress of the critical situation in the area [Central America]."[97] Seemingly, the administration was taking specific measures to prepare the nation to take whatever steps might be called for in the Western Hemisphere.

The other decisions Reagan made by signing the directive were to provide economic support to the countries in the region, to increase military assistance to El Salvador and Honduras, to provide military training for indigenous units, and to encourage cooperative efforts to defeat the externally supported insurgency. Regarding Nicaragua, trade and credit were to be maintained with the Sandinistas so long as they permitted the private sector to operate. Nevertheless, support was to be lent to the democratic forces in that country. Two components to that support were to come from military show-of-force operations and covert operations conducted against the Sandinistas. American newspapers reported the show of force operations as major exercises, while initially only members of the congressional intelligence committees were aware of the covert operations.[98]

On 1 December, Reagan signed a presidential finding authorizing William Casey's CIA to oversee covert operations, executed by foreign fighters, against the Sandinistas.[99] Specifically, the agency was authorized to create a commando force of up to 500 Latin Americans to conduct operations in Nicaragua from bases in Honduras. They were to destroy power plants, bridges, and other critical infrastructure to disrupt the Nicaraguan economy and the flow of arms into El Salvador. The plan also called for the United States to provide financial and logistical support to Argentina's military, which was training 1,000 Nicaraguan exiles.[100] The operations were to accomplish three goals: interdict arms from Nicaragua to El Salvador, get Nicaragua to focus inward, and make the Sandinistas amenable to negotiations.[101]

In reality Reagan's finding largely ratified a process that the administration had begun nine months earlier.[102] On 9 March, the president had signed his first finding, which channeled $19.5 million to the CIA to expand a program begun by President Carter to support moderate opponents of the Sandinistas. The document also provided funds to stop the flow of weapons from Nicaragua to guerillas in El Salvador. In the end, the finding proved significant because it allowed CIA agents to lay the groundwork for covert operations against the Sandinistas, operations that were a key component, though not the sole component, of the administration's overall strategy for the region.[103]

Director of the Central Intelligence Agency William Casey and Chairman of the Joint Chiefs of Staff Gen. David Jones, confer at the administration's first National Security Council meeting. Courtesy Ronald Reagan Library.

When Reagan entered office, one of his top priorities was to develop a comprehensive strategy for dealing with communist activities in Central America. The administration considered Central America the nation's third border and felt that American freedom of action around the world depended in part on the region's stability. Officials were psychologically ready to use all the tools of statecraft, even military power, in order to restore democracy and freedom to Central America by minimizing communist influence and by providing assistance to nations such as El Salvador.

Nevertheless, the administration's freedom to use military power to carry out its policy objectives was constrained by the nation's domestic political reality. The negative response from allies, the public, and congressional leaders to proposals to send a small number of military trainers to El Salvador made it clear to administration officials, with the exception of Alexander Haig, that they would not have the support necessary to use force in a decisive manner against Cuba. Instead, a more-modest strategy would have to be adopted until the administration could garner more political support.

Seeking to gain such backing, the administration informed the public and Congress of what it saw as the critical situation in the region. Over time, officials hoped that these groups would become convinced that vital national interests were involved, thus warranting action to prevail decisively over Castro and his supporters. Until that support could be gained, however, the administration's strategy was to take as much action as domestic political realities allowed. Thus, it provided economic support for El Salvador and other nations and adopted a modest role for military power. In addition to providing military assistance and training to indigenous forces in Central America, the administration planned to pressure the Sandinista government by conducting show-of-force operations and lending support to proxy fighters. These measures were possible because the show-of-force operations would not trigger the War Powers Resolution, and the covert operations would be supported with funds appropriated by members of the congressional intelligence committees, who had received the presidential finding.

Existing scholarship characterizes Reagan's decision to adopt a covert strategy in Central America as one largely forced upon the administration because more-aggressive action against Cuba was politically unavailable. Robert Kagan, for example, quotes Haig on the administration's embrace of covert operations as a "decision almost by default."[104] Roy Gutman, who studied the evolution of the policy, found neither substantial support for covert operations nor a single triggering event or a single point of decision.[105] Dario Moreno has explained that senior administration leaders accepted the proxy-force plan because it accounted for the political realities they faced.[106]

A different argument can be made that the Reagan administration worked very hard to adopt strategies that acknowledged those constraints while at the same time seeking to inform the public and congressional leaders of the need to take more-decisive action. These were consciously crafted, and the administration's decision to use proxy forces was not taken by default.[107] With this strategy in Central America, officials sought to retain options for more-assertive action in the future should political opposition subside. Their understanding of the relationship between national political objectives, the use of American military power, and the political realities of the time would evolve yet again as senior leaders sought to devise a viable policy for a second region, the Middle East.

4

❧

THE PENTAGON DOCTRINE

Using American Military Power
Decisively in Lebanon

E VEN AS THE REAGAN administration wrestled with policy
for Central America, it also faced decisions for a different region halfway around the world—the Middle East. In keeping
with his promise to provide leadership on the international stage, in June
1982, President Reagan decided to get involved in the war being fought
in the small nation of Lebanon. Israeli, Syrian, and Palestinian forces, as
well as separate factional militias, were fighting on Lebanese soil. Reagan
adopted two policy goals for Lebanon: withdrawal of all foreign forces
and establishment of a stable central government. To ensure these ends,
he also adopted a third policy objective: a secure border for Israel.

To develop and execute a strategy for achieving those ambitious
political objectives, senior administration officials needed to account
for the relationship between national political objectives, the use of
military power, and political realities both at home and abroad. Secretary of Defense Weinberger and Gen. John W. Vessey, chairman of the
Joint Chiefs of Staff, clashed with recently appointed Secretary of State
George Shultz and Reagan's special envoy to the Middle East, Philip
Habib, over how US forces ought to be used in Lebanon.

To understand the events leading up to the call for US military assistance and the subsequent reaction from Congress, the American public, and the Pentagon, one must analyze the historical context of US policy toward the Middle East in the 1970s and the policy the Reagan administration inherited. The commitment of forces in Lebanon illustrates conditions under which military power might be deployed decisively, conditions later encapsulated in the Weinberger Doctrine by the end of the administration's first term.

Background on the Middle East

ON 16 JANUARY 1979, the shah of Iran, Mohammad Reza Pahlavi, abdicated his authority to the revolutionary forces gripping his nation and departed for the United States.[1] Two weeks later, on 1 February, Ayatollah Ruhollah Khomeini, exiled since October 1964, returned to Iran and by year's end had used the shah's absence (for medical treatment in the United States) and the seizure of American hostages as an opportunity to take power and impose a theocratic regime.

The shah's fall undermined the policy that had undergirded US strategy in the Middle East since the early 1970s. This "twin pillar" policy, first adopted by President Nixon, made provisions for the supply of military arms to Iran and Saudi Arabia. In return the two nations were to serve as pillars of strength and stability in the Persian Gulf region, though neither the support nor the expectations for each pillar was the same.[2] While Iran was guaranteed access to some of the most sophisticated non-nuclear technology in the US military arsenal, American support for the Saudis was much more modest.[3] Additionally, Iran was expected to provide proxy resistance to the Soviets and other sources of regional instability, whereas the Saudis were expected to help keep oil prices low and promote moderation in the Arab-Israeli dispute.[4]

The impetus for the twin-pillar approach can be traced back to two sources: the Arab-Israeli War of 1967 and the British withdrawal from east of the Suez in 1971. During the 1967 conflict (known as the

Six Day War), the Soviets broke relations with the Israelis and began
supporting the Palestinian Liberation Organization (PLO). In turn, the
United States replaced France as Israel's largest benefactor. The decision by the superpowers to pair off on opposing sides to gain leverage
in the Middle East transformed the Arab-Israeli dispute from a regional
issue into a global affair.[5]

Initially, the United States relied heavily on the British to provide
a foothold for Western interests in the region.[6] But on 16 January 1968,
known as "Black Tuesday," Prime Minister Harold Wilson announced
that Britain would relinquish its remaining holdings east of the Suez
Canal by 1971. On 1 December 1971, Great Britain completed a withdrawal from the region it had begun in the late 1940s, with a departure
from Greece, Turkey, India, and Palestine, followed by the Suez Canal
in 1956. The United States responded to each step with policies intended to ensure that the vacuum left by the British was not filled by
the Soviets. President Truman promised economic and military aid to
Greece and Turkey, while President Eisenhower offered further military assistance to keep nations out of the Soviet sphere of influence.[7]

Like his predecessors, Nixon needed to thwart the Soviets from filling the vacuum left by "Black Tuesday." But his administration believed
that for a new policy to be effective, it had to account for two sets of
constraints: those generated by domestic political realities largely tied
to the Vietnam War and those generated by foreign political realities
largely shaped by radicalism, colonialism, and the Arab-Israeli conflict.
To accommodate these, Nixon relied upon surrogates, such as Iran and
Saudi Arabia, as a way to look after US interests in the region.

While the War Powers Resolution had not yet been enacted, many
of the same domestic political calculations that drove the Reagan administration to rely upon proxy forces in Central America drove Nixon's
officials to rely upon surrogates in the Middle East. Specifically, the
experience of Vietnam eliminated any chance that Congress or the
American people would tolerate replacement of departing British forces
in the Middle East with US troops. This was not the first time Nixon
faced the challenge of meeting American strategic interests while heed-

ing domestic political constraints. In July 1969, while the nation was still engaged in Vietnam, he announced what came to be called the Guam Doctrine, later known as the Nixon Doctrine. In recognition of the American experiences in the Korean and Vietnam Wars, the Nixon Doctrine promised that the United States would continue to keep its treaty commitments but called on other nations to take responsibility for their own security. Many authors have described the twin-pillar policy as the Nixon Doctrine applied to the Middle East.[8] But there was a key difference between the two, as the twin-pillar approach made an additional demand of its recipients: they were expected to take overt action to help protect American interests.[9]

The Nixon administration's second set of constraints was radicalism in the region, the legacy of colonialism, and the Arab-Israeli conflict. American strategic planners considered subversion and political instability brought on by Arab radicalism one of the most dangerous threats to Saudi Arabia and Iran. They did not want to inflame that menace by building bases in the region, which would serve as a reminder of the colonial past and provide opportunities for pro-Soviet and other radical groups to gain influence. Instead, US interests would be better served by relying upon regional actors to pursue the desired ends.[10] Additionally, Nixon and National Security Advisor Henry Kissinger believed that until the Arab-Israeli conflict could be resolved, using Iran and Saudi Arabia as surrogates was one of the few ways for the United States to improve its position in the Arab world.[11]

The first challenge to the Nixon Doctrine came in 1973, when Middle Eastern nations led by Saudi Arabia declared an oil embargo on the United States. On 6 October, Egypt had launched a surprise attack against Israel, initiating the Yom Kippur War, and prompting the United States and the Soviet Union to respond with massive arms airlifts to their respective clients. The Arabs, however, did not respond in their usual, uncoordinated way. The oil-producing nations of Saudi Arabia, Kuwait, Abu Dhabi, Bahrain, Qatar, Iraq, Syria, Egypt, Algeria, and Libya collectively agreed to implement an oil embargo on the West. Initially they cut production by 5 percent, but when their demands for a full Israeli withdrawal from Arab territories occupied since 1967 were not met, a 25-percent cut in production followed, and eventually all shipments of oil to the United States and Israel stopped.

Though Saudi participation in the embargo could have undermined the twin-policy pillar, it had the opposite effect. Official support for the Saudis increased significantly throughout the remainder of the 1970s, as each administration embraced two premises: first, the Saudis were critical to gaining Arab support for the Arab-Israeli peace process and for securing reasonable oil prices; second, their assistance could be gained through enticements of additional weaponry. So while the United States issued warnings and developed contingency plans for a intervention to occupy Saudi oil fields if necessary, plans also were formulated for Saudi investments in US weapons as well as airfield and port improvements.[12] Despite the oil embargo, American policy in the region continued to rest upon a Saudi pillar.

Instead it was Iran, the pillar deemed most critical to US strategy in the Middle East due to its military capability, that collapsed first. When the Carter administration entered office in January 1977, it had taken up the "twin pillar" policy despite the fact that Carter had campaigned on limiting arms sales abroad and despite the signs that the shah's control over Iran was becoming tenuous.[13] Regardless of whether Carter could have or should have done more, the shah's departure from Iran signaled the end of the American approach of reliance upon a surrogate to provide for American security interests in the Middle East.

The Carter administration backed into the adoption of a new policy. Two years earlier Carter had approved the concept for a rapid-deployment force (RDF) in a presidential directive (PD-18) that called for "a deployment force of light divisions with strategic mobility independent of overseas bases and logistical support, which includes moderate naval and tactical air forces, and limited land combat forces."[14] These units were to be capable of taking action against local or Soviet militaries in the Middle East, the Persian Gulf, or Korea.[15]

Yet until the shah departed Iran, very little progress was made in implementing the concept due to resistance from both the State Department and the Department of Defense.[16] On the one hand, State fought the concept on the grounds that an increased US military presence would lead to increased anti-American sentiment and pose more challenges for regimes that were perceived to be aligned with Washington. On the other hand, Defense opposed the concept on the grounds that the RDF would take forces away from planned European contingencies. The Pentagon also believed the RDF might be asked to carry out missions the military wished to avoid, such as helping secure the internal stability of a Middle Eastern nation.[17] The shah's departure from Iran cut through such misgivings and ended the departments' resistance. The fact that the United States had lain "strategically naked beneath the thin blanket of Iranian security" for so long was exposed for the world to see.[18]

Events in Iran were followed by the Soviet invasion of Afghanistan in December 1979. One historian has noted that "the obvious weakening of the US position in the region . . . may have influenced the decision of the Soviets to move in."[19] The invasion signaled that Russian influence in the Middle East, which had been minimal since the 1973 war, again would need to be taken into account.[20]

The Carter administration, working for months to correct the problems exposed by the shah's overthrow, capitalized upon the renewed threat from the Soviets to resolve the political challenge of publicizing the RDF concept.[21] In his State of the Union address delivered on 23 January 1980, Carter announced: "Let our position be absolutely clear: An attempt by any outside force to gain control of the Persian Gulf region will be regarded as an assault on the vital interests of the United States of America, and such an assault will be repelled by any means necessary, including military force."[22] Five weeks later, on 1 March 1980, the Rapid Deployment Joint Task Force was activated at MacDill Air Force Base in Tampa, Florida. It consisted of 261 personnel from all three services charged with responding to any contingency that threatened US vital interests.[23] These actions signaled that Carter was no longer going to depend upon surrogates to defend the nation's interests in the Middle East. When the Reagan administration came into office in January 1981, it embraced this "Carter Doctrine" and the RDF concept.

Five days into his job, though, Defense Secretary Weinberger received a memorandum from a subordinate that identified thirteen different issues that needed to be addressed by the administration in order to build a viable response for the Persian Gulf region.[24] Neither the nation's ability nor its true willingness to deploy military force to the Middle East would be tested until 2 July 1982. On that day, Lebanon's president, Bashir Gemayel, requested that an international peacekeeping force, to include US troops, be dispatched to his nation.[25]

The Call for American Military Power

THE ROOTS OF GEMAYEL'S request can be traced back to the Arab-Israeli war of 1948–49, when tens of thousands of Palestinians entered Lebanon after fleeing northern Palestine.[26] Their numbers grew during the Six Day War, when many more left their homes in the West Bank and Gaza Strip. Finally, the last large influx occurred in 1971, when 150,000 Palestinians were expelled from Jordan.[27] The PLO established its headquarters in Beirut, organized the refugees living in the camps, and launched raids from southern Lebanon against Israel and against Israeli targets outside of the Middle East.

The Lebanese government's weakness precluded it from stopping the Palestinians from forming a veritable state within its borders. The first challenge to Lebanese sovereignty came in December 1968, when the Israelis conducted a raid on the Beirut International Airport in retaliation for a Palestinian attack on an Israeli plane in Greece. The second followed in November 1969, when the government signed the Cairo Agreement with the PLO. Intended to maintain Lebanese sovereignty while providing the PLO with some autonomy, the agreement served to legitimize PLO freedom of action and ultimately allowed the Palestinians to gain control over large portions of southern Lebanon by the mid-1970s.

The third challenge came in May 1976, not from the Israelis or Palestinians, but from the Syrians, who entered Lebanon to restore order and stop the civil war that had been under way there since April 1975. They were by and large successful, winning the consent of the Lebanese government as well as the Arab League to remain in the country as part of an Arab peacekeeping force.[28] In July 1977, Syria, the Lebanese government, and the PLO signed the Chtaura Agreement, under which the PLO would pull back from the border with Israel and allow units from the reconstituted Lebanese army to move in to restore the government's authority over the border region. Days before the handover was to occur, the plan was thwarted when a Christian militia group, supported by Israel, attacked the PLO, and the renewed fighting prevented the Lebanese army from occupying positions in the south.[29]

In 1977, Israelis voted into power the right-wing Likud coalition, under the leadership of Menachem Begin. During the election campaign, Begin had promised to take a tougher stand against the PLO in Lebanon. Following through on that pledge in March 1978, the Begin government deployed 25,000 soldiers across the border to establish a security zone six miles deep into Lebanon. The United Nations immediately passed resolutions calling for an Israeli withdrawal and for the UN Interim Force in Lebanon (UNIFIL) to help the government reestablish control of the southern border. But the Lebanese were again prevented from restoring complete control when the Israelis turned over the final tracts of land to the same Christian militia group that had prevented the national army from occupying positions a year earlier.[30]

In 1981 the Israelis aided Christian militiamen, engaged in fighting the Syrians in northern Lebanon, by downing two Syrian helicopters. That June they also conducted air strikes on PLO positions in Lebanon, one of which hit the group's headquarters in downtown Beirut. Syria responded by emplacing ground-to-air missiles in Lebanon, while the PLO stepped up attacks into northern Israel. The United States sent retired Undersecretary of State Philip C. Habib to serve as a special negotiator to work on both issues. Habib could not convince the Syrians to remove their missiles, but he successfully negotiated a ceasefire between the Israelis and the PLO on 24 July 1981.

The ceasefire was tenuous at best, and the Israelis looked for a prov-

ocation to justify an attack against the PLO.[31] On 3 June 1982, that prov-
ocation came when a group of Palestinians, who were not organization
members, attempted to assassinate Israel's ambassador to Great Britain.
The Israelis charged the PLO with breaking the ceasefire agreement
and retaliated by bombing targets in Lebanon, which in turn prompted
PLO bombings of northern Israel.[32] Both parties were exhorted by the
United States and others to refrain from violence, but to no avail as the
Israelis invaded Lebanon on the sixth.[33]

The Israeli cabinet issued a statement indicating that the purpose of
the incursion, named "Peace for Galilee," was to "place all civilian population of the Galilee beyond the range of the terrorist fire from Lebanon."[34] To that end, they announced plans to clear a forty-kilometer
zone but not to engage Syrian forces. By 9 June, however, the Israelis
had pressed well beyond this region, attacked Syrian SAM (surface-to-
air missile) batteries, and shot down some twenty Syrian MiGs with no
losses.[35] Two days later the Israelis were within sight of Beirut. They
proceeded to lay siege to PLO forces trapped inside the city and to Syrian forces cut off outside, announcing their goals:

(1) All foreign armies (including the PLO) withdraw from
Lebanon.
(2) A new Lebanese Government be formed.
(3) The new government sign a peace treaty with Israel.[36]

Ambassador Habib, who was on his way to the Middle East when
the fighting began, arrived in Jerusalem for talks on 7 June. On the
twenty-second, Secretary Weinberger advised President Reagan: "Thirteen days ago, Israel invaded Lebanon to push the PLO and its artillery
back 40 kilometers. Israel's army has now advanced 80 kilometers to
encircle the PLO in Beirut. The low-key U.S. reaction has upset our
Arab friends, who are questioning our motives. Israel once again has
demonstrated its overwhelming military superiority and, for the time
being, has positively secured its only porous border. The effect upon our
security interests is not as positive. Turbulence, hatred and confusion

among 120 million Arabs do not enhance stability in the vital Gulf region or the influence of the West."[37] Weinberger pushed for a US policy that would preserve American standing in the Arab world.

To that end, he recommended that the president direct Habib to negotiate with the Palestinians to lay down their arms and withdraw their fighters from Lebanon. Weinberger emphasized that "a face-saving, *political* role for the PLO . . . be salvaged [his emphasis]." He also recommended that America "reiterate our long-time offer to recognize the PLO, deal with it and win a place at the peace table for it, *if* it unequivocally endorses Resolution 242, and commits itself to a negotiated peace with Israel working with the Camp David agreements [his emphasis]."[38] He further noted: "This position would give us enormous leverage with the Gulf States where we have vital interests that are now in peril as a result of our reactive support of Israel's use of force." Weinberger then concluded: "Under these circumstances, the international force for Southern Lebanon might include Egyptian, Saudi and Jordanian forces as well as our own, the French and others. We must carefully link our participation in such a force to broader agreements about the peace process and the Government of Lebanon. . . . In the absence of an agreement, we must not deploy U.S. troops in a continuing hostile situation."[39] The international force for southern Lebanon, to which the secretary referred, was a force that had not yet been assembled. Nevertheless, everyone could agree that the Israelis would not leave Lebanon until they received some type of security guarantee for their northern border. Thus, it would be necessary to have some force interposed between the Israelis and their enemies.

One option was to expand the role of the UNIFIL already located in southern Lebanon, but the idea that the administration favored most was to construct a separate multinational force (MNF). In his memoir, Shultz summarized some of the reasons why the administration believed this was justified: "A multinational force separate from the United Nations could be formed more quickly and would be composed of forces from major countries whose involvement the ever-bargaining Lebanese regarded as advantageous." Additionally, he noted that the

Israelis "would have nothing to do with a UN role in any form for Beirut, a view traced back to 1967, when the United Nations pulled its peacekeeping troops out of the Sinai at Gamal Abdel Nasser's demand, a step toward the war that followed."[40] Another reason why the administration did not favor a UN role was that it left open the potential for the Soviet Union to demand participation for its forces.[41]

The inclusion of US troops in the MNF, if and when it was formed, was an issue that would challenge administration leaders. Secretary Weinberger and General Vessey did not think that it was a good idea to include US soldiers, arguing that the mission might trap the United States in a long-term peacekeeping mission in which its troops might have to kill Israelis, Arabs, or civilians.[42] This was particularly worrisome to leaders in the Pentagon because they were charged with providing credibility to the RDF concept and needed access to facilities and logistical support in the Persian Gulf states to do so. As Weinberger told reporters, the United States needed a "number of friends" in the Middle East, and US participation in a peacekeeping force that excluded the Palestinians from southern Lebanon would not serve that end.[43] Indeed, US military involvement had the potential to present "immense diplomatic and political problems" with the Arab nations.[44] Weinberger wanted the administration to avoid actions that might anger important states such as Saudi Arabia.[45]

Nevertheless, Weinberger's June memorandum demonstrated that leaders in the Department of Defense could conceive of deploying soldiers as part of the MNF so long as that force was tied to securing a larger peace plan for the region. Such a policy would improve American relations with the Arab states, which in turn would help with relations with Persian Gulf states in which Pentagon leaders wanted to secure basing rights.

Later, Secretary of State Shultz would charge Pentagon leaders with being too hesitant in using military power, which left him and other State Department officials to conduct diplomacy without the advantage of being backed by credible force. But, in fact, Pentagon leaders were supportive of using the military, such as in the case of providing security to PLO fighters, when that power could be used to secure an important political objective. Hesitancy on the part of the Pentagon only came in the absence of a plan that related military power to political objectives to serve the nation's vital interests in the region.

On 30 June 1982, the administration announced the US objectives for Lebanon: withdrawal of all foreign forces, a stable central government, and a secure border for Israel.[46] Throughout the remainder of June and into July, Ambassador Habib worked to achieve a new cease-fire that would help set the stage for America to exert its leadership in the region and work toward meeting those objectives. Early on 2 July, Habib returned to the State Department to report significant progress: Yasser Arafat, chairman of the PLO, had agreed to depart Lebanon with his fighters so long as the Palestinian refugees left behind would be protected.

The Lebanese government recognized that assistance from an international force was necessary to give such a guarantee. Thus, officials sent word back through Habib to Reagan that they would request that an international force, to include the United States, be sent to Lebanon.[47] Habib gave his report to Walter Stoessel, deputy secretary of state, and Lawrence Eagleburger, undersecretary of state for political affairs, because Haig, having just recently resigned, was staying at an isolated resort in West Virginia in order to avoid the media.[48] Nevertheless, Haig was immediately notified about Habib's breakthrough as the president wanted him to continue to manage the Lebanon crisis until his replacement, George Shultz, could be confirmed. *The New York Times* reported that later that evening, Reagan, Haig, Shultz, and other key leaders in secrecy made the decision to allow US troops to participate in an international force for Beirut.[49] While Weinberger and Vessey had concerns about the mission, they supported it.

The force was directed "to assist Lebanese armed forces in the orderly and safe departure from Beirut of armed personnel, and to assist in the transition of authority to the Lebanese government in Beirut."[50] Although Reagan's announcement was only an agreement in "principle," the die was cast. The administration's intention to commit US military power was met with a range of reactions from leaders in Congress, the American people, and Pentagon officials.

Domestic Political Reality

AT THE BEGINNING of July, when the deployment of American troops to Lebanon was still conjecture, congressional reaction was mixed. Leaders of both parties expressed "doubts" and "deep concern" over the administration's plan.[51] For example, Senate Majority Leader Howard H. Baker Jr. (R-Tenn.) argued: "It is not wise to introduce American fighting men in the Lebanese conflict." Likewise, Rep. Clement J. Zablocki (D-Wisc.), chairman of the House Foreign Affairs Committee, had "serious reservations regarding the proposal."[52] But two Democratic leaders from key House subcommittees lent their support to the administration's plan.[53]

One fact-finding trip to Beirut by two senators from the Foreign Relations Committee captured the feelings of congressional leaders about the issue. Sen. Christopher J. Dodd (D-Conn.) told reporters that before the trip, he favored using marines as part of an international force, but he had changed his mind when he came to realize how many factions did not want peace and would view the marines as opportune targets. In contrast, his traveling companion, Carl Levin (D-Mich.), stated that he was still in favor of the deployment but added several caveats. He said those troops should be invited by all parties, deploy as part of a multinational force, be charged only with assuring the safe exit of the PLO fighters, and remain for only a limited time. Levin argued that further expansion of the conflict posed a greater risk to US interests than a deployment of American forces.[54]

Unlike the news reports in 1981, when the administration planned to send a small number of military advisors to El Salvador, coverage of this proposal avoided the words "quagmire" or "another Vietnam."[55] Additionally, there were no protest marches, large volumes of mail to the White House and Congress, or pressure on congressional leaders to

President Reagan meets with the chairman of the Senate Foreign Relations Committee, Republican Charles Percy, and the chairman of the House Foreign Affairs Committee, Democrat Clement Zablocki. Courtesy Ronald Reagan Library.

block the administration's plans. Congress, however, did ask Reagan to abide by the War Powers Resolution.

Though the president promised he would, he did not specify under which provision of the law he would report.[56] Section 4 (a) (1) required the president to report to Congress when US forces were introduced "into hostilities or into situations where imminent involvement in hostilities is clearly indicated by the circumstances." If the president reported under that section, he would be required to withdraw the forces within sixty days unless Congress declared war or extended the time, or he could demonstrate that an "unavoidable military necessity" demanded an extension of an additional thirty days. Section 4 (a) (2) simply required that the president report to Congress when American

forces were introduced "into territory, airspace or waters of a foreign nation, while equipped for combat."[57] If Reagan chose to report under that
provision, he could dispatch troops to Lebanon without a time limit.

Congressional leaders wanted Reagan to report under the stricter
section so that they would be involved in deciding when US forces
would come home. Nonetheless, many privately admitted that the mission was unlikely to extend beyond sixty days unless the administration
decided to move beyond providing a screen for the PLO. To assuage
the concerns of troubled critics such as Senate Majority Leader Baker,
administration officials repeatedly stressed that the mission would not
extend beyond thirty days.[58]

Additionally, days before making the final decision to deploy eight
hundred US Marines to Lebanon, recently confirmed Secretary of State
Shultz held sessions with congressional leaders over the better part of
three days to get their views on the Palestinian issue. One participant
was reported as saying: "It was a classic case of what consultations should
really be about. . . . Shultz showed he had an understanding of the need
to stroke members of Congress and make them feel as if they are really
part of the process, even if in the end he doesn't use their ideas at all."
Another quipped, "I don't know whether to admire him for soliciting
our advice, which no Secretary has done before, or be nervous if he
really is looking to us for creative thoughts."[59] Shultz's efforts were apparently appreciated and may have been one reason why congressional
leaders allowed Reagan a measure of latitude in the deployment.[60]

Reported in *The Washington Post* on 19 July, a Harris poll found
that 54 percent of Americans disapproved of the administration's plan to
deploy marines to Lebanon as part of the MNF.[61] Surprisingly, 40 percent said that dispatching US forces was a good decision. This considerable support from the public, which flew in the face of the Vietnam
syndrome, may have several explanations.

In the early 1980s, three out of four Americans held a positive
image of Israel. Because of shared values and traditions and the large
American-Jewish population, over the years a special relationship had
formed between the two countries. While most polls showed that most

were not interested in foreign affairs, the issue that consistently attracted the attention of American citizens was Israel and the Arab-Israeli conflict. This interest is reflected in media coverage throughout the 1960s and into the early 1980s, in which Israel received almost as much attention in the media as any domestic issue.[62] In October 1980, 86 percent of Americans questioned supported a statement describing Israel as "a small, courageous, democratic nation which is trying to preserve its independence."[63] This pro-Israeli sentiment may have helped mute some of the concerns the public had about sending troops as peacekeepers.

A majority of Americans believed that the nation had a vital interest in Israel's security. In a poll conducted in late 1981, Americans were asked whether they felt the United States did or did not have a vital interest in any of twenty-four countries. At 81 percent, Israel ranked as the second-most-important nation in terms of "American vital interest there," trailing only Saudi Arabia at 84 percent.[64] The Arab nations had already demonstrated their ability to disrupt Western economies by imposing an oil embargo, and if matters in the Middle East were allowed to escalate further, America might again be punished for the aggressive actions of its ally Israel in Lebanon.[65] The premise underlying the Carter Doctrine was that military forces might have to protect US vital interests in the region. Deploying marines to "rescue" the PLO from the Israelis seemed a relatively straightforward way to demonstrate the credibility of the nation's doctrine and to gain favor with Arab states.[66]

Many Americans may have been influenced by graphic imagery on television and in newspapers of innocent civilians killed or maimed in Beirut and Israel. Shultz wrote in his memoir, "[t]he symbol of this war has become the baby with its arms blown off," referring to a picture in *The Washington Post* of a nurse feeding a seven-month-old baby who had lost both arms and was severely burned when an Israeli jet accidentally hit a residential area in East Beirut.[67] Another graphic picture showed a young child bent down at a dripping faucet with the caption: "A Lebanese child scrounges for a few drops of water in West Beirut after Israeli forces cut off water and power."[68]

Lastly, American newspapers throughout the month of July portrayed intervention as a last resort: broken ceasefires that halted or slowed Ambassador Habib's diplomatic efforts; concerns of epidemics due to the Israeli siege and shortages of basic services in the city; Israeli intransigence against UN resolutions demanding the provision of electricity, food, and medical care; and the growing divide between the Reagan and Begin administrations over the tactics to expel the PLO from Beirut. By the end of the month, many Americans may well have felt the same way as the commander in chief. Reagan was asked by a reporter: "Are you losing patience? Are you frustrated?" The president answered, "I lost patience a long time ago."[69] And the minutes from a NSC meeting held on 4 August 1982 noted: "The President closed meeting at 10:02 by stating that he was extremely tired of a war whose symbol had become a burn baby with no arms."[70] Thus, it is not surprising that, like their congressional leaders, most Americans remained quiet when the administration made its decision to deploy marines to Beirut.[71]

Regarding Central America, Caspar Weinberger resisted taking stern measures against Cuba because he did not believe the American people and their congressional leaders would support such action. He argued that Vietnam had demonstrated that Americans and their congressional leaders were unlikely to respond positively to using military power unless US vital interests were at stake. The response of congressional leaders and the public to the proposal to send military forces to Lebanon suggested acceptance, if not positive endorsement, with the caveats described by Senator Levin: do it quickly and limit the mission to only getting the PLO out. The senator's caveats of swift, decisive action and avoidance of long-term commitments echoed those of the mass public.

The Pentagon Doctrine

BOTH SECRETARY WEINBERGER and General Vessey supported the administration's plans because assisting the departure of the PLO was an explicit military objective aimed at securing an important political objective. The United States could point to this action as a gesture of goodwill toward the Palestinians in particular and the Arab world in general, thus serving the nation's vital strategic interests in the Persian Gulf region.[72] The mission was supported by the American public and their congressional leaders, and a decisive result could be achieved in a very short period of time and without impinging upon resources needed for other global challenges.

Nevertheless, General Vessey expressed his concern regarding the second portion of the administration's announced intent, which called for assistance in the transition of authority to the Lebanese government.[73] A critical component in that transition would be rebuilding the Lebanese Armed Forces (LAF) so that they could support the government. Vessey believed that the political situation there was more likely to constrain the capability of the LAF to reassert Lebanese authority than any shortage in equipment, arms, or training.[74]

In a memorandum written to Weinberger in late July, Vessey explained that while the Joint Chiefs of Staff agreed that a strong Lebanese army was essential to ensuring the sovereignty of the Lebanese government, they also believed "that any United States action to assist in the strengthening of the LAF must be taken only after careful consideration of pertinent political and military factors bearing on the situation." The general went on to describe the constraining political situation: "The PLO and Syrian elements remaining in Lebanon have not yet agreed to accept Lebanese government authority in areas still under their control. Perhaps most significantly, the LAF itself is still beset with religious factionalism which makes their utility for governmental objectives doubtful in the absence of a political consensus." Thus, Vessey cautioned against sending a large influx of arms and equipment into Lebanon until "suitable political conditions can be achieved."[75] His concern also applied to the notion of keeping American soldiers deployed in Lebanon after the PLO had departed. The small, lightly armed MNF, which the administration had agreed to deploy, was not disposed to exert pressure on any of the parties to reach a political settlement. Vessey, who was supported by Weinberger, wanted the administration to make it very clear to all parties involved that US forces would redeploy as soon as the PLO fighters had left.

The influence of Weinberger and Vessey is manifest in the announcement that explicit conditions would need to be met before the administration would officially consider dispatching troops to Lebanon. Officials wanted a formal request from Lebanon and demanded assurances from the involved parties that the peacekeeping forces would be accepted and protected. Another country needed to participate along with the United States, for the role of US troops would be limited by geography and time.[76] Each condition was meant to gain support for the mission both domestically and internationally.

Weinberger took every opportunity to emphasize these points when talking to reporters and during television interviews.[77] While on *Meet the Press*, he stressed that American forces would be in Lebanon only for the period of time it took to evacuate the PLO forces, which he predicted could be done in a matter of days. With regards to assistance in the transition of authority in Beirut, Weinberger said that US forces would not remain in country waiting for the full restoration of the Lebanese government's authority because that would lead to a "totally open-ended, indefinite commitment." The secretary noted, "our acceptance of the use of U.S. troops is for the very limited purpose of getting the PLO out."[78]

At that time there was no official comment from the White House regarding the Weinberger interpretation of the mission. After a month, on 20 August, President Reagan formally announced that eight hundred marines would deploy to Lebanon in accordance with Weinberger's interpretation of their mission: "Our purpose will be to assist the Lebanese Armed Forces in carrying out their responsibility for ensuring the departure of PLO leaders, officers, and combatants in Beirut, from Lebanese territory under safe and orderly conditions. The presence of U.S. forces also will facilitate the restoration of the sovereignty and authority of the Lebanese Government over the Beirut area. In no case will our troops stay longer than 30 days."[79] Clearly, the Pentagon had helped shape the president's orders to the marines in the MNF. His statement emphasized the mission of helping evacuate the PLO members. The second portion of the administration's previously announced intent, restoring the sovereignty and authority of the Lebanese government over the Beirut area, was limited in scope, to be accomplished by the mere "presence" of US forces (both on land and offshore).

In deciding to send the military into the Middle East, the administration did not face the same domestic political constraints when it considered using military power to blockade Cuba or quarantine Central America. Congress and the American people were generally supportive of the announced policy, stemming from a perception that if the matter was allowed to get further out of hand, far greater risk to US vital interests might result. The conditions placed on deployment were designed to help the administration account for the two constraining factors: domestic political realities driven by the American experience in Vietnam and foreign political realities driven by radicalism, colonialism, and the Arab-Israeli conflict.

The administration took specific actions in order to mitigate each of those constraints. First, it submitted a report consistent with the War Powers Resolution and consulted with Congress regarding strategy in the region. Second, it did not take action until it had received a formal request from the Lebanese government and ensured that another nation (in this case, France) would be involved in the operation. Lastly, the administration planned to keep its involvement limited to the clear objective of removing the PLO within a thirty-day time span.

A Decisive Use of American Military Power

ON 18 AUGUST 1982, the Lebanese government presented to the American ambassador its formal request for a MNF. Two days later the United States responded favorably.[80] On the twenty-fourth, President Reagan reported to Congress "consistent with the War Powers Resolution" on the deployment and mission of the marines.[81] Since his report did not specify that he was under Section 4 (a) (1), no time limit was placed on the deployment other than the administration's self-imposed public promise to redeploy after thirty days.[82]

On 21 August, the French contingent of the MNF began arriving in Lebanon, joined four days later by the 32nd U.S. Marine Amphibious Unit. According to their mission statement, the marines were to "[s]upport Ambassador Habib and the MNF committee in their efforts to have PLO members evacuated from the Beirut area; occupy and secure the port of Beirut in conjunction with the Lebanese Armed Forces; maintain close and continuous contact with other MNF members; and be prepared to withdraw on order."[83] Regarding the evacuation, the chief Department of Defense spokesman said the US role was expected to be "totally pacific." He stated that "the presence of the Americans . . . will be seen as a guarantor and as a safety mechanism that will make the Palestinians feel comfortable in a withdrawal situation."[84]

The mission statement did not direct the force to help restore the sovereignty and authority of the Lebanese government over Beirut. Nonetheless, that aspect of the administration's intent had not been forgotten by members of the media or by Habib. In regards to this aim, the Defense Department spokesman said: "There won't be anything, as far as I understand it, specific done to help restore Lebanese authority except the very key first step, which is to remove the PLO fighters from the Lebanese capital. That in itself will contribute to the restoration of the authority of the Lebanese Government."[85] One reporter summarized the entire press conference by asking: "Have I got this right? Eight hundred marines wearing camouflage field uniforms and carrying M-16s are going to get on boats and helicopters and go into the port area of Beirut and set up tents. That is all you've told us they are going to do in the course of 30 days, isn't it? Have you told us a single thing that they are going to do while they're there?" The spokesman answered: "You are quite correct. I have not told you a single thing that they are going to do while they are there because it is, at this stage of the game, quite simply impossible to know in advance precisely what it is going to be."[86]

On the ground in Lebanon, Habib did have plans for how to use the marines to help the Lebanese restore their authority. Specifically, he wanted them to take up the positions vacated by Palestinian forces under Syrian command along the "Green Line," which divided Christian East Beirut from Muslim West Beirut. The Palestinians wanted to turn their positions over to the Americans because they believed that the Lebanese army was too weak to stand up to the Christian militias that might attack the civilians they left behind. As a significant negotiating point, Habib had "given assurances for the safety of the camps after the PLO fighters departed" and wanted the American forces to enforce that pledge.[87]

Weinberger, though, refused to allow the marines to leave the port compound. Shultz went to Reagan on the matter, but the president, according to Shultz, "did not want to intervene with his secretary of defense on matters of tactical deployment of troops." Shultz also related that "Habib sent a blistering cable to Weinberger arguing for an active marine role along the Green Line. Cap would not hear of it."[88] Weinberger noted in his memoir that the MNF had been "sized and equipped" for a "single mission."[89] Clearly, he saw a relationship between the first and second aspects of the mission as described by his department's spokesman. Getting the PLO out would promote the conditions for the Lebanese government to establish its sovereignty again, but other than helping with this evacuation, the marines had not been sized or equipped to play any further role in the process.

Secretary Weinberger and General Vessey supported the decision to use US military power to help provide security for the PLO fighters because it supported important political objectives and could be accomplished despite the challenging situation in Lebanon. Beyond this, the two Pentagon leaders argued that there was no further usefulness for American forces in Lebanon until the military and political situation there changed. The small, lightly armed MNF was not disposed to exert pressure on any of the parties to reach such a political settlement or to change the military situation on the ground. Leaving American servicemen there would only put them at risk of being killed or injured or killing or injuring Israelis or Arabs. Any such developments would hurt the administration's political interests at home and strategic interests in the region.

On 1 September, the last PLO elements departed Lebanon, and from 10 to 16 September, the US Marines followed suit. Weinberger took the lead in extracting American forces as soon as possible.[90] Yasser Arafat, who was counting on the MNF to protect the Palestinian civilians left behind, complained that the United States was withdrawing prematurely and sent word through intermediaries urging the administration to remember the promise made through Habib about the safety of the refugees.[91] The Lebanese government also wanted the MNF to stay on longer to help provide security and stability to the broken city during the transition.[92]

But from Weinberger's perspective, the marines had completed their mission and needed to depart. Of this decision, he later wrote: "Frequently in the case of such special forces, there is not a sufficiently clear-cut objective, so no one can tell when the objective has been secured (whether or not we had 'won'); and thus when it is time to leave. In this case we had not only secured our objective, but agreed with our associates that after ten quiet days following the departure of the PLO forces, it was time to leave, and we left." Weinberger further noted: "I judged the MNF action to be a complete success because with virtually no losses, we had not only taken out the PLO army, one of the principal magnets for an Israeli house-to-house attack through Beirut, but we had removed a principal cause of instability in Lebanon itself."[93]

At a 21 September press conference, Shultz seemed to agree with Weinberger's assessment. The secretary of state was asked if he agreed with the assertion made by many that the marines had departed too early, to which he replied: "No, I don't agree. The situation was stable, and the new GOL [government of Lebanon] was in the process of taking over. The President, Bashir [Gemayel], was in the process of bringing about reconciliation. So the conditions that were presumed at the time we came in had been met, and so we left, and I think properly so."[94] But writing later in his memoir, Shultz captured both sides of the issue. "To Arafat the MNF meant protection for civilians but, in fact, the MNF's stated mission—to achieve the safe departure of the PLO—had been completed."[95]

On 17 and 18 September, Arafat's concerns became reality when a bloody massacre in the Palestinian refugee camps of Sabra and Shatila resulted in the deaths of an estimated seven hundred to eight hundred unarmed Palestinian civilians. As the Reagan administration was pressed by the military and political situation in Lebanon, its stance would again have to evolve on when and how to use military power in the Middle East.

5

THE SHULTZ DOCTRINE

Using American Military Power
to Support Diplomacy

IN 1981, during the early weeks of the Reagan administration, Secretary of Defense Weinberger argued that domestic political realities made it unwise to use military power to overtly coerce Cuba. Specifically, he contended that public and congressional support would be absent because the military forces were not being called upon to secure a vital national interest. A year later, in 1982, the circumstances in Lebanon were such that the administration did have domestic support for deploying military forces to Beirut. Still, Weinberger argued that domestic political realities in that instance supported only a very limited use of military power and that political realities in the region were such that the nation should exercise caution in deploying forces lest it threaten its vital strategic interests in the Persian Gulf. In the end, the administration deployed US Marines in pursuit of a narrow and clearly articulated objective—to lend support to the Lebanese government as it escorted PLO fighters out of its territory—and the unit was to be redeployed as soon as that objective was met. Weinberger's concerns regarding domestic political realities, limited mandates, and vital strategic interests for the use of military power would be overshadowed by the massacres at the PLO refugee camps in September 1982.

The second round of US involvement in Lebanon further developed the evolution of the Reagan administration's doctrine regarding the relationship between national political objectives, the use of American military power, and political realities in terms of strategic reappraisals.

The administration deliberated whether to return the marines to Lebanon amid the political objectives sought in the region and the relationship between military power and policy objectives. It soon came to recognize that its original strategy was unlikely to succeed and that it needed to reappraise how it planned to use US diplomatic, economic, and military strength to achieve its objectives. What transpired was a series of strategic reappraisals beginning in October 1982 regarding strategy toward Lebanon, followed by another strategic appraisal almost a year later in September 1983. Each provides insight into how the administration sought to account for domestic and international political realities when deciding upon the use of military power in support of political objectives, marking further steps toward the promulgation of the Weinberger Doctrine.

Relating American Military Power to Policy Objectives

THE CHAIN OF events leading to the massacre in the Palestinian refugee camps on 17 and 18 September 1982 began four days after the US Marines, having overseen the evacuation of the PLO from Lebanon, departed from Beirut.[1] On 14 September, Bashir Gemayel, the Lebanese president-elect, was assassinated, prompting the Israelis to occupy West Beirut. The United States and the UN Security Council immediately demanded that the Israelis return to their previous positions, but their calls went unheeded.[2] The actual perpetrators of the massacre were Phalangist Party militiamen, but many observers blamed the Israeli Defense Forces (IDF) for allowing them to enter the camps.[3] French officers who arrived shortly after the murders reported horrific carnage and were told by survivors that Israeli bulldozers had come in to push rubble over the bodies.[4]

After the reentry of the Israelis into Beirut and the massacre of the Palestinian refugees, many senior administration officials felt morally obligated to do something.[5] Publicly, however, Reagan did not accept responsibility: "I don't think that specifically there could [be] assigned a responsibility on our part for withdrawing our troops. They were sent in there with one understanding. They were there to oversee and make sure that the PLO left Lebanon. And that mission was completed, virtually without incident, and they left. Then, who could have foreseen the assassination of the President-elect that led to the other violence and so forth."[6] Nonetheless, the Arab League accused the United States of being "morally responsible for the massacre" and supported the PLO's demand that a new international force be sent back into Beirut.[7]

Key administration leaders reached a similar conclusion and supported the assignment of US forces to a new MNF. During a conference call on 18 September, a recommendation by Secretary of State Shultz to reconstitute the MNF was backed by Edwin Meese, William Clark, and William Casey but opposed by Weinberger and Vessey.[8] Regardless, Reagan's desire to go back and resolve the problems in Lebanon left little space for disagreement. He explained to his advisors that the nation had "inherited a responsibility."[9]

The decision to redeploy the marines as part of the reconstituted MNF was made relatively quickly. Robert McFarlane, who was working at the time as National Security Advisor William Clark's deputy, wrote that "the Marines were sent in out of guilt and compassion, purely as moral support, without clarity or analysis beyond that level."[10] Prior to the redeployment, Clark did not solicit formal opinions from any government agencies. Nor did Weinberger request a formal clarification of the purpose or end date of the redeployment prior to the return of forces to Lebanon.[11]

Yet to characterize the administration's actions as devoid of analysis, as McFarlane did, is not completely accurate. Senior officials did consult with the president, articulate political objectives for American

President Reagan meets with key advisors in the Situation Room to discuss the crisis in Lebanon. Courtesy Ronald Reagan Library.

policy in Lebanon, and consider several different options for the use of the marines in support of those objectives. Additionally, as the deployment progressed, the administration carried out two deliberate strategic reappraisals in which the disposition of the force was considered in relationship to US political and military objectives and in relationship to political realities at home and abroad.

The Objectives

On 19 September, the morning after learning of the refugee massacres, Reagan met with his chief advisors in the White House Situation Room.[12] The president wanted US military forces returned to Lebanon for the immediate purpose of protecting the Palestinians, but he also wanted American policy to accomplish much more. "We should go for

broke," Reagan told his closest advisors. As he recorded in his diary entry
for September 19: "We are asking the Israelis to leave Beirut. We are asking Arabs to intervene and persuade Syrians to leave Lebanon at which
time we'll ask Israelis to do likewise. In the meantime, Lebanon will
establish a govt. & the capability of defending itself. No more half way
gestures, clear the whole situation while the M.N.F. is on hand to assure order."[13] One objective Reagan did not record in his diary, but that
was included in his announcement regarding the MNF reconstitution
the next day, was to provide security for Israel's northern population.[14]
Thus, the administration publicly articulated three policy goals: departure of all foreign forces from Lebanon, a stable Lebanese government,
and security for Israel's northern border.[15]

Consensus was not difficult to reach. Members of the administration
and even members of Congress were in agreement that it was in keeping with US strategic interests to remove foreign forces from Lebanon
and establish a stable, sovereign government there.[16] The real problem
was deciding how best to relate military power to US policy objectives
and to current political realities.

The administration considered three options. First, a large force
could be sent, akin to the 7,000 troops that President Eisenhower deployed in 1958 to help Lebanese president Camille Chamoun maintain
order after he illegally tried to seek another term.[17] Convincing the Israelis to leave Lebanon would be easier if a large force was in place to secure its border and also compel the Syrians, still severely weakened from
skirmishes with the Israelis over the summer, to depart the country.

McFarlane favored this large-force option. "At this stage of the
game," he later wrote, "Syria was on its knees. It was the moment to
take heed of W. C. Fields' admonition: 'Never kick a man unless he's
down.' There was a need to act quickly to force the Syrian troops out
of Lebanon before they had time to rearm and dig in their heels." Yet
neither Shultz nor Weinberger supported this position.[18] In addition to
the lessons of Vietnam, they shared other concerns that drove them to
different solutions.[19]

Shultz favored a second option: sending in a small multinational force, similar to the first MNF, to stabilize the situation in Beirut.[20] Supported by Special Envoy Philip Habib, Shultz believed that after a ceasefire was achieved in Beirut, the State Department could proceed with diplomacy and thereby achieve the administration's objectives. His reasoning was captured comprehensively by a senior officer involved in planning the deployment of US forces to Lebanon: "A small force seemed prudent and sufficient for the immediate task of stabilizing the situation in Lebanon's capital city. Additionally, a small force could be deployed more quickly than a large one; it would be less likely to provoke a U.S.-Soviet confrontation; and it would be simpler to introduce and less costly to support. It would also keep the U.S. contribution in proportion to the French and the Italian contributions, thus fostering perceptions that the interpositional forces were truly multinational and neutral with respect to the military and political interests of the factional antagonists."[21] Nevertheless, the success of the small-force plan rested upon three critical assumptions: the Israelis would leave as soon as there was a satisfactory security arrangement with the government of Lebanon; the Lebanese would be strong enough to enforce such an agreement; and the Saudis would and could convince the Syrians to withdraw as soon as the Israelis agreed to leave.[22]

Not everyone was convinced that diplomacy would go smoothly even if a ceasefire was upheld in Beirut. McFarlane argued that the approach ignored "the implausibility of the [Amin] Gemayel government enforcing such an agreement" and demonstrated "a grave lack of analytical depth in the career foreign service."[23] The Shultz plan depended on what one writer described as an "astounding reliance on a best-case scenario."[24] For diplomacy to be successful, the Lebanese would need to form a government of reconciliation out of factions that had warred for years, the Israelis would need to be convinced that the Lebanese government could secure their mutual border, and the Syrians would have to allow the balance of power in the region to shift in favor of Israeli and American interests.

Questioning the soundness of the Shultz plan, Weinberger argued for a third option: holding off reintroduction of American forces until all foreign forces departed Lebanon, then deploying a US force large

enough to "form a giant cordon around the entire perimeter of Lebanon's borders and coastline so that the Lebanese army would be undis-
turbed as it retook control of internal security." Weinberger believed
that it was far too risky to return to Beirut and "simply hope for the
best."[25] Specifically, he thought it foolish to deploy US forces into Lebanon before the Israelis and Syrians had agreed to withdraw or before the
Christian and Muslim factions warring in Beirut had formed a government of reconciliation.[26]

Shultz responded heatedly to Weinberger's condition of the removal
of all foreign forces before the introduction of the US military. He declared in his memoir: "I was, under this 'plan,' supposed to conduct
diplomacy without strength, with no military backup—and in pursuit of
a ludicrously impossible ideal."[27] Determining how to relate diplomacy
and military power proved to be a constant challenge for the top leaders
in the Reagan administration. This would not be the last time Shultz
and Weinberger would reach different conclusions over how best to relate those two aspects of American power to achieve policy objectives.

In order to gain a diplomatic voice in the region, Reagan believed
in the importance of deploying US forces to demonstrate the nation's
willingness and resolve to assert leadership in the region. Yet for years
it has seemed that the military and political situation in Lebanon and
the Middle East was so challenging that only a dramatic or drastic effort
could affect matters. The administration did not want to embark on such
a venture because top officials believed that such action would cause the
Soviet Union to get involved more heavily in the region, a development
to be avoided. Additionally, they did not support the Israelis as proxies
in that role because of American interests in the Persian Gulf.[28]

The Shultz Doctrine

THE OUTLOOK CHANGED in the fall of 1982, when Reagan,
joined by Habib and Shultz, thought that a window of opportunity had
opened in Lebanon, making political change possible without the in-

troduction of a large military force. The Syrians were badly beaten, the Israelis wanted to avoid urban fighting or a long occupation, and the Palestinian leaders had escaped with their political dignity intact so they could conceivably engage in a larger Middle East peace process. Weinberger and Vessey disagreed, believing it was risky to stick one's hand into the proverbial hornets' nest until there was more proof that a political solution was possible and would be embraced by all parties. From the perspective of the Israelis and Syrians, the overall weakness of the Lebanese government lent itself just as well to partitioning the country as to Reagan's plan for a sovereign authority created out of the factions vying for power.

Partitioning Lebanon was supported by neither the administration nor its European partners in the MNF, who believed a parceled Lebanon would invite more violence down the road. Instead, Reagan thought that long-term stability depended on achieving a sovereign Lebanese government strong enough to secure its borders and provide the Israelis with a security agreement. It was essential that the LAF be able to demonstrate success and provide security to Beirut and its inhabitants. Pres. Amin Gemayel believed that to be successful in achieving those ends, his army would initially need assistance and requested the American, French, and Italian MNF be redeployed.

In consultation with the US government, the Lebanese government specified that the purpose of the "MNF will be to provide an interposition force at agreed locations and thereby provide the Multinational *presence* requested by the Lebanese Government to assist it and the Lebanese Armed Forces (LAF) in the Beirut area."[29] That in turn was translated by the US military chain of command into a marine mission "to *establish an environment* which will permit the Lebanese Armed Forces to carry out their responsibilities in the Beirut area."[30] On 29 September, a force of 1,200 marines began landing and taking over vacated Israeli positions at the Beirut International Airport.[31]

It is worth noting that the marine mission statement did not require them to attack, defend, police, or protect anyone or anything during their estimated sixty-day deployment. The Lebanese government and the LAF were responsible for providing security to Beirut. In their "presence" role, the marines were to remain neutral and, technically, would not be allowed to respond forcefully even if another massacre began. Instead, their mission was to serve as a "symbolic presence designed to alter the psychology of confrontation and fear then rampant in Beirut."[32]

Robert McFarlane of the NSC staff further described this role: "The MNF was a political signal [of American support] to the government of Lebanon as well as to the Arabs in the context of the peace process. The deployment of the MNF was a political act . . . not a military act, and if we didn't do it, we would lose credibility in the Middle East and any hope of success with the president's peace initiative."[33] Reagan appeared to be quite optimistic that American resolve demonstrated by the redeployment of the MNF would quickly convince all foreign forces to leave. At a press conference held the day before the marines reentered Lebanon, the president was asked if the marines would remain until all foreign forces were withdrawn. "Yes," he answered, "because I think that's going to come rapidly."[34] On the same day, Weinberger publicly supported the president with his own optimistic statement. On the ABC News program *This Week*, the secretary of defense said he expected the Israelis and Syrians to be out of Lebanon by Christmas, adding: "I would certainly hope they would be out long before that. There's no reason they couldn't get out in less than a week."[35] Unfortunately, the "presence" of the MNF failed to achieve the administration's goals and forced a strategic reappraisal of its policy.

A Strategic Reappraisal: NSDD-64, "Next Steps in Lebanon"

ALTHOUGH IT IS AN ARTIFICIAL construct to describe a strategic reappraisal as a single event occurring within a set period of time, the term is used here to denote the span of time when the Reagan administration devoted attention to the strategic issues regarding its policy in Lebanon, decided to change course, and codified that change of course by publishing a national-security decision directive (NSDD). The first instance occurred less than a month after the MNF reentered Lebanon.

In the summer of 1982, Israel announced three objectives for its military drive into Lebanon: all foreign armies must be withdrawn from Lebanon; a new Lebanese government must be formed; and a peace treaty must be signed between Israel and the new government. The plan did not rely solely upon the use of military force to achieve these goals but also upon diplomacy. The Israelis had supported the presidential aspirations of Bashir Gemayel, commander of the Phalangist Party militia, the largest and best-armed force in the country, with the expectation that as soon as he was elected in August 1982, he would sign a peace treaty with Israel.[36]

That plan was disrupted when the newly elected Gemayel proved unwilling to sign such a treaty and instead pursued his own vision for his country. On 1 September, while Secretary Weinberger was visiting American service members deployed in Beirut, Gemayel approached him and requested that the United States consider using Lebanon as a strategic outpost in the Middle East. Weinberger described Gemayel's vision: "Lebanon was not quite to be our fifty-first state, but its relationship with us [the United States] might not have been altogether dissimilar."[37] The president-elect must have hoped that a large US troop presence in his country would prevent Syria and Israel from ignoring its borders and sovereignty in the future.

The day after his discussion with Weinberger, Gemayel was whisked to Jerusalem by helicopter at the behest of Menachem Begin, who berated him for his ingratitude and demanded that he sign a peace treaty with Israel immediately.[38] Gemayel told the prime minister that he could not, claiming that such an agreement would be unacceptable to the Muslim citizens of his nation and would result in its isolation from other moderate Arab nations. Recommending that the two neighbors exercise patience and consider negotiating a treaty in six to twelve months, Gemayel promised to keep the borders open and encourage trade between the two countries.[39]

Gemayel's resolve in the face of Begin's demands was undoubtedly helped by President Reagan's nationally televised announcement the previous night, 1 September, of his plan for achieving peace in the Middle East.[40] One portion of his proposal was to support the Lebanese in rebuilding and reviving their nation into a stable state. While the administration would not accept the strategic-outpost concept, Gemayel would have known when he faced Begin that the United States would support his desire to obtain national autonomy from Israel and Syria.

In Reagan's Middle East policy address to the nation, one can hear a refrain of the themes he campaigned upon in 1980. "Our involvement in the search for Mideast peace is not a matter of preference; it's a moral imperative. The strategic importance of the region to the United States is well known, but our policy is motivated by more than strategic interests. We also have an irreversible commitment to the survival and territorial integrity of friendly states."[41] The president called for international assistance in Lebanon, self-government by the Palestinian inhabitants of the West Bank and Gaza in association with Jordan, a settlement freeze in those areas by Israel, unchallenged legitimacy for Israel within the community of nations, and an undivided Jerusalem, with its final status to be decided through negotiation.[42]

While Reagan's policy was supported by Congress, the press, and America's allies in Europe and in the Arab world, it was repudiated by Israel. Begin wrote directly to the president: "A friend does not weaken his friend; an ally does not put his ally in jeopardy."[43] Shultz related the shock the peace initiative must have had on the psyche of the Israelis:

What we have announced as a Middle East initiative must be shattering for Begin and the group around him. In recent days they must have felt at the height of their power. They have proven again the invincibility of their military machine. They have secured their southern border in a peace treaty with Egypt. They believe they have just devastated their bitter enemy, the PLO, and most of southern Lebanon is their playground. They think they have the power and influence to establish whatever kind of government they want in Beirut. They are wrong about that, but they see the road open to a unilateral implementation of restricted autonomy in the West Bank. Jordan is cowering. All of this has brought Israel, in their eyes, to a supreme position. As they see it, we have suddenly pulled the rug out from under them.[44]

On 14 September, twelve days after his tense meeting with Begin, Bashir was assassinated, and the responsibility to move Lebanon toward greater autonomy and stability fell upon his older brother, Amin.

Amin Gemayel, like his brother, had no interest in signing a peace treaty with Israel nor in being beholden to the Syrians, but he was considered more open to Muslims and Syrians than Bashir had been. Yet the most important difference between the two had to do with their relationship with Lebanon's largest martial force, the Phalangist Party militia. Bashir had been its commander, and while its fighters were fiercely loyal to him, they did not consider Amin their new commander in chief. If he was to reestablish a working central government, enforce law and order, and put an end to factional violence in Lebanon, the new president would need a credible fighting force of his own.[45] Unfortunately, in the fall of 1982, the Lebanese army was in no condition to take on such a responsibility.[46]

Thus, as one of his first actions, President Gemayel traveled abroad to visit Western and Arab governments and ask for promises of economic and military support.[47] Specifically, he hoped to convince the international community to send a force of 30,000 soldiers to Lebanon to help him stabilize the nation, remove all foreign forces, and give him time to rebuild the LAF. His first stop was in New York, where he told the UN General Assembly that Lebanon was "like a phoenix rising out of its own ashes" and vowed to lay "the foundations of a strong, independent and democratic state." Next he traveled to Washington to visit Reagan and his top cabinet officers.

On 19 October, Gemayel had breakfast with the president, lunch with Shultz, and tea with Weinberger.[48] The visit had been initiated by

President Reagan eats breakfast with Pres. Amin Gemayel of Lebanon.
Courtesy Ronald Reagan Library.

the administration and was intended to allow officials to let Gemayel
know that the United States shared his desire for the prompt withdrawal
of all foreign forces and for a strong, independent Lebanon. Following their discussion, Reagan and Gemayel came forward with official
remarks regarding the meeting. Reagan stated that he had "reaffirmed
the U.S. support for the sovereignty, unity, territorial integrity, and freedom of Lebanon."[49] It was time to get serious about getting the foreign
forces to leave and helping the Lebanese prepare to manage their own
internal affairs.

    Reagan's words were immediately backed by action, for by the next
day, plans to put an early end to the marine presence in Lebanon were
held in check and interagency staffs in Washington began working on
contingencies for positioning an expanded (15,000-man) MNF in the

areas from which Israeli and Syrian forces were expected to withdraw.[50] The president's call for action was officially codified a week later with NSDD-64, "Next Steps in Lebanon."[51]

While the text of the directive was classified, three days earlier during a press conference, Shultz had laid out its central point: "We have set in our minds an objective of trying to get the foreign forces out of Lebanon by the end of this year [1982]."[52] Additionally, three days after the directive's publication, a White House aide indicated another major aspect of NSDD-64: Reagan might be willing to commit more military force if necessary to help Lebanon. The aide stated: "The President believes the 'Viet Nam syndrome' has put ridiculous restraints on peace keeping, even when it is in American interests. He is disturbed at the reluctance to use American military force when it can be a useful adjunct of our foreign policy."[53]

The cover letter on the decision directive sent to Shultz, Weinberger, and Vessey, among others, made this point explicitly:

> It is clear that negotiations must take place before the full range of politico-military requirements for implementing the withdrawal of Syrian, Israeli and Palestinian forces are known. Only then will it be possible to define the precise size and composition of the requisite military forces. However, we do have sufficient knowledge at hand to postulate notional force packages which would be essential to the support of alternative missions and dispositions. Consequently, it is requested that the necessary analysis be performed to facilitate timely responses in the upcoming negotiations with the parties. The analysis should be premised on the understanding that to reach agreement we will probably need to agree to the expansion of the MNF and that it may have to be deployed into any of several areas of Lebanon (northern, central or southern). While we should generally seek to broaden international participation, we must accept that the measures of U.S. leadership relies on our own willingness to contribute.[54]

The directive itself concluded: "I recognize that there are substantial risks in these undertakings which will confront our forces and those of our friends. However, mindful of the recent tragic history of this traditionally friendly country and the opportunity which now exists to further the cause of peace between Israel and all its neighbors, we cannot let this historic moment pass. Clearly, our initiatives and our commitment to Lebanon's independence will further strengthen our credibility and demonstrate our determination to continue the progress we have already made."[55] With his 1 September speech and the signing of NSDD-64, Reagan demonstrated his willingness to exert American leadership on the international stage in the Middle East and to use military power as part of that solution. The president counted on his cabinet officers to develop the specific diplomatic strategy and supporting plans to achieve his objectives given the political realities faced domestically and overseas.

On 3 November, five days after NSDD-64 was signed, Shultz and Weinberger sent a memorandum to the president in which they laid out a series of strategies for Reagan to consider.[56] This document remains classified, but it can be freely noted that the marines deployed to Lebanon in early November were sent in with a different mission than those deployed in late September.

Starting in early November, the marine contingent of the MNF was charged with establishing a larger presence in Beirut and conducting presence patrols in East Beirut.[57] While out in the streets, the marines were to warn infiltrators to turn back and avoid any decisive involvement, though the responsibility for physically turning back infiltrators was to rest solely upon the Lebanese army. Even though the Americans were patrolling in a new and expanded area, their "presence" mission remained the same as it had been during the first deployment.

The East Beirut patrols were carried out to help achieve two political ends. First, they were meant to support Gemayel's efforts at reconciliation by demonstrating not only an evenhandedness in patrolling both Muslim and Christian areas but also the willingness of the LAF to exert authority over areas that had been controlled by the Phalangist militia. Second, they were to serve as a rehearsal for the time when the LAF, supported by an expanded MNF, would extend its responsibility to areas outside of Beirut after the Israelis and Syrians departed. Although the Joint Chiefs had been against the idea of redeploying American forces into Lebanon, they supported expanding the presence mission beyond the international airport into East Beirut to help Gemayel assert his power.[58]

Also in November, a small group of military officers opened the Department of Defense's Office of Military Cooperation in Beirut to rebuild and train the Lebanese army.[59] Weinberger and the Joint Chiefs of Staff did not believe the best way to support diplomatic initiatives in Lebanon and Gemayel's drive for reconciliation was to man the borders with larger forces, as Gemayel had proposed to Reagan during his October visit.[60] Instead, they favored redoubling the efforts to train the LAF so it in time could take over all of Lebanon's security responsibilities. Opening the office was an important first step in getting the LAF trained.

With the benefit of hindsight, the key players involved and historians have identified the fall of 1982 as the period of time in which the administration had the best prospect for achieving its political objectives in Lebanon.[61] Israel and Lebanon were soon expected to begin negotiating the terms of an Israeli withdrawal, and Syria was still severely weakened from the earlier fighting. Syria's foreign minister had met with Shultz and pledged to withdraw his nation's forces from Lebanon if the Israelis withdrew rapidly and unconditionally.[62]

During his overseas travels, Gemayel found his request for assistance received favorably by the leadership in France, Italy, Great Britain, and Morocco. He returned home with numerous promises for assistance, though each was typically prefaced with the condition that he secure an Israeli withdrawal based upon terms that were acceptable to Arab leaders, especially Syrian president Hafez al-Assad. Additionally, Gemayel needed to demonstrate that he was making progress toward reconciling the Christian, Druze, and Muslim demands for political change. His efforts would be helped by the fact that he could tell the parties that further international support was conditioned upon demonstrated steps toward achieving a unified government.[63]

Even the challenge of rebuilding Lebanon's army appeared surmountable. In early October, shortly after the second MNF went ashore, a team of American military specialists went to Lebanon to assess the LAF. The group's report, released on 1 November, recommended creation of a force of four 70-percent operationally ready infantry brigades by February 1983. Four undermanned and underequipped infantry brigades could not defend Lebanon's sovereignty, but the Lebanese Army Modernization Program, as the initiative was called, was expected to produce a nucleus for a larger, more capable military by 1986 or 1987.[64]

Unfortunately, a host of issues cropped up to slow the agreement process for the departure of the Israeli forces, the first step in getting Syria to withdraw. Shultz recounted some of the problems in his memoirs: Israeli defense minister Ariel Sharon tried to negotiate a peace treaty with Lebanon on his own without US involvement, which only served to hinder the process; Ambassador Habib's health was poor, and he convinced Shultz that his deputy could handle the negotiations, which as Shultz said, "sent a signal to the region that Lebanon had been relegated to a lower level of priority"; and Shultz said he misjudged Prime Minister Begin and the Israelis' "stomach for sustained political engagement in or with Lebanon."[65]

In late October 1982, with the publication of NSDD-64, the administration committed itself to getting all foreign fighters out of Lebanon and helping the government gain control of its territory. In reality it may be more accurate to say that administration leadership *recommitted* itself to those goals, for NSDD-64 did very little to change the basic premise under which the administration had operated when it decided to send the marines back to Lebanon as part of the second MNF: that if the United States demonstrated leadership and resolve by keeping American military forces present to support and train the LAF, the Lebanese government would have an opportunity to achieve stability and foreign forces would agree to leave. NSDD-64 simply expanded the area of the presence mission—into East Beirut—and set a definitive timeline for success—the end of the year.

In the end, 1982 closed without any of the parties agreeing to a withdrawal. For almost another year, the Reagan administration would continue to follow the strategy laid out in NSDD-64 and adhere to the notion that the mere presence of US military forces would be enough to support diplomatic efforts and achieve its political objectives. Officials would not change their strategy toward Lebanon until September 1983, though movement in that direction had begun earlier that year.

A Strategic Reappraisal: NSDD-103, "Strategy for Lebanon"

IN EARLY FEBRUARY 1983, in an effort to move Israel to an agreement for withdrawal, Ambassador Habib returned to the negotiating table with approval from Reagan and Senate Democrats to offer more American troops to help secure the Israeli-Lebanese border. This gesture was meant to eliminate the Israeli demand to keep IDF outposts in southern Lebanon. Shultz was also working to gather support from more nations for an expanded 15,000-man MNF mission in southern Lebanon, while the Joint Chiefs of Staff were working to determine what role US forces would play in such a force.[66] Domestic politics in the United States did not preclude the deployment of additional military forces.

On 21 March, these efforts were rewarded when the Israelis finally agreed to Habib's proposal to rely on US and Lebanese outposts in southern Lebanon, and matters finally seemed to be progressing.[67] Less than a month later, however, on 18 April, the US embassy in Beirut was bombed, killing seventeen Americans. The very next day Congress voted to place restrictions on the size, disposition, mission, and employment of the marines unless Reagan obtained further approval. Additionally, congressional leaders suggested that the president might need to reassess his determination that hostilities were not imminent, but they did not try at this time to force him into reporting under the War Powers

Resolution. Congressional and public support still existed for Reagan to respond to the bombing, provided his response was reasonable, but the decision to place restrictions on the disposition and employment of the marines constrained the military support Habib could promise as he continued to work for a diplomatic solution.[68]

Additionally, the apparent progress made with Israel the previous month had evaporated. On 21 April, Shultz wrote to Reagan: "Phil Habib has concluded that we have reached a basic decision point in the Israel-Lebanon negotiations. We can either push forward to bring them to an early conclusion, or accept the prospect of an impasse followed by protracted negotiations. I believe it is vitally important to our interests in the region that we not allow these negotiations to drag on. Both sides, however, have frozen their positions on the major outstanding issues; some new impetus will be required to force the pace of decision."[69] Shultz believed that he could provide the "impetus" required to reenergize the political process by personally visiting the Middle East and received permission to do so.

On 27 April, Reagan signed NSDD-92, "Accelerating the Withdrawal of Foreign Forces from Lebanon," which directed Shultz to visit the Middle East and provided the secretary with his marching orders. While part of the document is still classified, enough is unclassified to hear Reagan's strident tone toward the Israelis and to recognize that he was committed to obtaining a withdrawal of all foreign fighters from Lebanon: "[W]e should make clear to the Government of Israel my strong wish to restore our good relations and to indeed deepen the relationship in a manner befitting allies. Secretary Shultz should make it clear that we have in effect two courses of action. One is to restore and enhance the relationship and that is a very high priority of this Administration. *The other course leads inevitably to a fundamental reappraisal of the entire U.S.-Israeli relationship.* We clearly prefer the former course, but we are also committed to obtaining the withdrawal of foreign forces from Lebanon [author's emphasis]."[70]

By 17 May, Shultz had accomplished his mission. Israel and Lebanon finally signed a peace accord that included an agreement from

Israel to withdraw to its borders. The cost of Israeli support was high, though, as the United States agreed to a Trilateral (U.S.-Israel-Lebanon) Security Arrangements Commission from which the Israelis were allowed to remain in Lebanon until the Syrians agreed to withdraw as well.[71] Thus, the next step in the process was to get an agreement from Damascus to leave Lebanon. But eight months had passed since the Syrians had indicated that they would be willing to depart Lebanon, and much had changed.

The Syrians, with Soviet assistance, had taken advantage of the long lull in activity to rearm. They no longer believed that it was in their best interest to leave and were able to find support for that stance from Lebanon's Muslim and Druze factions and their militia forces. These factions, which had initially supported Gemayel because they believed he would satisfy their demands for economic and political reform, by the spring of 1983 were ready to accept Syria's support and guidance in fighting against the government, the Lebanese army, and even the US Marines in the MNF if necessary.[72] From their perspective, Gemayel had not made any reforms and would be even less likely to do so once he established control with an army equipped and trained by the United States. These factions wanted to resist any further expansion of the LAF until there were guarantees for reform.[73]

In the summer of 1983, the conflicting interests of all parties erupted in the Shuf Mountains of Lebanon, a stronghold of the Druze militia but occupied by the Israelis in the summer of 1982. The Israelis allowed Phalangist Party militia into the area, hoping to use it as a proxy force against the Syrians. Begin, struggling to maintain support at home for the extended occupation, could no longer afford the regular casualties that were occurring in the Shuf from ambushes and bomb attacks. He made plans to pull the IDF out of the mountains into more defensible positions in the south. But who would control the Shuf after the Israelis departed? Would it be the Druze, who had filled that role historically; the Phalangist militia, who were no friends of the Druze and held those positions only through the help of the Israelis; or the forces from Gemayel's national army?

From the perspective of Gemayel and Reagan, the answer had to be the LAF. From the perspective of the Druze, however, there was little difference between the Lebanese army and the Phalangist militia—both needed to be thwarted until a government of reconciliation was formed. The Druze leader, Walid Jumblatt, turned to the Syrians for help and thus came to be considered their proxy.[74]

For the Reagan administration, Israel's plan to pull out of the Shuf presented a number of problems. The unilateral pullback could be taken as a sign of success by Syria and the Druze forces, giving them additional impetus to oppose the May 17 agreement. The United States was also uncertain if the LAF was prepared to decisively engage the Druze. If the army suffered defeat at the hands of the militia, it would surely lead to the downfall of Gemayel and provide the Israelis additional justification for their continued occupation of southern Lebanon. Essentially, such a defeat would guarantee the partitioning of Lebanon, which the administration wanted to avoid. Lastly, the Shuf Mountains were tactical high ground, overlooking the marine position at the Beirut International Airport; whoever controlled that land could easily rain down fire on the American positions.

Between 21 June and 20 July, the administration held three national-security planning group meetings (NSPGs) to develop contingencies for how to respond should Israel conduct a partial and unilateral withdraw and in order to prepare for an impending Gemayel visit to Washington.[75] The president's talking points from those meetings indicate that he was willing to involve the MNF as part of the administration's overall calculus. At the 15 July NSPG, one talking point went: "As to the MNF, we should indicate our readiness, together with the others, to help the Lebanese army. I would like to anticipate what President Gemayal will ask of me next week and to develop a plan of action which is cautious but responsive to what he thinks he needs."[76] While at the 20 July meeting, Reagan's talking points stated: "We can expand and redeploy the MNF in ways we, the Lebanese, and our co-contributors agree are helpful. I think we should develop plans here in-house and with our European friends to reassure the Lebanese that we stand with them. Let the Lebanese do the police work, but let's not be afraid to stand—and be seen as standing—with them."[77]

On 22 July, President Gemayel returned to Washington to visit President Reagan and to request additional military assistance from the United States. During the visit, Reagan promised to do all he could to quickly increase military assistance to the LAF. He dispatched General Vessey to assess the ability of the Lebanese army to absorb more aid and to determine what additional role the marines might be able to play on the ground to assist Gemayel. On the twenty-seventh, Reagan announced that he was willing to consider expanding the MNF presence into the Shuf if an agreement could be reached between the Lebanese government and the Druze. In the meantime, the Joint Chiefs of Staff worked to develop a plan to reinforce the marines with an additional battalion so they could maintain contact with the IDF during the withdrawal to new defensive positions in the south.[78]

Events in August did not favor the administration and its policies. On 10 August, sparked by concern that the president might be dragging the nation into a quagmire, Congress placed a rider on a supplemental appropriations bill that prohibited any significant change to the size, mission, or location of the marines without prior approval. That rider warned of the difficulty ahead for the administration if it wanted to send in the additional battalion that the Joint Chiefs had under consideration. Additionally, it greatly reduced the chances that Reagan would obtain support for expanding the MNF mission into the Shuf.

Hoping to gain additional time for opening negotiations with the Druze and turn them away from Syrian influence, Washington sent a flash cable on 28 August to Prime Minister Begin requesting a delay of the IDF withdrawal from the Shuf. Begin agreed to wait until 4 September. On 3 September, the administration held another NSPG on the situation in Lebanon, and Reagan called the Israelis to ask that they delay their withdrawal by several more days.[79] The president explained: "The [Lebanese] Army is now concluding its operations in West Beirut, and has extended its activity into East Beirut to demonstrate it is an army of all the Lebanese people. However, the army will not physically be able to move into the Shuf for several more days. It is vital to the success of your redeployment that the LAF move into the Shuf in an orderly, coordinated fashion."[80] The Israelis replied that their forces were already on the move and could not be delayed further.[81]

The administration's plans to achieve its political objectives in Lebanon seemed to be unraveling. With Israel's unilateral withdrawal, it would be very difficult to convince Syria to do the same. Furthermore, five days earlier, American resolve and credibility had seemingly become ensnared in a congressional debate over the marines continued deployment.

On 29 August, Druze rocket, artillery, and mortar attacks had killed two marines and wounded fourteen others. That action triggered debate over whether Reagan should file a report under the War Powers Section 4 (a) (1) regarding imminent hostilities, which would place a time limit of sixty days on the deployment unless the House and Senate approved an extension.[82] The next day, Reagan submitted a report to Congress "consistent with Section 4 of the War Powers Resolution."[83]

During testimony before the House Foreign Affairs Committee, Secretary Shultz warned that an early departure of the marines would undermine American leadership and credibility abroad. "The simplest and first thing that I think you have to keep in mind," he argued, "is that when the world sees that when America sends its forces to perform a legitimate mission asked for by the legitimate government involved and it does so and then the minute some trouble arises we turn tail and beat it, I think that sends a gigantic message around the world that is very undesirable and totally incompatible with our role as a defender of freedom and justice around the world and as a great power with interests around the world."[84]

In the end, the administration was able to persuade Congress to allow US forces to remain in Lebanon for eighteen months.[85] Nevertheless, Shultz believed that the debate had weakened the standing of the marines as a lever in American diplomacy:

Our marines, or the multinational force as a whole, cannot tip the balance of forces alone—and it is not their mission to do so. But their presence remains one crucial pillar of the structure of stability. As a former marine . . . I will not allow anyone to cast doubt on how formidable even this small number of marines can be. They are an important deterrent, a symbol of the international backing behind the legitimate Government of Lebanon, and an important weight in the scales. To remove the marines would put both the government, and what we are trying to achieve, in jeopardy. This is why our domestic controversy over war powers has been disturbing. The uncertainty about the American commitment only weakens our effectiveness; doubts about our staying power can only cause the aggressors to discount our presence—or to intensify their attacks, in hopes of hastening our departure.[86]

In order to offer additional protection to the MNF during this debate, Reagan held the carrier USS *Eisenhower* off Beirut and brought 2,000 marines from Egypt to stand by offshore.[87] Furthermore, at the NSC meeting held on 6 September, officials considered also sending an additional carrier battle group (the USS *Carl Vinson*) to the region.[88] The day prior to this, Reagan had dutifully called the parents of the two marines killed in Lebanon. In his 7 September diary entry, the president recounted: "I can't get the idea out of my head that some F14s off the Eisenhower coming in at about 200 ft. over the Marines & blowing hell out of a couple of artillery emplacements would be a tonic for the Marines & at the same time would deliver a message to those gun happy middle east terrorists."[89]

Robert McFarlane, who began serving as the president's personal representative in the Middle East on 22 July, shared Shultz's and Reagan's concerns about how the United States was expressing its resolve and commitment to both friends and adversaries. He returned to Washington for the 3 September NSPG strategy session and later sent cables back for consideration by those who attended the NSC meeting on

10 September, during which Lebanon was discussed.[90] It was in these discussions that the administration abandoned the basic premise underlying its strategy for Lebanon: the "presence" of US military forces would be enough to move diplomacy along in Lebanon. Instead of presence, they adopted an operational concept called "aggressive self-defense," an idea largely shaped by the political realities the administration faced at home and abroad.

At the 3 September strategy session, McFarlane reported on what he had learned while in the Middle East. The Syrians were determined to maintain influence over Lebanese policy and would likely achieve that goal due to their overwhelming military power unless a major third country decided to intervene. He recommended that the administration do so with a credible display of military force to convince the Syrians that a withdrawal was in their best interest.[91] As Reagan's special negotiator on the ground, McFarlane wanted to be able to call upon the power of the Sixth Fleet, which was deployed to the Mediterranean. Shultz and Clark agreed; the administration's diplomatic efforts toward Syria needed to be backed with a display of credible force.

General Vessey also agreed on the importance of constructing an American strategy that was more influential with the Syrians. In a memorandum to Secretary Weinberger sent three days earlier, he emphasized that it was important to "find solutions to the root causes of the current confrontations." Many of Syria's opportunities for meddling in Lebanon came from the fact that Gemayel had yet to build a government of reconciliation. Thus, Vessey advised that "the focus should continue to be on diplomatic initiatives aimed at the achievement of a viable political accommodation between the GOL [government of Lebanon] and the Lebanese factions."[92]

Vessey's memorandum recommended that, in addition to obtaining Syrian cooperation, there were "a number of parallel efforts that should be undertaken" to move Lebanon toward a reconciliation government. Those efforts were to convince Gemayel that this move was imperative, to persuade the Druze to support the reconciliation effort, to demand that the Israelis control factional artillery firing from areas under their control, and to warn the Soviets that any US-Syrian confrontation would have detrimental effects on US-Soviet relations. Additionally, he recommended that the LAF "undertake a series of confidence building measures," such as sending advance parties into the Shuf to establish factional support for their later arrival. Furthermore, he suggested that the administration be prepared to demonstrate its resolve by positioning US forces to protect or reinforce the MNF and to consult with other members of the MNF about expanding the mission and/or size of the current forces.[93]

Regarding Syrian cooperation, the general noted, "there are very few political and military levers that can be employed."[94] Constructing a credible American threat to them would be no easy task given the domestic political realities in the beginning of September 1983. The administration was locked in debate with Congress over whether or not the marines would remain in Lebanon.[95] Additionally, it remained constrained by the 10 August rider that prohibited any significant change to the size, mission, or location of the marines without prior congressional approval.[96]

In response, on 10 September the administration published NSDD-103, "Strategy for Lebanon."[97] The language of the directive attempted to hew a fine line between using military force and avoiding a War Powers dispute. The end of the MNF's "presence" mission was harkened by a concept of operations called "aggressive self-defense" in which the Americans, French, and Italians would coordinate their supporting naval and air forces to respond to hostile fire, to gather intelligence, and to conduct reconnaissance activities. Such action was meant to demonstrate credible resolve to the Syrians until more could be done to gather up third-party support for the Lebanese. Reagan also approved Secretary Weinberger's recommendation to dispatch the battleship USS *New Jersey* to the Mediterranean to lend additional fire support.[98]

The strategy developed at the beginning of September was only an interim measure until the administration had time to adopt a more deliberate and longer-term approach.[99] In many ways, this is reminiscent of its actions in Central America, where a strategy of covert operations was employed with the intent of demonstrating US leadership, will, and credibility until domestic political realities shifted to allow a more overt presence. In the case of Lebanon, NSDD-103 called for the MNF contingents to adopt aggressive self-defense to give diplomatic efforts more time.

On 11 September, McFarlane sent a flash cable back to Washington informing key administration leaders of "a serious threat of a decisive military defeat which could involve the fall of the Government of Lebanon within twenty-four hours." He believed that the LAF was one battle away from being broken, which in turn would lead to the collapse of Gemayel's government and the administration's hopes for Lebanon. McFarlane asked that Reagan consider modifying the rules of engagement to allow the marines to fire in support of the Lebanese army in addition to their own self-defense.[100] Essentially, aggressive self-defense as codified in NSDD-103 would be extended to include the defense of the LAF. In his diary, Reagan recounted the situation: "NSC is meeting without me on Lebanon re a new Cable from Bud MacFarlane [sic]. Troops obviously PLO & Syrian have launched a new attack against the Lebanese army. Our problem is do we expand our mission to aid the army [LAF] with artillery & air support. This could be seen as putting us in the war. George S.[hultz], Bill C.[asey,] & Jim Baker have just left me . . . to get more info. on what is happening and where our partners in the MNF stand."[101] After being briefed by his key leaders, the president decided to order the use of naval gunfire to support the LAF units defending Suq al-Gharb.

This decision was captured in an addendum to NSDD-103 published on 11 September: "It has been determined that occupation of the dominant terrain in the vicinity of SUQ-AL-GHARB by hostile forces will endanger Marine positions. Therefore, successful LAF defense of the area of SUQ-AL-GHARB is vital to the safety of U.S. personnel. . . . As a consequence, when the US ground commander determines that SUQ-AL-GHARB is in danger of falling as a result of attack involving non-Lebanese forces and if requested by the host government, appropriate U.S. military assistance in defense of SUQ-AL-GHARB is authorized."[102] Of the decision, Reagan wrote at the time: "My reasoning is that this can be explained as protection of our Marines hoping it might signal the Syrians to pull back. I don't think they want a war with us. If it doesn't work then we'll have to decide between pulling out or going to Congress & making a case for greater involvement."[103]

Clearly Reagan hoped to use naval fire as a signal to the Syrians of American determination in hopes that this would ultimately move along talks and convince them to accept the 17 May agreement and withdraw from Lebanon. Shultz and McFarlane agreed with the president's decision and felt that in order for diplomacy to work, the nation needed to demonstrate both the will and the means necessary to change the balance of power in Lebanon. Both also favored air strikes on the Syrian surrogates fighting the LAF.

But Weinberger and Vessey believed that supporting the Lebanese with American firepower might lead to retaliations, which the marines were not properly disposed to repel.[104] Therefore, they argued that the mission should not change until the force's disposition on the ground was also changed to afford adequate protection, since the marines were lightly armed as peacekeepers.[105] Additionally, they were not convinced that such measures would truly bear any diplomatic fruit without support from Congress or the American public for a conflict with Syria. Based on that political reality, the most force the administration could bring to bear was gunfire from the Sixth Fleet, and since Assad could rely upon proxy forces to do his bidding in the Shuf, such fires were unlikely, as Weinberger believed, to convince the Syrian leader to leave Lebanon or stop meddling in its political affairs.[106]

Between 19 and 26 September, the Syrians were given a display of what form aggressive self-defense would take. On 19 September, strikes were called in to support Lebanese forces defending Suq al-Gharb. Three days later the French conducted a retaliatory air strike on Syrian and Druze elements in the Shuf. Then on 26 September the *New Jersey* arrived off the coast, signaling additional resolve on the part of the United States, a point McFarlane made deliberately with Assad. American negotiating positions had been further strengthened on 21 September, when Congress extended the MNF mission for another eighteen months.[107]

On the day the *New Jersey* arrived, the Syrians agreed to sign a ceasefire agreement with the Lebanese. While it is difficult to know exactly why Assad made that decision, from the perspective of Shultz and McFarlane, American diplomacy had succeeded because it had been backed by a credible show of military strength. But another factor may have been at work. The Druze had been unable to overrun the LAF, which was well armed by the United States and remained intact rather than breaking along confessional lines as many had believed it would. By signing the ceasefire, Assad signaled that he did not want to commit his forces to the fighting, and a stalemate had been reached. Neither the United States nor Syria was willing to take the next step militarily, clearing the way for diplomacy.[108]

In the aftermath of the ceasefire agreement, Weinberger and Vessey hoped to reduce the number of forces ashore.[109] They believed that the supporting fire from the Sixth Fleet had put the marines in the difficult position of appearing to have sided with the Lebanese government and Phalangist militia. Nevertheless, Weinberger and Vessey were cognizant that such a withdrawal had to be done in a way so as not to disrupt the delicate diplomatic dance being managed following the ceasefire.[110]

Officials had just begun their deliberations of when and how to adjust the US military posture on the ground when a suicide terrorist bombed the marine barracks at the Beirut International Airport, killing 241 Americans. The 23 October attack further spurred the administration to conduct a reappraisal of how and when military force should support American diplomatic efforts.

6

THE WEINBERGER DOCTRINE

A New Pattern for Civil-Military Relations

A S THE REAGAN ADMINISTRATION worked to relate military power and diplomacy to achieve its policy
objectives in Lebanon, a formal reappraisal of its strategy
occurred in two instances, resulting in adjustments to the manner in
which force was used. With the first strategic reappraisal, officials expanded the area of the multinational force's presence mission to improve Lebanon's chances for building a reconciliation government.
With the second reassessment, they changed the MNF's operational
concept from presence to aggressive self-defense in order to steer Syria
back to the negotiating table. Each reappraisal was greatly influenced
by the political realities both at home and in the Middle East.

Although tragic, the barracks bombing did not end the resolve of administration leaders to overcome the Vietnam syndrome and to provide
American leadership on the international stage, nor did it undermine
their belief in the efficacy of military power as a tool of statecraft. Instead, the attack provided the impetus for crafting a major policy speech
in which the administration would codify six principles for deciding
when and how to use military power. These six principles, which would
come to be known as the "Weinberger Doctrine," are representative of

a pattern of civil-military relations that synthesized the administration's concerns about potential threats and requirements of world involvement with domestic political realities and social norms.

The doctrine's principles are symbolic of one plank in the bridge that Reagan and his cabinet built for Americans to carry the nation from its sour Vietnam experience to its future need to respond in a legitimate and decisive manner to gray-area challenges, such as irregular warfare and state-sponsored terrorism. Not wanting to make the use of military power an election-year issue, however, the speech, while mostly completed by April 1984, was not delivered until after the November general election.[1]

Challenging the Vietnam Syndrome with Action: Grenada

AT THE TIME OF the barracks bombing, the administration was already developing plans to invade Grenada.[2] The events leading up to this action began in 1979, when Maurice Bishop, the leader of a Marxist group called the New Jewel movement, took control of the island nation in a coup d'état. Bishop immediately aligned Grenada with Cuba and, in turn, with the Soviet Union and other Eastern-bloc nations. The Reagan administration became concerned about Grenada in early 1983, when intelligence reports indicated that approximately eight hundred Cuban soldiers and technicians were constructing a 10,000-foot jet runway there. This runway was considered much larger than anything the country would need for its tourist industry, and it did not have an air force, thus leading US officials to conclude that the island was being transformed into a Soviet-Cuban base for military operations. The most significant concern was that the Soviets could send long-range bombing missions from the island or Cuba could ship supplies to and from Libya and Angola.[3]

In a defense address to the nation on 23 March 1983, Reagan showed pictures of the runway construction and expressed his concerns:

President Reagan, Secretary of State George Shultz, and National Security Advisor Robert McFarlane discuss the situation in Grenada at the Eisenhower Cabin, Augusta National Golf Club, on 23 October 1983.

On the small island of Grenada, at the southern end of the Caribbean chain, the Cubans, with Soviet financing and backing, are in the process of building an airfield with a 10,000-foot runway. Grenada doesn't even have an air force. Who is it intended for? The Caribbean is a very important passageway for our international commerce and military lines of communication. More than half of all American oil imports now pass through the Caribbean. The rapid buildup of Grenada's military potential is unrelated to any conceivable threat to this island country of under 110,000 people and totally at odds with the pattern of other eastern Caribbean State, most of which are unarmed.

The Soviet-Cuban militarization of Grenada, in short, can only be seen as power projection into the region. And it is in this important economic and strategic area that we're trying to help the Governments of El Salvador, Costa Rica, Honduras, and others in their struggles for democracy against guerrillas supported through Cuba and Nicaragua.[4]

On 7 June, Bishop visited with National Security Advisor William Clark and Deputy Secretary Kenneth W. Dam, who encouraged him to moderate his actions, which had included jailing political opponents and denouncing the United States. Bishop's response was not positive: "His [Bishop's] response led us to conclude that we should review United States policy toward Grenada and also to start thinking what we should do if the Americans in Grenada were threatened or taken hostage."[5]

The trip to Washington left Bishop vulnerable to attack from a more-radical faction in Grenada, which charged that he did not truly support the revolution's Marxist-Leninist program. He was overthrown in a coup and placed under house arrest by members of that faction on 13 October. Although freed six days later by a crowd 3,000 strong, Bishop and five of his cabinet officials were caught again and this time assassinated by members of the Grenadian armed forces. Amid the ensuing chaos and turmoil, a twenty-four-hour curfew was issued, with a warning that anyone found in public would be shot. Diplomats from the US embassy in Barbados attempted to travel to Grenada, but all flights to the island were cancelled.

While Bishop was no friend of the West, the unrest following his assassination greatly concerned the United States and members of the Organization of Eastern Caribbean States (OECS), who were joined by Jamaica and Barbados as well. On 22 October, the OECS unanimously decided to form a multinational Caribbean force to remove what they considered an outlaw regime and restore democracy in Grenada. That same day Dominican prime minister Eugenia Charles, acting on behalf of the OECS, requested help from the United States to accomplish those objectives.

President Reagan, Secretary of State George Shultz, and National Security Advisor
Robert McFarlane discuss Grenada with Prime Minister Eugenia Charles
of Dominica. Courtesy Ronald Reagan Library.

Reagan responded positively, offering three justifications for his decision. First, approximately 1,000 US citizens lived on Grenada, of whom 800 were medical students, and he did not want to face a hostage situation like the one in Iran in 1979. Second, the president wanted to follow through on his commitment to support democracy and freedom. As Secretary of State Shultz later cast the issue: "What kind of a country would we be, he [Reagan] asked, if we refused to help small but steadfast democratic countries in our neighborhood to defend themselves against the threat of this kind of tyranny and lawlessness?"[6] Finally, Reagan wanted to eliminate further Cuban intervention in Grenada.

On the twenty-third, the president signed NSDD-110A, "Response to Caribbean Governments' Request to Restore Democracy on Grenada," which outlined these three policy objectives.[7] Reagan received unanimous support from his cabinet officers and from the Joint Chiefs of Staff.[8] The support of the latter stemmed from their view that intervention in Grenada would be "a clearly defined mission for which United States forces have been trained and armed," and the assigned "objectives . . . were realistic and could be achieved by military forces and power."[9]

In considering how to relate military force to its policy objectives, the administration had to address the three issues of when the force should be sent, what size the force should be, and how the administration should handle the political realities that would come into play. Regarding commencement of operations, most agreed that it should be done as soon as possible to capitalize on surprise and improve the chances of rescuing the Americans. Weinberger and Vessey recommended delaying the operation until at least 25 October to give the Defense Department time to gather additional intelligence for the operation. Weinberger noted: "My original instructions to the Joint Chiefs had been that we should plan to begin the operation at the soonest possible time consistent with the maximum safety to our forces, and consistent with the actual time needed to assemble both the forces and supplies for a successful action."[10]

Regarding the size of the force, Weinberger and Shultz were of one mind: the force should be twice as large as the Pentagon recommendation. Shultz later recounted: "I suggested to the president that he call Jack Vessey . . . and ask him what the numbers of troops were that would be required for this operation. 'After he has told you, Mr. President, I suggest that you tell him to double it.'"[11] Similarly, Weinberger also related that his "invariable practice was to double, at least, any Joint Chief recommendations as to the size of a force required." He noted that this reasoning was based on his belief that one of the "major problems" with the 1979 hostage rescue attempt in Iran was that the Pentagon sent "too few helicopters."[12]

It is clear from reading his memoirs that Weinberger's thinking was also greatly influenced by the manner in which the nation conducted the Vietnam War. He explained: "The war in Vietnam, with our 'limited objectives' and yet unlimited willingness to commit troops, reinforced my belief, which I expressed many times when I was the Secretary of Defense, that it was a very terrible mistake for government to commit soldiers to battle without any intention of supporting them sufficiently to enable them to win, and indeed without any intention to win."[13] He further stated: "I . . . felt keenly that we should not wander into any situation of conflict unless we felt it was important enough to win. We should define our mission carefully—and then go in with overwhelming force to ensure victory."[14] In the end, American forces in the Grenada operation outnumbered the island's defenders by ten to one.[15]

Regarding political realities, the administration did its best to manage the perception of congressional leaders, allies, and the public regarding the operation. The day prior to initiating the invasion, the Joint Chiefs presented Reagan with the final plan. During that discussion, General Vessey strayed away from providing strictly military advice and warned the president of possible problems with public opinion because of what had happened to the marines in Lebanon.[16] While the general was correct and Reagan did face criticism, the administration took a number of actions to keep that opposition within manageable limits.

On 20 October, Reagan directed his counselor for legislative affairs, Kenneth Duberstein, to develop a strategy for consultation with leaders on Capitol Hill. Implementation began the evening before the invasion when the president invited the House and Senate majority and minority leaders and the Speaker of the House to the family quarters of the White House so he could "consult" with them regarding the invasion. Although Reagan had already given the final approval for the mission, he and other administration leaders pointed to this meeting as fulfillment of the requirement in the War Powers Resolution for consultation with Congress. They all believed that the president had followed the intent of the law because he had the power to abort the mission if he had deemed it necessary after this discussion.

Still, congressional leaders did not believe that they had been truly consulted. Thomas P. "Tip" O'Neill, the Speaker of the House, characterized the meeting as one in which they were "informed," and Senate Majority Leader Baker said they were "advised." The meeting took place after the daily news cycle in order to prevent any leaks that might jeopardize the secrecy of the mission. A second part of Duberstein's plan was for Reagan and his advisors to "consult" with the entire leadership in Congress. Thus, at 8:15 A.M. the following day, three hours after the invasion had begun, the president and his key advisers conducted a briefing for legislative leaders.[17]

Congressional reaction to the invasion was divided—Republicans rallied around the decision, while Democrats split over whether or not to support the president. Speaker O'Neill, who had not supported the invasion when he was "consulted" at the White House, nevertheless lent his support while American soldiers were in action on the island, arguing that the president deserved bipartisan support in a time of crisis.[18] Not everyone was as generous. Sen. Daniel Patrick Moynihan (D-N.Y.) called the attack "an act of war" and questioned whether "you restore democracy at the point of a bayonet." Sen. Alan Cranston (D-Calif.) called Reagan "a trigger-happy president," and Rep. Ted Weiss (D-N.Y.) characterized the invasion as "immoral, illegal, and unconstitutional."[19]

On 27 October, seventeen House Democrats introduced a concurrent resolution that called upon the president for immediate removal of US military forces from Grenada. The following day, nine Democrats and nine Republicans introduced a joint resolution requiring an immediate withdrawal, asserting that the president had violated the constitutional prerogatives of the Congress. Neither resolution left the Foreign Affairs Committee.[20] On 1 November, the House approved a measure making the War Powers Resolution operative from the day of the invasion, 25 October, but this also failed in the Senate.[21] All these legislative actions carried little weight because few in Congress or the administration believed that the operation would last over sixty days.[22]

Reagan officials worried not only about the perceptions of Congress but also those of its European allies. American nuclear missiles would begin deployment into Western Europe in December 1983, and the administration was concerned that Grenada might give antimissile groups an opportunity to argue that the United States was irresponsible

The chairman of the Joint Chiefs of Staff, Gen. John W. Vessey Jr., briefs a
bipartisan group of congressional leaders about the situation in Grenada.
Courtesy Ronald Reagan Library.

and should not be trusted with nuclear weapons in Europe. Additionally, the administration was counting on continued support in Lebanon from the French and Italians, despite the bombing there and the
American actions in Grenada. To manage the perceptions of the allies,
George Shultz traveled to Europe on 27 October to meet with the British, French, and Italian foreign ministers.[23] All three nations expressed
criticism and were joined by most Latin American countries as well. On
28 October, the UN Security Council approved a resolution "deeply
deploring" the US-led invasion as a "flagrant violation of international
law."[24] While the United States vetoed the resolution, the invasion left
America isolated, supported only by the eastern Caribbean nations who
had requested US assistance.

In addition to opposition from American allies, the administration worried about the support of the American public. Officials tightly controlled what information the public received, and camera crews were kept off the island for four days. In the interim, the administration released sanitized videotapes of the operation to news organizations and justified its actions by claiming the military necessity for secrecy. By the time the press was allowed to report unhindered on Grenada, public opinion on the invasion had been successfully shaped.[25]

In addition to controlling news coverage from the island, the administration presented its rationale for the operation to the public. Now almost three years into his administration, Reagan continued to believe, as he had while running for office, that the American people would accept the responsibility to spread freedom and defend peace so long as the nature of the challenge was conveyed to them. On 27 October, he addressed the nation to explain that even though Grenada and Lebanon were oceans apart, they were closely related by the fact that Moscow had encouraged violence in both countries and provided support through a network of surrogates and terrorists. He stated: "You know, there was a time when our national security was based on a standing army here within our own borders and shore batteries of artillery along our coasts, and, of course, a navy to keep the sealanes open for the shipping of things necessary for our well-being. The world has changed. Today, our national security can be threatened in faraway places. It's up to all of us to be aware of the strategic importance of such places and to be able to identify them." Regarding US interests in Grenada, Reagan offered three reasons for the invasion: approximately 1,000 US citizens were at risk of being taken hostage or killed, the United States had received a legitimate request from the OECS to help restore order and democracy, and there was a real threat of the island becoming a Soviet-Cuban colony.[26] Following the president's speech, polling showed that respondents were more receptive to the presence of American forces in Grenada than the previous night. Yet it also indicated that the change could be attributable more to news accounts than to the speech.[27]

In examining the popularity of the Grenada invasion with the public, one cannot overlook the reactions of the medical students evacuated from the island. Upon return to American soil, one student fell to his knees and kissed the runway asphalt, an event covered widely on all three major networks. Shultz recounted: "The TV anchormen kept trying to push the students to say that they were never in danger; it didn't work. Suddenly I could sense the country's emotions turn around. Our effort in Grenada wasn't an immoral imperialist intervention: it was an essential rescue and a job well done."[28] A *New York Times* article on the students' return reported: "With tears and expressions of relief, scores of American students evacuated from Grenada told yesterday of days and nights of terror on the strife-torn island and praised the Reagan administration and United States invasion forces for bringing them safely away."[29]

Additionally, news reports showed warehouses full of weapons, ammunition, and communications equipment, which implicated Cuba in using Grenada as a military base to spread communism in the Caribbean and Africa. A poll conducted on 26 and 27 October showed men, by a margin of 62–29 percent, approved of Reagan's decision to send troops to Grenada.[30] Similarly, a November ABC–*Washington Post* survey showed Americans 71 percent in favor and only 22 percent opposed to the invasion.[31] With such strong public support, concerns about congressional reaction were largely negated.

Kai Schoenhals and Richard Melanson, while examining a series of polling data taken following the Grenada operation, found an "overwhelmingly pragmatic nature . . . [to] the public's reactions." They concluded: "Despite the administration's elaborate efforts to portray the Grenada intervention as a humanitarian rescue mission, a compassionate response to an urgent request for help by small, friendly, democratic neighbors, and the successful foiling of a Soviet-Cuban colony, the U.S. public supported the action because it was swift, conclusive, and relatively free of cost." While November polling portrayed Americans as strongly in favor of the operation, a *Newsweek*-Gallup canvass showed a majority favoring a withdrawal as soon as US citizens were

secured, rather than maintaining forces until the formation of a democratic government. Furthermore, 47 percent of these polled believed
that Reagan was too quick to employ US forces (43 percent supported
the timing).[32] While the president may have earned support from the
American people for Grenada, he had not convinced them to support
his broader plans to advance democracy in the region through aggressive action against the Soviets and their proxies.[33]

Nonetheless, the administration viewed Grenada as a defining moment in American history. Reagan proclaimed: "A period of self-doubt
is over. . . . History will record that one of our turning points came on a
small island in the Caribbean where America went to take care of her
own and to rescue a neighboring nation from a growing tyranny."[34] Years
later Shultz explained why he believed the administration had made the
right decision to use military force in Grenada:

> Often one hears the argument "Force should be used only as the
> last resort." This makes people feel good, and it sounds states-
> manlike. In fact, I feel strongly that it is poor public policy and
> an unsound application of the law. The use of force, and the
> credible threat of the use of force, are legitimate instruments
> of national policy and should be viewed as such. Waiting to
> use force as a last resort would have meant possibly enduring
> hostage taking and having to use force then. The use of force
> obviously should not be taken lightly, but better to use force
> when you *should* rather than when you *must; last* means *no
> other*, and by that time the level of force and the risk involved
> may have multiplied many times over.[35]

Weinberger similarly had positive remarks regarding the operation: "In
many ways, it was the complete model for future such activities, should
our armed forces be called upon to undertake them at such short notice
as we were in Grenada. If the measure of success is attaining our political
objectives at minimum cost, in the shortest possible time, then the Grenada operation has to be judged to have been a complete success."[36]

In its handling of Grenada, the administration further incorporated lessons that would ultimately become its policy describing US military power as a tool of statecraft. Yet it recognized that while responding to Cubans in Grenada was one matter, dealing with terrorism, like that which had occurred at the marine barracks in Beirut, presented an entirely new set of challenges.

The Vietnam Syndrome Redux

FOLLOWING THE ATTACK on the marine barracks, Secretary of Defense Weinberger convened the DoD Commission on the Beirut International Airport Terrorist Act of 23 October 1983, the Long Commission for short.[37] The commission reported to Weinberger: "The 23 October 1983 attack on the Marine Battalion Landing Team Headquarters in Beirut was tantamount to an act of war using the medium of terrorism. Terrorist warfare, sponsored by sovereign states or organized political entities to achieve political objectives, is a threat to the United States that is increasing at an alarming rate. The 23 October catastrophe underscores the fact that terrorist warfare can have significant political impact and demonstrates that the United States . . . is inadequately prepared to deal with this threat."[38] The administration believed the only way to confront terrorism was to be willing to respond militarily, though also recognizing that the challenge raised a host of questions for a free society. Americans would undoubtedly, and justifiably, have many concerns about when and how preemptive, preventative, or punitive action would be taken against known terrorist groups. What evidence would the public insist upon having before sanctioning forceful action, and what action would they consider appropriate?[39]

Given the national preference to reserve military power as a last resort when all else has failed, the administration recognized the challenge of developing a sound counterterrorism program.[40] Shultz explained their concerns: "As the [terrorist] threat mounted—and as the involvement of such countries as Iran, Syria, Libya, and North Korea had become more and more evident—it had become increasingly important that the nations of the West face up to the need for active defense against terrorism. Once it becomes established that terrorism works—that it achieves its political objectives—its practitioners will be bolder, and the threat to us will be all the greater. The lesson of Vietnam was continually being cited to reject any use of military force unless in exceptional circumstances and with near total public support in advance."[41] In a speech to the Trilateral Commission on 3 April 1984, Shultz addressed the administration's position on the lessons of Vietnam:

> It is often said that the lesson of Vietnam is that the United States should not engage in military conflict without a clear and precise military mission, solid public backing, and enough resources to finish the job. This is undeniably true. But does it mean there are no situations where a discrete assertion of power is needed or appropriate for limited purposes? Unlikely. Whether it is crisis management or power projection or a show of force or peacekeeping or a localized military action, there will always be instances that fall short of an all-out national commitment on the scale of World War II. The need to avoid no-win situations cannot mean that we turn automatically away from hard-to-win situations that call for prudent involvement. These will always involve risks; we will not always have the luxury of being able to choose the most advantageous circumstances. And our adversaries can be expected to play rough. . . . It is highly unlikely that we can respond to gray-area challenges without adapting power to political circumstances. . . . This is just not the kind of reality we are likely to be facing in the 1980s, or 1990s, or beyond.[42]

In addition to the threat of state-sponsored terrorism, the administration's foreign-policy setbacks in the Middle East and Central America also added to a desire to enunciate clear principles for deciding when and how to use military power.

Following the Beirut bombing, legislative leaders began to reconsider their earlier decision extending the marines' MNF deployment for eighteen months. Rather than risk facing a certain political defeat when Congress returned to session in January 1984, the administration started making plans in December 1983 to remove US forces.[43] By February, the marines were aboard ships, and by March they had left the Mediterranean completely. Despite this outcome, Reagan still believed that the nation needed to be prepared to conduct similar peacekeeping missions in the future.

The administration struggled in Central America as well to combine military force with its diplomatic efforts. In 1981 Reagan had asked for and received support from congressional leaders to aid Contra insurgents in Nicaragua in an effort to pressure the Sandinistas into diplomatic negotiations. By the end of 1982, however, some legislators became concerned that the administration might be funding the overthrow of the Sandinista regime and engaging in activities that could draw the nation into a war in Central America. To express its concern, on 8 December 1982 by a vote of 411–0, the House of Representatives passed the Boland Amendment, which prohibited the Department of Defense and the CIA from providing military equipment, training, or advice for the purpose of overthrowing the Nicaraguan government.[44]

A story related by Shultz shows that going into its third year, the administration was just as concerned about Central America as it had been during its first, but that it was well aware of the political challenges it faced at home in pursuing a coherent policy in the region. The secretary wrote:

> On December 21, 1982, just back from a trip to solidify relations with our European allies and with a new U.S. peace initiative under way in the Middle East, I was feeling reasonably good about our progress in dealing with thorny foreign policy problems. I was startled to be assaulted by CIA director Bill Casey just after finishing a meeting in the Roosevelt Room of the White House. Bill cornered me as I was leaving and unloaded:

"The American people are not behind our policy in Central America," he growled. "Our support in Congress is fading. We're in danger of losing on what is by far the most important foreign policy problem confronting the nation. You shouldn't be traveling around Europe. You should be going around the United States sounding the alarm and generating support for tough policies on the most important problem on our agenda. Force is the only language the Communists understand."[45]

Shultz agreed: "the situation in Central America was a problem of immense importance to the United States, and I knew we had to confront it." Nevertheless, he also noted: "The Soviets knew full well that Central America and the Caribbean was the region where the American press and American public opinion were the most sensitive to the possibility of 'another Vietnam.' Trying to forge policy was like walking through a swamp."[46]

Challenging the Vietnam Syndrome with Words: Public Diplomacy

FROM THE ADMINISTRATION'S perspective, congressional interference was undermining its strategy both in the Middle East and in Central America. Reagan and his advisors believed that public and congressional support were critical components to using military force as an effective tool of statecraft and to constructing a foreign policy that was able to address the multitude of threats the nation faced. Thus, in January 1983, the Reagan administration took action with NSDD-77, "Management of Public Diplomacy Relative to National Security."[47]

The directive explained: "Public diplomacy is comprised of those actions of the U.S. Government designed to generate support for our national security objectives." It called for a special-planning group under the NSC to be established under the chairmanship of National Security Advisor William Clark. According to the directive, the group was "responsible for the overall planning, directions, coordination and monitoring of implementation of public diplomacy activities." As secretaries of state and defense respectively, Shultz and Weinberger would be members of the special-planning group. Additionally, four interagency standing committees were established and ordered to report to it.[48] One of these was the Public Affairs Committee, charged with "the planning and coordination of major speeches on national security subjects and other public appearances by senior officials."[49]

Four speeches from this time are of particular importance to the development and articulation of the Weinberger Doctrine: "Power and Diplomacy in the 1980s," given by Secretary Shultz before the Trilateral Commission on 3 April 1984; "American Leadership is Back," delivered by President Reagan before the Center for Strategic and International Studies on 6 April 1984; "The Uses of Military Power," delivered by Secretary Weinberger before the National Press Club on 28 November 1984; and "The Ethics of Power," given by Shultz before the convocation of Yeshiva University on 9 December 1984.[50]

While it is uncertain whether these were part of the administration's public-diplomacy campaign as managed by the Public Affairs Committee, they do contain three common themes and were intended to convince the public of the importance of those ideas. First, the security and protection of vital interests demanded that the nation be prepared to deploy military force to respond to a conflict or crisis. Second, for diplomacy to be effective, it needed to be backed by military force, both direct and indirect. Third, a better system than the present one was needed to ensure that the nation legitimately used all the tools of statecraft and achieved a consistent, coherent, and determined foreign policy.

In their speeches, Reagan, Schultz, and Weinberger explained that US security depended on providing leadership within the community of nations. They maintained that isolationism was no longer an option because America's strength was needed to protect all democratic nations' vital interests, including peace, justice, sources of energy, minerals, and free markets. This was a theme that the administration had promoted throughout its first three years in office, yet this time it was paired with an insistence that military force may very likely be required to carry out that leadership responsibility. As Weinberger explained: "While we do not seek to deter or settle all the world's conflicts, we must recognize that, as a major power, our responsibilities and interests are now of such scope that there are few troubled areas we can afford to ignore. So we must be prepared to deal with a range of possibilities, a spectrum of crises, from local insurgency to global conflict. We prefer, of course, to *limit* any conflict in its early stages, to contain and control it—but to do that our military forces must be deployed in a *timely* manner, and be fully supported and prepared *before* they are engaged, because many of those difficult decisions must be made extremely quickly."[51] He, Reagan, and Shultz noted the fine line the nation could walk as it carried out this responsibility. In their speeches, by invoking the memory of the European democracies' early appeasement of Hitler, they justified the need for involvement, whereas by invoking the memory of Vietnam, they emphasized that any involvement must be handled in a prudent manner to prevent unnecessary forfeiture of blood, treasure, and spirit to meet that responsibility.

All three characterized the threats to peace as covering a full spectrum, from individual acts of terrorism to nuclear war. They warned that gray-area threats, such as state-sponsored terrorism and wars fought by proxy forces, were particularly challenging for the United States because they fell somewhere in the continuum between war and peace. In a democracy, the decision to use military force comes easily when one's own soil is attacked, but knowing when and how to respond to all other significant, yet different, events is much more challenging. Weinberger expressed his concern: "We find ourselves, then, face to face with a modern paradox: The most likely challenge to the peace— the gray area conflicts—are precisely the most difficult challenges to which a democracy must respond. Yet, while the source and nature of today's challenges are uncertain, our response must be clear and understandable."[52] These speeches emphasized that it was in the nation's best interest to become committed to smaller events in order to prevent them from spinning out of control and leading to total war. Such commitments were described not only in terms of military force but also in terms of economic aid, security assistance, and diplomatic mediation.

The concept of diplomatic mediation led to their second point: for diplomacy to be effective, it needed to be backed by both direct and indirect military force. In support of negotiations, this force might include direct involvement in localized military actions as in Grenada, show-of-force operations as conducted in Central America in the summer of 1983, or peacekeeping operations as in Lebanon. Military force could also be indirect in nature, such as support for proxy forces in Central America or military assistance to allies to help in their defense.

While both Weinberger and Shultz agreed on the importance of relating military power to diplomacy, they parted company over when and how US military forces were to be coupled to the diplomatic effort. Weinberger believed that the nation should preserve its combat soldiers as a last resort and instead rely upon what he in later years called "other currencies of power" to promote US interests and to shape outcomes.[53] Thus, he supported economic aid, political support, military aid, sales and training, and covert action to advance American interests and believed that those actions, if carried out successfully, could preclude the need for combat forces. Weinberger argued that soldiers put into harm's way as pawns in a diplomatic chess game were likely to have lower morale and be less effective.[54]

Shultz, like Weinberger, was supportive of using "other currencies of power" whenever possible, however, he was more inclined to believe that the presence of American forces on the ground was important in demonstrating the nation's resolve and lent credibility and strength to diplomatic efforts. Weinberger countered and cautioned against basing US diplomacy on the ability to deploy forces because it ignored the possibility that domestic constraints could preclude such leverage. For Shultz, military forces on the ground linked with diplomatic efforts represented *power*; those forces were the physical embodiment of national resolve and support for the diplomacy at hand. His ideas reflected a gradualist, or incremental, approach like that popularized in the 1960s by

Secretary of Defense Robert McNamara and by limited-war theorists.[55] This line of thought argues that military force is one instrument of national power that can be combined simultaneously with others in order to achieve policy ends.[56] Thus, the use of military force should operate on a continuum of coercion to achieve strategic advantage, and if the desired response is not forthcoming, then one has the option to add more force. In this approach, military force is a direct extension of policy.

Weinberger was adamantly opposed to the gradualist approach, which he associated with the Korean War, the Vietnam War, and the Reagan administration's efforts in Lebanon. Because this approach ignored domestic political realities, it was fatally flawed: "Gradualism is inherently attractive to some [sic] almost always mistaken. It exaggerates the illusion of control, violates the strategic principle of concentration of force, and encourages underestimation of the domestic political costs entailed by any use of American military forces abroad."[57] He believed that how and when military force was coupled to US diplomacy ultimately determined the ability or power of that force to serve as an effective instrument. In his classic *On War*, Carl von Clausewitz contended, "If you want to overcome your enemy you must match your effort against his power of resistance, which can be expressed as the product of two inseparable factors, viz. *the total means at his disposal and the strength of his will.*"[58]

In a democracy like the United States, Weinberger recognized a slightly different formula was required since the convoluted political and bureaucratic systems adversely affect how will and means are coupled to a military force. Therefore, rather than define power like Clausewitz as a product of all the will and means at a nation's disposal, Weinberger conceptualized power as the product of the will and means actually coupled to the military instrument on the ground. When the will and means of the American people are tied to a military unit, it represents *power* and as such can accomplish challenging military and political objectives. Yet without that coupling, a military unit is merely a *force*, with an effectiveness limited to the reach of its weapons. The six principles the administration codified in November 1984 seem designed to maximize the will and means coupled to a military force by capitalizing on the strengths of American ideals and accounting for domestic political realities.

The first test emphasizes that the nation should not commit forces to combat unless vital interests are at stake, and the fifth test calls for having reasonable assurance of the support of the American people. Additionally, the sixth test limits the use of military force only as a last resort. Taken together, these three tests work to ensure that power exists with the force on the ground because the will of the American people would be linked to vital interests such as self-preservation or moral issues like freedom and liberty.[59]

In order to account for domestic political realities, Weinberger's second test calls for commitment of enough military force to quickly achieve one's political and military objectives, which his third test calls for developing clearly. Unmistakably defined objectives would prevent mission creep, while their rapid achievement minimized the opportunity for any congressional debate that might hinder the leverage a military force could exert. Lastly, the administration sought to account for domestic political realities with the fourth test, which called for constant reassessment. Through continual reevaluation, any degradation in the will or means coupled to the military force could be recognized quickly to allow appropriate adjustment of objectives. Thus, the six tests seek to root the will and means coupled to a military instrument in moral concerns and alleviate the affect of domestic political realities.

A subset of the Shultz and Weinberger debate on the proper relationship of power and diplomacy was the disagreement over how the administration ought to respond to terrorist attacks.[60] Shultz believed that Weinberger and Pentagon leaders had a "deep philosophical opposition to using . . . military for counterterrorist operations." He elaborated: "There was the Joint Special Operations Command (JSOC), a group of commandos trained to rescue Americans held by terrorists. But Cap [Weinberger] set down conditions that must exist before the JSOC could be employed that were so restrictive as to mean that they would virtually *never* see action."[61]

Weinberger, for his part, charged members of the State Department with favoring an "unfocused" or "revenge" approach that called for bombing a Syrian or Iranian city if the United States suspected a terrorist attack originated from either of those nations. Arguing against such a policy, Weinberger believed it failed to focus on the terrorists themselves and would lead to an unnecessary cycle of violence. Instead, he favored a "focused" approach that held off action unless the terrorists' origins were confirmed and then only responded in a manner that was appropriate to the terrorist action and would discourage future attacks. The administration's response to the bombing of a discotheque in Berlin served as Weinberger's example of a successful focused approach.[62] When Libyan linkage to the bombing was exposed, the response involved attacks on various targets in Libya associated with terrorism. Despite the differences, the administration believed that the United States could abide by the rule of law and effectively counter terrorists if a more-active means of defense was developed.[63]

Most contemporary journalists focused on these differences of opinion between Shultz and Weinberger rather than on the larger message each speech imparted—the executive branch needed to be allowed to exercise its prerogative to use military power as a tool of statecraft.[64] A piece written by Sen. J. William Fulbright and Seth Tillman proved to be an exception to this rule. In their article, "Shultz, Weinberger Nondifferences," they argued: "there may be less to their apparent difference than meets the eye. . . . [W]hile they may differ as to when and how it should be used, both regard military force as the primary instrument of American foreign policy."[65]

Examining the Shultz and Weinberger speeches in a larger context shows the similarity in their support for the executive branch's use of military power as a tool of statecraft. Military actions demonstrated the nation's strength and resolve to pressure adversaries to negotiate, but unfortunately this demanded a balanced and sustained approach that had proven difficult for the United States following its experience in Vietnam.

Accordingly, the third point for the administration was the importance of mitigating challenges to consistency, coherence, and determination in American foreign policy. Reagan explained that a web of restrictions on executive action embedded in federal laws made it very difficult to maintain a coherent policy: "In the 1970s we saw a rash of congressional initiatives to limit the President's authority in the areas of trade, human rights, arms sales, foreign assistance, intelligence operations, and the dispatch of troops in time of crisis. Over a hundred separate prohibitions and restrictions on executive branch authority to formulate and implement foreign policy were enacted." Reagan argued: "If we're to have a sustainable foreign policy, the Congress must support the practical details of policy, not just the general goals." While not mentioning the War Powers Resolution by name, for his part Weinberger said:

> Once a decision to employ some degree of force has been made, and the purpose clarified, our government must have the clear mandate to carry out, and continue to carry out, that decision until the purpose has been achieved . . . The issue of which branch of government has authority to define that mandate and make decisions on using force is now being strongly contended. Beginning in the 1970s Congress demanded, and assumed, a far more active role in the making of foreign policy and in the decision-making process for the employment of military forces abroad than had been thought appropriate and practical before. As a result, the centrality of decision-making authority in the executive branch has been compromised by the legislative branch to an extent that actively interferes with that process.[66]

According to Shultz, that interference also stemmed from what he called "alibis for inaction." The first alibi argued that another nation should not be helped if it did not meet the human-rights standards required to receive assistance; the second saw conflict in another country as stemming from deep social and economic problems that must be resolved before United States involvement; and the third presumed that

America was a guilty party having nothing good to offer. Administration leaders insisted that the nation must overcome these concerns over the legitimacy of American action.

Reagan, Shultz, and Weinberger believed that events had demonstrated that the legislative branch's capability to restrict the president's freedom of action was detrimental to the nation's security. The current system to ensure that military force was for legitimate purposes and used in a legitimate manner needed reconsideration, Shultz argued: "Congress has the right, indeed the duty, to debate and criticize, to authorize and appropriate funds and share in setting the broad lines of policy. But micromanagement by a committee of 535 independent-minded individuals is a grossly inefficient and ineffective way to run an important enterprise. The fact is that depriving the President of flexibility weakens our country. Yet a host of restrictions on the President's ability to act are now built into our laws and our procedures. Surely there is a better way for the President and Congress to exercise their prerogatives without hobbling this country in the face of assaults on free-world interests abroad." In December 1984, he provided three tests that could be used to determine whether or not a use of power was legitimate: "The use of power is legitimate: *Not* when it crushes the human spirit and tramples human freedom, but when it can help liberate a people or support the yearning for freedom; *Not* when it imposes an alien will on an unwilling people, but when its aim is to bring peace or support peaceful processes; when it prevents others from abusing their power through aggression or oppression; and *Not* when it is applied unsparingly, without care or concern for innocent life, but when it is applied with the greatest efforts to avoid unnecessary causalities and with a conscience troubled by the pain unavoidably inflicted."[67]

With their speeches, Reagan, Shultz, and Weinberger expressed deep concern over the nation's current pattern of civil-military relations. They questioned whether it was adequately meeting the military-security needs of the nation. Was the pattern that had developed out of the nation's experience in the Vietnam War serving its role to bridge the gap between the nation's military-security needs and its social norms governing the use of violence? Was it instead, as they believed, leaving gaping holes through which the nation was falling?

The Weinberger Doctrine

ON THE EVENING OF 28 November 1984, Secretary of Defense Weinberger took the podium in front of the National Press Club in downtown Washington. Even when not holding a strong hand, Weinberger always found ways to appear certain and in command. That night, however, there was no need to bluff. The newsmen and women in his audience surely remembered the reports they had filed just three weeks earlier announcing to the American public and the world that Ronald Reagan had won a landslide reelection as president of the United States. It would not be necessary to remind his audience that Reagan had carried forty-nine of the fifty states or won the highest number of electoral votes ever received by a presidential candidate, 525 out of 538. Nor would the secretary have to flout that Reagan, having earned over 58 percent of the popular vote, surely earned a mandate from the American people to continue the course he had set four years earlier. His message would be delivered without explicitly stating such credentials.

Weinberger got right to the point: "I want to discuss with you perhaps the most important question concerning keeping the peace. Under what circumstances, and by what means, does a great democracy such as ours reach the painful decision that the use of military force is necessary to protect our interests or to carry out our national policy?" He explained that a pluralist democracy like the United States could easily decide upon military force when its own territory was under attack or to refrain from using the military to "invade, conquer or subjugate other nations." What was problematic was gaining and maintaining a consensus of support for less-apparent cases: "The extent to which the use of force *is* acceptable remains unresolved for the host of other situations which fall between these extremes of defensive and aggressive use of force."[68] He then offered his six tests as a way to think about using force given a fragmented US political system and international challenges that were nearly always in this gray area. (The six tests are enumerated in the preface.)

Just days after the secretary's address, William Safire wrote an editorial essay on the speech entitled "Only the 'Fun' Wars." The columnist contended: "Secretary Weinberger's purpose in enunciating the doctrine of only-fun-wars is to undermine Secretary of State Shultz's position in the battle for President Reagan's strategic soul." Safire said that the speech expressed "the world according to the most Vietnam-traumatized elements in the Pentagon," explaining:

> Secretary Weinberger's stunning doctrine suggests that we take a poll before we pull a trigger. No more unpopular wars—if the public won't hold a big parade to send us off, we're not going. And, no more of the "gradualist incremental approach," goes this Pentagon ultimatum—if we can't win in a week by pulverizing the place, it's not worth jeopardizing our men's lives or all the expensive equipment. Finally, our interest must be "vital"—we fire only when we see the reds of their eyes. . . . No wonder the epitome of a military operation in the mind of Pentagonians has become Grenada, the quick crushing of a lightly armed gang of thugs by a huge task force operating in the dark for a few weeks. Oh, what a lovely war."[69]

Safire concluded that these tests represented the dominant view of lessons from Vietnam and emerged as part of the ongoing dispute between Weinberger and Shultz over how to use military force to counter terrorism and support the nation's diplomatic efforts in places like the Middle East.

While Weinberger and Shultz did have significant disagreements over how to use military force, Safire's characterization of the speech uses too narrow a lens. Weinberger speechwriter K. T. McFarland stated that "The Uses of Military Power" address had its origins following the marine barracks bombing in 1983.[70] President Reagan and Secretary Weinberger discussed writing a speech outlining the conditions under which the administration would use military force, with the intent of it being a major policy speech. McFarland began work on the text in the fall of 1983 and had it completed by April 1984, but the White House asked that the speech be held up because they did not want to make the use of military force an election-year issue.[71]

Adm. John Poindexter, who was serving as the deputy national security advisor at the time that the address was staffed at the NSC, expressed uncertainty that Weinberger was asked by Reagan to write the speech. His recollection was that the defense secretary had written it to reflect his own views and that it was simply shaped by the NSC staff to come into line with the views held by the president.[72] When one examines the changes Poindexter made to the text during staffing, one can appreciate how he came to have that view.[73]

Weinberger's calendar for the day of the National Press Club address show him consulting with Gen. Colin Powell, his senior military assistant, in the morning regarding the NSC's proposed changes, then calling McFarlane regarding his meeting with Powell. Additionally, the secretary had breakfast with Shultz and talked with him about the speech. The calendar also indicates that following his meeting with Shultz, Weinberger called McFarlane back "re meeting with Shultz & further changes in speech."[74]

Materials from the Reagan Presidential Library show that a copy of Weinberger's speech arrived at the NSC on 27 November and was circulated for comment.[75] A routing form indicates that General Powell sent the text to Admiral Poindexter and was received by Karna Small, deputy assistant to the president and senior director for the NSC Public Affairs Directorate. She sent copies to Robert McFarlane; Donald Fortier, special assistant to the president and senior director of political-military affairs on the NSC; and Robert Kimmitt, deputy assistant to the president, executive secretary, and general counsel. During the staffing process, changes were recommended and incorporated into the final version of the speech.

A review of the changes and differences in the draft versions, markups, and final speech adds considerable insight and support to the contention that the six tests emerge from more than an intense ideological struggle. One example serves to illustrate this point. In Weinberger's version of the speech, the sixth test originally was written: "the commitment of U.S. forces to combat should be a last resort to be used only when other means have failed or clearly have no prospect of success." During the staffing process, Poindexter crossed through "to be used only when other means have failed or clearly have no prospect of success" and noted in the margin of the draft: "This leaves open the possibility of combining diplomatic and military force as a last resort."[76]

When asked about his comment, Poindexter remarked: "What I obviously meant rather than 'open' was 'out.' This leaves OUT the possibility. See, Cap was taking the position that the military should be used as a last resort after diplomatic action had been taken. But it was the view of a lot of us and I think of the President that we should often consider a combined diplomatic and military response to add credibility and weight to the diplomatic effort."[77] Poindexter wanted to make certain that the sixth test did not preclude using military power in conjunction with other tools of statecraft.

While the original speech was crafted by Weinberger and his speechwriter, they received input not only from generals in the Pentagon but also probably from the president, other cabinet members, and members of the NSC staff, which led to changes in the text and a version of the six tests that represented a synthesized policy by the administration that included Shultz's views.

Conclusion

RONALD REAGAN began challenging America's pattern of civil-military relations while campaigning for the presidency in 1980. He questioned the legitimacy of the Vietnam syndrome and contended that Americans in the 1980s were no less willing than their forefathers to use their power or make sacrifices to keep their "rendezvous with destiny." Reagan repudiated President Carter's claim that the United States was suffering from a crisis of confidence and instead argued that Americans were suffering from a crisis of leadership. At the heart of Reagan's platform lay a promise to renew the nation's confidence to pursue its interests and to lead on the international stage.

Campaigning under the slogan "peace through strength," Reagan envisioned a world hospitable to American society and its liberal-democratic ideals in which the United States and its allies were free from the threat of nuclear war and had access to vital resources. He believed that such peace could only be achieved by rebuilding America's strength both economically and militarily, pursuing reductions in nuclear arms, and actively working to roll back communism and to spread freedom and democracy.

In his first term as president, Reagan sought to provide the leadership he felt the nation needed by rebuilding its strategic and conventional military forces, dispatching military advisors to help the government of El Salvador overcome an insurgency supported by Cuba and the Soviet bloc, and expending an immense amount of political capital and funding to build the Contra proxy force to fight the communist-led government in Nicaragua. He also sent marines to Lebanon to encourage the withdrawal of foreign forces, to help achieve a stable government there, and to promote a secure northern border for Israel. When American lives and the safety of the Caribbean region were threatened by events in Grenada, the president deployed military forces to remove those threats. Reagan was a leader who wanted peace and did not want to use military force, however, his actions indicate that he did see the efficacy of military power as a tool of statecraft if it was used properly.

With each instance that Reagan and his administration sought to use military power, they recognized that they had to account for the nation's values, beliefs, laws, and unique political system, which influenced when and how force could be used. These political realities were born in the American experience of recent wars, but with each exercise of military power as a tool of statecraft, the administration's understanding of the relationship between the nation's political objectives, the use of force, and political realities evolved.

When Secretary Weinberger took the podium in front of the National Press Club on 28 November 1984, he enunciated six principles that represented a new pattern of civil-military relations for the nation that emerged from a combination of historical lessons, hard experiences, intense ideological and political struggle, and a need to respond to gray-area challenges. Considering the six tests in the overall context of the speech and the administration's experiences in the years previous, the Weinberger Doctrine was not promulgated to serve as a barrier against US efforts to defend and foster freedom abroad. Rather, the doctrine codified principles Reagan and his officials had followed throughout their first term to decide when and how to use military force.

The Weinberger Doctrine was a pattern for civil-military relations that synthesized the administration's concerns about potential threats and requirements for world involvement with domestic political realities and social norms. It was a pattern indicative of Reagan's "higher realism" in that it promised to ensure that the strengths of American ideals were fully leveraged while at the same time accounting for the peculiarities of America's domestic political realities. It was a pattern that promised to build a bridge capable of carrying Americans from their past use of military *force* to their future use of military *power*.

NOTES

Preface

1. Ronald Reagan, "Peace: Restoring the Margin of Safety," Veterans of Foreign Wars Convention, Chicago, 18 Aug. 1980, The Public Papers of President Ronald W. Reagan, Ronald Reagan Presidential Library, http://www.reagan.utexas.edu/archives/reference/8.18.80.html (accessed 28 Aug. 2010).

2. Weinberger, *Fighting for Peace*, 441–42 [Weinberger's emphasis].

3. Richard Halloran, "U.S. Will Not Drift into a Latin War, Weinberger Says," *New York Times*, 29 Nov. 1984.

4 J. William Fulbright and Seth P. Tillman, "Shultz, Weinberger Nondifferences," *New York Times*, 9 Dec. 1984 (online archive, accessed 3 Aug. 2006). Fulbright and Tillman used the term "Weinberger Doctrine" in their article, written eleven days after the secretary's speech. Leslie H. Gelb referred to the concepts captured in the speech as "Mr. Weinberger's defense doctrine." "Weinberger's War Guide: Follow the Direct Route," *New York Times*, 2 Dec. 1984.

5. Weinberger, *Fighting for Peace*, 434.

6. Kissinger, *Diplomacy*, 39.

7. Arthur S. Link, *The Higher Realism of Woodrow Wilson and Other Essays* (Nashville, TN: Vanderbilt University Press, 1971), 130. In a 1962 address to the Presbyterian Historical Society in Philadelphia, Link described President Wilson to his audience as a "supreme realist." He explained: "A realist . . . is one who faces life and its situations without illusions, in short, one who can see realities or truth through the fog of delusion that normally shrouds the earth-bound individual." Specifically, Link argued that Wilson's view of both domestic political realities and the global situation was indicative of a "higher realism" because it was "more perceptive, more in accord with ultimate reality, more likely to win the long-run moral approval of societies professing allegiance to the common western, humane, Christian traditions." This concept is very apt for describing President Reagan and many of the leaders in his cabinet as well.

Chapter 1

1. Isaacson, "America's Incredible Day," 9. Also see Steven R. Weisman, "Reagan Takes Oath as 40th President," *New York Times*, 21 Jan. 1981 (online archive, accessed 26 Jan. 2007); and James Reston, "Washington: Reagan's

Dramatic Success," *New York Times*, 21 Jan. 1981 (online archive, accessed 26 Jan. 2007).

2. Deaver, *Different Drummer*, 84–85. Deaver actually had to wake up the president-elect. He remarked that he would never doubt Reagan's ability to handle pressure.

3. Weinberger, *In the Arena*, 3–4.

4. Terence Smith, "A Weary Carter Returns to Plains," *New York Times*, 21 January 1981 (online archive, accessed 26 Jan. 2007).

5. Ronald Reagan, "Inaugural Address," 20 Jan. 1981, American Presidency Project, http://www.presidency.ucsb.edu/ws/index.php?pid=43130 (accessed 20 Nov. 2007). In 1999 John Woolley and Gerhard Peters collaborated to establish The American Presidency Project at the University of California, Santa Barbara. Their archive contains over 76,000 documents related to the study of the presidency and was the primary source for the presidential speeches referenced herein.

6. Reagan's message also contrasted sharply with Carter's inaugural address given four years earlier: "We have learned . . . that even our great Nation has its recognized limits, and that we can neither answer all questions nor solve all problems. We cannot afford to do everything." Jimmy Carter, "Inaugural Address," 20 Jan. 1977, American Presidency Project, http://www.presidency.ucsb.edu/ws/index.php?pid=6575 (accessed 20 Nov. 2007).

7. Carter's address was the product of a remarkable twelve-day period in the history of his administration. The president had planned to give an energy speech to the nation on 5 July. Yet on 4 July he decided it needed to be broadened to include other national concerns. Therefore he scrapped the original text and called in advisors to help him pull together a domestic summit at Camp David. Over the next six days, 150 people were shuttled by helicopter from Washington for sessions of varying length with the president. The participants included governors, cabinet members, former defense secretaries, educators, union leaders, clergymen, bankers, and civil-rights leaders. Carter also left the confines of Camp David to visit the homes of two families in middle America. His decision to hold a summit and give a broader speech was not spontaneous. Instead, it was influenced by concern over opinion-poll numbers, which had been dipping since the winter, and concerns over the mood of the American public found by his pollster Pat Caddell in the spring. For a more detailed narrative of this period in the Carter presidency, see Carter, *Keeping Faith*, 114–22; Kaufman, "A Growing Sense of Crisis," in *Presidency of James Earl Carter*, 133–50; and Bourne, *Jimmy Carter*, 441–46.

8. Jimmy Carter, "Address to the Nation on Energy and National Goals:

'The Malaise Speech,'" 15 July 1979, American Presidency Project, http://www
.presidency.ucsb.edu/ws/index.php?pid=32596 (accessed 4 Sept. 2010). In his
speech, Carter said:

> We were sure that ours was a nation of the ballot, not the bullet, until
> the murders of John Kennedy and Robert Kennedy and Martin Lu-
> ther King, Jr. We were taught that our armies were always invincible
> and our causes were always just, only to suffer the agony of Vietnam.
> We respected the Presidency as a place of honor until the shock of
> Watergate.
>
> We remember when the phrase "sound as a dollar" was an ex-
> pression of absolute dependability until 10 years of inflation began
> to shrink our dollar and our savings. We believed that our Nation's
> resources were limitless until 1973, when we had to face a growing
> dependence on foreign oil.

9. Ibid.; Carter, *Keeping Faith*, 118–20. Also see William K. Stevens, "Basic U.S. Shifts Foreseen," *New York Times*, 1 July 1979 (online archive, accessed 15 Feb. 2007). Stevens's article, published two weeks before Carter's
speech, discussed the potential psychological and sociological effects that the
energy crisis might have on the American public. Stevens seemed to accept
that there was no way around the tyranny of limitations the United States began
to encounter in the 1970s. He cited the following: "First there was Vietnam,
convincing many Americans that their country could no longer automatically
have its way in the world. Then there was the Arab oil embargo of 1973–4,
demonstrating to Americans that they no longer had a special claim to the
world's resources. Next, soaring inflation sapped Americans' long-standing conviction that they could get ahead if they worked hard. And now the energy crisis
of 1979 appears to be crystallizing it all, according to some experts." Stevens
asked whether Americans would learn to sacrifice while preserving a "spirit of
can-do optimism," or if instead they would adopt a more pessimistic outlook.
Carter clearly believed Americans were beginning to adopt a more pessimistic
outlook. He wanted to check that trend and have citizens draw upon their
historical "can-do optimism" to help them accept sacrifices.

10. Carter urged the nation to never import more foreign oil than it did in
1977, to set import quotas, to commit funds and resources to develop America's
own alternative sources of fuel, to pass a law to make utility companies cut their
use of oil by 59 percent over the next decade, to create an energy mobilization
board, and to follow a bold conservation program.

11. Patterson, *Restless Giant*, 127–28.

12. Adam Clymer, "Speech Lifts Carter Rating to 37%," *New York Times*, 18 July 1979 (online archive, accessed 26 Jan. 2007).

13. Hedrick Smith, "Dismissals Taken as Pre-Campaign Move by Carter," *New York Times*, 20 July 1979 (online archive, accessed 14 Nov. 2007); Terence Smith, "Carter Offered Resignations by Cabinet and Senior Staff," *New York Times*, 18 July 1979 (online archive, accessed 14 Nov. 2007); "Carter's Great Purge," 10–16. The five cabinet members who resigned were Joseph A. Califano Jr., secretary of health, education, and welfare; Michael Blumenthal, secretary of the Treasury; James Schlesinger, secretary of energy; Brock Adams, secretary of transportation; and Griffin Bell, attorney general. In October Carter established the President's Commission for a National Agenda (PCNA), which was to serve as an extension of the discussions he had held in July at Camp David. The commission's report was made public in January 1981. It stressed challenges, limits, and the necessity of making choices, noting: "The nation faces a decade of difficult choices and priority-setting among many important and compelling goals; it has been the principal task of the Commission to draw national attention to the necessity of choice and to clarify the implications and consequences of the difficult choices before us." PCNA, *A National Agenda for the Eighties*, 1. For a detailed study of the report, see Robert H. Zieger, "The Quest for National Goals, 1957–1981," in Fink and Graham, *Carter Presidency*, 39.

14. A contemporary journalist, Howell Raines, reached a similar conclusion while interviewing Americans in early August 1979. He reported that people from around the country agreed with Carter's theory that Americans had lost confidence in the future; however, his interviews also revealed that even among Carter supporters, there was "widespread agreement that much of the country's crisis had to do with Mr. Carter's leadership." Raines, "Citizens Ask if Carter Is Part of the 'Crisis,'" *New York Times*, 3 Aug. 1979 (online archive, accessed 15 Feb. 2007).

15. "Ronald Reagan's Announcement for Presidential Candidacy," 13 Nov. 1979, The Public Papers of President Ronald W. Reagan, Ronald Reagan Presidential Library, http://www.reagan.utexas.edu/archives/reference/11.13.79.html (accessed 29 Dec. 2010).

16. Many other Americans also questioned whether the crisis had more to do with Carter's leadership and ability to govern than to some national malaise. See Raines, "Citizens Ask if Carter Is Part of the 'Crisis.'"

17. Gerald M. Pomper, "The Presidential Election," in Marlene Pomper, *Election of 1980*, 67. In addition to Reagan's impressive victory, the Republican

Party had remarkable success in 1980. In the US Senate, they gained a majority for the first time since 1954; in the House of Representatives, the Democratic majority was cut in half; and the GOP gained four governorships (Missouri, West Virginia, Washington, and Arkansas). See Ellis Sandoz, "Introduction: Revolution or Flash In the Pan," in Sandoz and Crabb *Tide of Discontent*, 2; Austin Ranney, "The Carter Administration," in *American Elections of 1980*, 1–3; and Pomper, "Presidential Election," 65–67.

18. "Reagan's Announcement for Presidential Candidacy," 13 Nov. 1979. In his speech, Reagan admitted, "It is true there is a lack of confidence, an unease with things the way they are."

19. The following offer insightful discussion as to whether or not the election brought about a party realignment similar to that which occurred in 1932 with Franklin D. Roosevelt's election: Sandoz and Crabb, "Electoral and Policy Realignment or Aberration," in *Tide of Discontent*, 191–209; William Schneider, "The November 4 Vote for President," in Ranney, *American Elections of 1980*, 249–62; Hedrick Smith, "A Turning Point Seen: Republicans Call Election Watershed—Look to Party Realignment," *New York Times*, 6 Nov. 1980 (online archive, accessed 15 Nov. 2007; "Some Old Ideas Were Buried in Creating a New Landscape: Four Analysts Examine the Implications of the Republican Landslide," *New York Times*, 9 Nov. 1979 (online archive, accessed 14 Nov. 2007).

20. See Schneider, "November 4 Vote for President," 247. Schneider cited a survey conducted by Yankelovich, Skelly, and White in January 1981. He also noted, "Even Republicans (54 to 34 percent) and self-described conservatives (57 to 30 percent) felt that the election was more a rejection of Carter than a conservative mandate." Also see Sandoz, "Introduction," 15. Sandoz cited a *New York Times*/CBS News exit poll that found that only 11 percent of respondents said their reason for voting for Reagan was because "he's a real conservative."

21. Adam Clymer, "The Collapse of a Coalition: Carter Failed in Groups that Backed Him in '76," *New York Times*, 5 Nov. 1980 (online archive, accessed 15 Nov. 2007).

22. "Some Old Ideas Were Buried," *New York Times*, 9 Nov. 1979.

23. See Sandoz and Crabb, "Electoral and Policy Realignment or Aberration," 194. For views that do not share the view that American political ideology had become more conservative in 1980, see James L. Sundquist and Richard M. Scammon, "The 1980 Election: Profile and Historical Perspective," in Sandoz and Crabb, *Tide of Discontent*, 19–44.

24. Cecil V. Crabb Jr., "The Reagan Victory: Diplomatic and Strategic

Policy Implications," in Sandoz and Crabb, *Tide of Discontent*, 158; "Mr. Reagan's 'Scary' Mandate," *New York Times*, 8 Nov. 1980 (online archive, accessed 15 Nov. 2007). Crabb argued: "As much as any national election in the United States can accurately be interpreted as a mandate, Ronald Reagan and his advisors had obtained overwhelming public endorsement for that goal [to make America great again]." Also see Yankelovich and Kaagan, "Assertive America," 1, 13–15; and I. M. Destler, "The Evolution of Reagan Foreign Policy," in Greenstein, *Reagan Presidency*, 129–30. Yankelovich and Kaagan offered three ways in which the Reagan mandate differed from the Carter mandate. First, the "vast majority of Americans now enthusiastically support stronger military power in the service of . . . national objectives." Second, "a solid 61 percent majority" supported US internationalism over isolationism. Third, "the moral self-doubt that characterized the Ford-Carter period" was "replaced by a powerful assertion of national pride" and a "desire to vindicate American honor." Destler said that the answer as to whether or not the 1980 election constituted a "mandate" for Reagan "must be mixed." But he offered that "the trend of American opinion on international issues was definitely running in Reagan's direction." In particular, Destler noted that Americans in larger numbers were supportive of greater defense spending, anti-Soviet efforts, and opposition to SALT II. Thus he concluded: "If Reagan did not have a foreign policy mandate, he did have a clear opening, an opportunity to press his tough line and see how far he could get."

25. See Key and Cummings, *Responsible Electorate*, 61–62. One analyst of the 1980 election concluded: "The voters were voting for a *change*, and they were certainly aware that the type of change Reagan was offering was going to take the country in a more conservative direction. They were willing to go along with that, not because they were convinced of the essential merits of the conservative program, but because they were willing to give conservatism a chance." See Schneider, "November 4 Vote for President," 248.

26. "Transcript of Reagan News Conference with Bush on Plans for Administration," *New York Times*, 7 Nov. 1980 (online archive, accessed 15 Nov. 2007). Also see H. Smith, "Turning Point Seen," *New York Times*, 6 Nov. 1980. Smith's article quoted Reagan's chief of staff, Edwin Meese III, as stating, "A new President has a mandate." During the Reagan transition into the White House, Meese became counselor to the president. In his memoir, Meese did not use the term "mandate," instead he described some of the advantages enjoyed by the administration to overcome political constraints in order to correct the nation's problems: "The President's victory, popular support, and communications skills gave us a powerful impetus coming out of the election. And a

Republican Senate and the potential support of the 'boll weevil' (conservative, mostly Southern) Democrats in the House gave us hopes of winning majorities for our legislation in Congress. Most important—the flipside of all these developments—was the widespread belief that the system was not working, that some kind of change was urgently needed. This configuration of forces by no means guaranteed victory. But it did give us a 'window of opportunity.'" *With Reagan*, 119.

27. The following works were useful resources for this section. In addition to Reagan's speeches, Skinner, Anderson, and Anderson, *Reagan, in His Own*, was invaluable to understanding Reagan's thoughts on a wide range of subjects. Another invaluable work to understanding the continuity of Reagan's thoughts was Schweizer, *Reagan's War*. Helpful edited works on the Reagan administration include Kengor and Schweizer, *Reagan Presidency*; Brownlee and Graham, *Reagan Presidency*; Hill, Moore, and Williams, *Reagan Presidency*; Haftendorn and Schissler, *Reagan Administration*; Greenstein, *Reagan Presidency*; Lees and Turner, *Reagan's First Four Years*; Boaz, *Assessing the Reagan Years*; Kymlicka and Matthews, *Reagan Revolution?*; Kyvig, *Reagan and the World*; and Schmertz, Datlof, and Ugrinsky, *President Reagan and the World*.

28. Much of the literature on Reagan conceptualizes his aim as rebuilding US economic and military strength in order to meet the dangers of international communism. See, for example, Chester J. Pach Jr., "Sticking to His Guns," in Brownlee and Graham, *Reagan Presidency*, 86. This work argues that Reagan did not believe rebuilding economic and military power on its own was enough, that there also needed to be a renewal of the American spirit and sense of purpose. Reagan enunciated that point in his speech accepting the Republican nomination for president in July 1980. See Ronald Reagan, "Republican National Convention Acceptance Speech," 17 July 1980, The Public Papers of President Ronald W. Reagan, Ronald Reagan Presidential Library, http://www.reagan.utexas.edu/archives/reference/7.17.80.html (accessed 29 Dec. 2010).

29. Meese, *With Reagan*, 126. Meese may have overstated one point. Apparently, not everyone on the Reagan team understood that the campaign playbook would be the same for running the administration. Donald T. Regan, Reagan's first Treasury secretary, acknowledged in his memoir that it took him some time to realize that the president "had meant what he said about federal spending and fiscal and monetary policy in his campaign speeches and his other public utterances." Regan, who served in the cabinet for four years, recounted that he never saw the president alone and was never told by him directly what he wanted to accomplish in economics. Regan recounted that

he eventually learned "to figure these things out like any other American, by studying [Reagan's] speeches and reading the newspapers." Regan, *For the Record*, 142. Without exception, scholars writing on the administration support Meese's claim of continuity between Reagan's campaign rhetoric and his actions upon taking office. One can see the continuity of his ideas regarding the problems facing the nation and proposals for resolving those issues by reading his writings from the 1960s and 1970s. See Skinner, Anderson, and Anderson, *Reagan, in His Own Hand*; Reagan, *Where's the Rest of Me*; and Reagan, *Creative Society*.

30. Cannon, *President Reagan*, 845n2. It seems that the administration did exceptionally well following Reagan's plan of action. Four years later, during a strategic planning session for the 1984 campaign, the president's chief strategist worried out loud about what the administration had to offer in way of a second-term agenda: "The Reagan administration fired all its bullets very early and very successfully in the first two years. . . . All their plans, all their priorities, all their programs. They've run out of ammunition." Mayer and McManus, *Landslide*, 4.

31. Reagan, "Republican National Convention Acceptance Speech," 17 July 1980.

32. For detailed narratives regarding the economic situation and policies during the Carter administration, see Bruce J. Schulman, "Slouching toward the Supply Side: Jimmy Carter and the New American Political Economy," in Fink and Graham, *Carter Presidency*, 51–71; and Hargrove, "Economic Policy Making," in *Carter as President*, 69–109. Also see Patterson, *Restless Giant*, 62–66; Edward Cowan, "Congress Unit Sees Recession: Blumenthal Now against Stimulus to Economy," *New York Times*, 21 July 1979 (online archive, accessed 20 Nov. 2007); Roger Wilkins, "Inflation in Price of Necessities Makes the Poor Choose Debt or Hunger," *New York Times*, 30 July 1979 (online archive, accessed 20 Nov. 2007), and "Buyer Confidence: 1-Year Low Found," *New York Times*, 2 Aug. 1979 (online archive, accessed 20 Nov. 2007).

33. Joseph J. Hogan, "Reaganomics and Economic Policy," in Hill, Moore, and Williams, *Reagan Presidency*, 135.

34. See "Reagan's Announcement for Presidential Candidacy," 13 Nov. 1979; Reagan, "Republican National Convention Acceptance Speech," 17 July 1980; and Reagan, "Five-Year Economic Program for U.S.," 738–44. These same themes are also captured in the 1980 Republican platform and the Carter-Reagan presidential debate, which was held on 28 October. See "Republican Party Platform of 1980," American Presidency Project, http://www

.presidency.ucsb.edu/ws/index.php?pid=25844 (accessed 20 Nov. 2007); and "Presidential Debate in Cleveland," 28 Oct. 1980, ibid., http://www.presidency.ucsb.edu/ws/index.php?pid=29408 (accessed 29 Dec. 2010).

35. Reagan, "Republican National Convention Acceptance Speech," 17 July 1980.

36. "Reagan's Announcement for Presidential Candidacy," 13 Nov. 1979.

37. Reagan, "Five-Year Economic Program for U.S."

38. Paul Craig Roberts recalled: "The term 'Reaganomics' originated, I believe, in the title that a copyeditor put on an article, 'Reaganomics: A Change?' that I wrote for the *New York Times* (November 9, 1980) a few days after the election of Ronald Reagan. . . . I did not like the copy editor's title because it seemed to imply that the President's economic program was an idiosyncrasy." Roberts, *Supply-Side Revolution*, 93.

39 For more-detailed discussions on Reaganomics, see Roberts, *Supply-Side Revolution*; Stockman, *Triumph of Politics*; Lowe, *Reaganomics*; Hogan, "Reaganomics and Economic Policy"; and Hugh Heclo and Rudolph G. Penner, "Fiscal and Political Strategy in the Reagan Administration," in Greenstein, *Reagan Presidency*, 21–47. After Reagan was elected, he selected David Stockman to serve as the director of the Office of Management and Budget. Stockman introduced two changes into the Reagan economic plan. The first was to focus on extensive reductions in nondefense spending rather than focus on the fraud, waste, and abuse as Reagan had championed during the campaign. The second was to make balancing the budget and eliminating the deficit a principal aim. While Reagan had campaigned on the promise he would balance the budget, it was to be the result of following supply-side theory and achieving economic growth. A balanced budget itself was not to serve as a principal aim or as a constraint in dictating economic policy, as Stockman proposed. See Hogan, "Reaganomics and Economic Policy," 140–42; and Roberts, *Supply-Side Revolution*, 90–92.

40. Roberts, *Supply-Side Revolution*, 89.

41. Reagan, "Inaugural Address," 20 Jan. 1981.

42. Ronald Reagan, "A Time for Choosing (The Speech—October 27, 1964)," The Public Papers of President Ronald W. Reagan, Ronald Reagan Presidential Library, http://www.reagan.utexas.edu/archives/reference/timechoosing.html (accessed 29 Dec. 2010).

43. Reagan, "Inaugural Address," 20 Jan. 1981.

44. Reagan, "Republican National Convention Acceptance Speech," 17 July 1980.

45. Meese, *With Reagan*, 73–74.

46. Reagan, "Republican National Convention Acceptance Speech," 17 July 1980. Also see "Reagan's Announcement for Presidential Candidacy," 13 Nov. 1979.

47. Reagan, "Republican National Convention Acceptance Speech," 17 July 1980.

48. "Reagan's Announcement for Presidential Candidacy," 13 Nov. 1979. These were themes that Reagan had enunciated for over twenty years. As early as 1952, he had delivered a commencement address at William Woods College in Fulton, Missouri, in which he discussed these ideals. See Schweizer, *Reagan's War*, 19.

49. Reagan, "Time for Choosing."

50. Reagan argued that the United States could coax and influence right-wing regimes to improve their human-rights records through positive dialogue and support. He spoke out against the double standard of backing left-wing dictators while often opposing right-wing regimes. For an example of one of Reagan's earlier ruminations on the subject, see "Ruritania, August 1975," in Skinner, Anderson, and Anderson, *Reagan, in His Own Hand*, 130. The president selected Jeane J. Kirkpatrick to serve in his cabinet as the US permanent representative to the United Nations. In an essay she had published in *Commentary* in November 1979, shortly after the start of the Iranian Revolution, she argued that the United States was undermining its strategic position in the world by forcing friendly autocratic governments, such as the shah's in Iran and Anastasio Somoza's in Nicaragua, to implement democratic reforms that served only to make conditions ripe for their downfall. Kirkpatrick believed that the United States, as well as the citizens in those nations, would be better served by following a more-moderate course of reform. This position was congenial to Reagan. See Kirkpatrick, "Dictatorship & Double Standards."

51. Neither Reagan nor the Republican platform were very specific regarding how this would be implemented. The platform sought to "pursue positive non-military means to roll back the growth of communism." Nevertheless, since the early 1950s Reagan had been involved in using nonmilitary means, such as radio addresses and movies, to challenge those who supported communism. For a more detailed description of Reagan's activities, see Schweizer, "You Too Can Be Free Again," in *Reagan's War*, 17–28.

52. See Quester, "Consensus Lost," 18–32. Quester argued: "What the United States lost in Vietnam was not so much the strong belief that communism was behind most of the world's problems and must be resisted, but something much more vital—the common agreement among Americans about what positive goals the United States could accomplish through its for-

eign policy. Lost in Vietnam, in other words, was agreement on what produces progress in the world." For discussions on the breakdown of consensus among foreign-policy decision makers in the United States, see Moreno, *U.S. Policy in Central America*, 4–8; Melanson, "In Search of Consensus," in *Reconstructing Consensus*, 1–32; and Holsti and Rosenau, *American Leadership in World Affairs*. Also see Ehrman, *Rise of Neoconservatism*. Ehrman's work provides an excellent history of the rise and fall of the liberal foreign-policy consensus in the United States.

53. See note 1. Vietnam is a historical phenomenon that hangs over this entire study. Its influence on US foreign policy is discussed in further detail in chapter 2.

54. "Reagan's Announcement for Presidential Candidacy," 13 Nov. 1979. In his speeches, Reagan borrowed and attributed that phrase to Franklin D. Roosevelt, who had used it in his speech to the Democratic nominating convention in July 1932. Also see Skinner, Anderson, and Anderson, *Reagan, in His Own Hand*, 24. The three editors made the following observation:

> Reagan also argues that the popular idea that a "Vietnam Syndrome" exists in the United States should be abandoned. Even though the fall of Saigon punctuated a painful period of American military failure, Reagan contends that America is not unwilling or unable to fight the cold war. America's destiny is to be a shining example and defender of freedom; it is a destiny that transcends the temporary setbacks of Vietnam, he says. The American people will accept the responsibilities of their country's destiny if the requirements of freedom and the nature of internal and international challenges are explained to them, but, Reagan charges, American leaders failed to do this during the Vietnam War.

55. "Reagan's Announcement for Presidential Candidacy," 13 Nov. 1979.

56. Reagan, "Republican National Convention Acceptance Speech," 17 July 1980.

57. Ibid.

58. Reagan's first secretary of state, Alexander Haig, did not conceptualize that spirit as constant; however, he reached the same conclusions as Reagan regarding the nation's readiness to use its power. In public addresses, he often said that in the wake of Vietnam and Watergate, the United States went through a period of confusion that he described as a time in which the nation questioned its values and purposes: "Did our democratic institutions still work? Were they

worth defending? Could we offer anything to the world? Was the dream over?" Haig went on to tell his listeners, the 1981 graduating class of Syracuse University, that he believed this period of "American introspection" had ended (though he never mentioned a specific date or event marking this). He stated: "We are more certain of ourselves today than we have been for a long time. A profound national consensus has emerged. Our Democratic institutions do work. They are worth defending. Our ideals and our liberty do offer a notable example to a world desperately searching for peace and prosperity. The dream lives." See Haig, "NATO and the Restoration of American Leadership," 11.

59. This list is not all inclusive. Reagan also argued that America's defense strength was at its lowest ebb in a generation when compared to the Soviets and that the nation's European allies had found US leadership lacking. Reagan, "Republican National Convention Acceptance Speech," 17 July 1980. Some scholars note that "most efforts to uncover a systematic relationship between world events and public opinion on national security issues have failed." See Russett and Deluca, "'Don't Tread on Me,'" 395. In their essay, Russett and Deluca explain that the Iranian hostage affair and the Soviet invasion of Afghanistan immediately preceded peaks in both the number of Americans who selected foreign affairs as the most important problem facing the country and the number of Americans favoring increased defense spending. Yet other events, like the oil embargo in 1973, the fall of the shah in January 1979, and the announcement of the Soviet combat brigade in Cuba in the summer of 1979, did not trigger a strong response.

60. Democratic senator Frank Church, chairman of the Foreign Relations Committee, went public with news of the brigade while campaigning in his home state of Idaho on 30 August 1979. Secretary of State Cyrus R. Vance held a news conference on the matter on 5 September, and President Carter gave a five-minute address to the nation two days later. See Carter, "Soviet Combat Troops in Cuba Remarks to Reporters," 7 Sept. 1979, American Presidency Project, http://www.presidency.ucsb.edu/ws/index.php?pid=32832 (accessed 2 Mar. 2008). The Kremlin claimed that the unit had been in Cuba for seventeen years and that its purpose was to train Cuban soldiers.

61. Kaufman, *Presidency of James Earl Carter*, 153, 156. Also see Bernard Gwertzman, "Vance Tells Soviet Its Troops in Cuba Imperil Ties," *New York Times*, 5 Sept. 1979 (online archive, accessed 20 Feb. 2007); "Storm over Cuba," 12–18.

62. AP, "Senator Church Charges Moscow Has a Brigade of Troops in Cuba," *New York Times*, 31 Aug. 1979 (online archive, accessed 20 Feb. 2007). The senator from Florida was Richard Stone.

63. Carter, "Soviet Combat Troops in Cuba Remarks to Reporters."

64. Jimmy Carter, "Peace and National Security Address to the Nation on Soviet Combat Troops in Cuba and the Strategic Limitation Treaty," 1 Oct. 1979, American Presidency Project, http://www.presidency.ucsb.edu/ws/index.php?pid=31458 (accessed 2 Mar. 2008).

65. Ibid. Also see "Carter Defuses a Crisis"; and Richard Burt, "Carter, Given Conflicting Advice, Chose a Middle Course on Cuba," *New York Times*, 3 Oct. 1979 (online archive, accessed 26 Feb. 2007). Burt reported that those advising the president urged two different courses: one side saw the "problem as serious but isolated," while the other saw it as "part of a global contest."

66. Between 1975 and 1980, the Soviet Union provided military assistance to and supported proxy forces as well as assigned advisers to aid insurgent activities in Ethiopia, South Yemen, North Yemen, Afghanistan, Cambodia, Nicaragua, and El Salvador. Proxy forces in Central America were typically Cubans. In Africa there were Cubans in Angola and Cubans and East Germans in Ethiopia. There were also Cubans and East Germans in South Yemen. In Asia Vietnamese forces were used to conquer Kampuchea. Finally, the Libyans, while not an official Soviet pawn, had occupied Chad and annually purchased an estimated $1 billion in arms from the Soviet Union. William Casey, Reagan's choice for director of the Central Intelligence Agency, claimed that it was not a coincidence that the eleven insurgencies being supported by the Soviets and their proxies were situated close to natural resources and choke points strategically vital to the United States and its allies. Persico, *Casey*, 320. The Libyan estimate is from Woodward, *Veil*, 94. These views are captured in the platform adopted by the Republican national convention on 15 July 1980. See "Republican Platform: A Preamble," American Presidency Project, http://www.presidency.ucsb.edu/ws/index.php?pid=25844 (accessed 4 Sept. 2010).

67. The written notes from those broadcasts have been preserved and demonstrate that the concerns Reagan expressed while on campaign in 1980 were concerns he had possessed for a number of years. The text of those broadcasts can be found in Skinner, Anderson, and Anderson, *Reagan, in His Own Hand*.

68. "Common Sense and the Common Danger: Policy Statement of the Committee on the Present Danger," in Tyroler, *Alerting America*, 3–5. For the full list of board members, see ibid., 5–9. Some of the more prominent CPD members were Ronald Reagan, Paul Nitze, Eugene V. Rostow, Dean Rusk, David Packard, James Schlesinger, Gen. (Ret.) Matthew Ridgeway, Gen. (Ret.) Andrew Goodpaster, Adm. (Ret.) Elmo Zumwalt, William Casey, Jeane Kirkpatrick, Richard Perle, Richard Pipes, Norman Podhoretz, George Shultz,

and Richard Allen. To see a full list of committee members who were appointed to the Reagan administration, see ibid., ix–xi.

69. Sanders, *Peddlers of Crisis*, 254–63.

70. Vance, *Hard Choices*, 349.

71. For full figures and more information, see Russett and Deluca, "'Don't Tread on Me,'" 381–99. Russett and Deluca note that the Soviet brigade in Cuba did not lead to greater calls for defense spending, though the seizure of the hostages in Iran and the Soviet invasion of Afghanistan seemingly did. Yet the authors note that since no poll was taken in between the two events, it is difficult to disaggregate the relative effect of each. Also see "In a Fiercely Hawkish Mood," 23.

72. Hedrick Smith, "Crisis Alters Attitude in U.S.," *New York Times*, 2 Dec. 1979 (online archive, accessed 12 Dec. 2007).

73. The general principles and goals of "peace through strength" were enunciated as Reagan campaigned and captured in the platform adopted by the Republican national convention. See "Republican Platform: A Preamble."

74. Elizabeth Edwards Spalding also uses this conceptualization of peace. See Spalding, "The Origins and Meaning of Reagan's Cold War," in Kengor and Schweizer, *Reagan Presidency*, 58.

75. The Soviet actions undermined the old conception of national security centered on détente, and the United States undertook a new assessment of the nation's vital interests and available capabilities. This reassessment process surfaced in January 1980 in Carter's State of the Union pronouncement that the Persian Gulf region was a vital interest to the United States and its allies and as such would be defended. The Carter Doctrine expanded the American sphere of responsibilities. Reagan and other key leaders in his administration accepted the underlying concept of the Carter Doctrine—a peaceful world was one in which the United States and its allies enjoyed unchallenged access to vital natural resources and transportation and communications routes. More evidence that this process was underway could be seen in the Carter administration's decision to expand the US sphere of responsibility by playing a more-constructive role in defeating leftists in the Third World. Secretary of State Edmund Muskie announced on the last day of Carter's presidency a decision to restore nonlethal aid and to send $5 million of lethal material to the Salvadoran armed forces fighting a leftist insurgency. Thus, in rather dramatic fashion, the announcement signaled not only the end of the Carter administration's role in foreign policy but also the end of a period in which instability and violence in the Third World were attributed to factors other than Soviet-American competition. See Moreno, *U.S. Policy in Central Amer-*

ica, 20–21. When viewed outside the context of the Cold War, the United States had been more inclined to give Third World nations the latitude to find their own way and experiment with systems of government that were less than democratic, or in the case of the Sandinistas, leftist. Such a nuanced approach became increasingly difficult to sustain in the face of evidence that arms were being sent from Cuba via Nicaragua to the guerillas fighting in El Salvador. Fearful of another Sandinista-style regime, Carter returned the United States to its traditional stance of blaming instability and violence in the Third World on the Soviets and their proxies. Like his call to defend American vital interests in the Persian Gulf, Carter's decision to expand the American sphere of responsibility by a more-active role in defeating leftists in the Third World was heartily accepted by the Reagan administration.

76. Because the focus is on the Reagan administration's use of military power as a direct tool of statecraft, this book does not fully describe its efforts to provide leadership on the international stage in regards to arms control and seeking an end to the Cold War. In both instances, the administration provided exceptionally decisive leadership. While on the campaign trail in 1980, Reagan made it clear that he supported nuclear-arms reductions but also made it clear that he would only negotiate with the Soviets from a position of strength. Yet given the abhorrence that most Americans had toward spending more on strategic weapons, regaining that position of strength required a great deal of political effort. Nevertheless, Reagan persevered and won congressional approval for increased defense spending throughout his first term. His efforts in arms control reached a climax in 1987, when he signed the Intermediate Nuclear Forces (INF) Treaty with the Soviet Union, which eliminated two classes of nuclear weapons. For more discussion on the administration's role in regards to arms control, see Lettow, *Reagan and His Quest to Abolish Nuclear Weapons*; John Lewis Gaddis, "The Reagan Administration and Soviet-American Relations," in Kyvig, *Reagan and the World*; Samuel F. Wells Jr., "Reagan, Euromissiles, and Europe," in Brownlee and Graham, *Reagan Presidency*, 133–52; Raymond A. Moore, "The Reagan Presidency and Foreign Policy," in Hill, Moore, and Williams, *Reagan Presidency*, 179–98; and Michael Paul, "The Reagan Administration's Strategic Arms Control Policy: The Meaning of 'Deep Cuts,'" in Haftendorn and Schissler, *Reagan Administration*, 231–49. On the actions the administration took in seeking an end to the Cold War, see Mann, *Rebellion of Ronald Reagan*; Gaddis, *Strategies of Containment: A Critical Appraisal of American National Security Policy during the Cold War*; Fischer, *Reagan Reversal*; Kissinger, "The End of the Cold War: Reagan and Gorbachev," in *Diplomacy*, 762–803; Gaddis, *Cold War*; Matlock, *Reagan and*

Gorbachev; Gates, *From the Shadows*; Schweizer, *Victory*; and Schweizer, *Reagan's War*. Also see J. M. Scott, *Deciding to Intervene*; and Mark P. Logan, *The Reagan Doctrine: Sources of American Conduct in the Cold War's Last Chapter* (Westport, CT: Praeger, 1994).

77. "Republican Platform: A Preamble."

Chapter 2

1. Secretary of Defense Weinberger used the term "political realities" in an essay he wrote for *Foreign Affairs*. See Weinberger, "U.S. Defense Strategy," 190.

2. Huntington, "Soldier and the State in the 1970s," 13–14.

3. Melanson, *Reconstructing Consensus*, 4–7.

4. Ehrman, *Rise of Neoconservatism*, 10–24.

5. Destler, Gelb, and Lake, *Our Own Worst Enemy*, 18.

6. Melanson, *Reconstructing Consensus*, 13.

7. William Schneider, "Public Opinion," in Nye, *Making of America's Soviet Policy*, 11.

8. See I. M. Destler, "Congress," in ibid., 42–43.

9. For more discussion about the nation's strategy of containment, see Gaddis, *Strategies of Containment: A Critical Appraisal of Postwar American National Security Policy*.

10. Ibid., 107.

11. See Destler, "Congress," 41–44.

12. Schneider, "Public Opinion," 13.

13. See Destler, "Congress," 42–43.

14. Schneider, "Public Opinion," 18.

15. Ibid., 11–13.

16. Melanson, *Reconstructing Consensus*, 14–15.

17. Schneider, "Public Opinion," 14; Arnson, *Crossroads*, 3.

18. Ehrman, *Rise of Neoconservatism*, 18–20.

19. Ibid.

20. Ibid., 13; Destler, Gelb, and Lake, *Our Own Worst Enemy*, 20.

21. Moreno, *U.S. Policy in Central America*, 4; Holsti and Rosenau, "The Three-Headed Eagle: Three Perspectives on Foreign Affairs," in *American Leadership in World Affairs*, 108. Holsti and Rosenau use the terms "conservative internationalism," "liberal internationalism," and "non-internationalism." Schneider uses the similar terms "conservative internationalists," "liberal internationalists," and "noninternationalists." "Public Opinion," 16–17.

22. Moreno, *U.S. Policy in Central America*, 4–5; Holsti and Rosenau,

"Three-Headed Eagle," 108–39; Schneider, "Public Opinion," 16–18. Rhetoric from the 1980 campaign would label Reagan as a Cold War internationalist. During his run for president, Reagan prepared for question-and-answer sessions with a briefing book, which reveals his views on the Soviet threat. To the question "Is it your view . . . that the Soviet Union underlies *all* the unrest that's going on?" Reagan answered:

> If you are familiar with the currently popular rating scale, is that in a rating of threat and troublemaking the Soviet Union is a true *10*, while all others are *5* or less. My view is that the primary challenge, by far, to our security and interests, and to the security of others, comes from the Soviet Union. That does not imply exclusivity, but dominance— it is the threat that most dominates our security concerns. This does not mean that I am unaware of all the various sources of international unrest, many of which are indigenous and of ethnic, economic, or social causes; but it is a fact, which we cannot ignore, that the Soviet Union feeds on, exacerbates, and attempts to exploit such sources of unrest or instability—particularly in areas of strategic and economic importance. If this view seems "simplistic" to you, I might point out that nearly 200 of the nation's leading intellectuals and statesmen— prominent professors and university presidents; men of vast government experience; labor, business, and financial leaders—a wholly bipartisan or multipartisan group—have subscribed to the statement: "The principal threat to our nation, to world peace, and to the cause of human freedom is the Soviet drive for dominance based upon an unparalleled military buildup."

Weinberger Papers, Library of Congress, container I:572, folder "Transition Papers, Campaign Defense Policy Briefing Book, 1980, by William Van Cleave." The briefing book consisted of a series of defense-related questions and answers that Reagan used while on the campaign trail. William Van Cleave was the administration's transition-team leader and the director of defense and strategic studies at the University of Southern California. Additionally, he was a founding member of the Committee on the Present Danger. The 200 "leading intellectuals and statesmen" were members of the committee, a group that scholars classify as Cold War internationalist. See Holsti and Rosenau, "Three-Headed Eagle," 108–109.

23. Schneider, "Public Opinion," 14, 30.

24. Ibid., 30.

25. Melanson, *Reconstructing Consensus*, 17.

26. Arnson, *Crossroads*, 3, 9.

27. Ehrman, *Rise of Neoconservatism*, 23.

28. Arnson, *Crossroads*, 9.

29. John Tower, "Congress Versus the President," in *The Reagan Foreign Policy*, ed. William G. Hyland (New York: New American Library, 1987), 152.

30. Melanson, *Reconstructing Consensus*, 11.

31. "Gulf of Tonkin Resolution," http://www.luminet.net/~tgort/tonkin .htm (accessed 13 Mar. 2008).

32. "War Powers Resolution of 1973," Almanac of Policy Issues, http:// www.policyalmanac.org/world/archive/war_powers_resolution.shtml (accessed 13 Mar. 2008).

33. Arnson, *Crossroads*, 13.

34. Samuel Huntington explained that "until the 1950s the prevailing American view on the use of military force emphasized the distinction between war and peace." He argued that President Truman's conflict with General MacArthur and the declaration of massive retaliation by the Eisenhower administration caused the "traditional dichotomy between war and peace, force and diplomacy," to be "replaced by a new stress on a continuum of conflict from war to peace and on the role of force as an instrument of policy and diplomacy." "Soldier and the State in the 1970s," 18.

35. Morris Janowitz used the terms "absolutist" and "pragmatist" to distinguish between the two groups. *Professional Soldier*, 257–79. Richard Betts used those terms as well in his work *Soldiers, Statesmen, and Cold War Crises*. David Howell Petraeus also used these terms in his "The American Military and the Lessons of Vietnam: A Study of Military Influence and the Use of Force in the Post-Vietnam Era," (PhD diss., Princeton University, 1987). It is common to see the terms "overwhelming" or "decisive force" associated with absolutists. General MacArthur was one of the more famous absolutists, while Gen. Maxell Taylor was one of the more famous pragmatists.

36. Huntington, *Soldier and the State*, 69–70, 79.

37. Ibid., 69.

38. Betts, *Soldiers, Statesmen, and Cold War Crises*, 4–5.

39. Michael R. Gordon, "The Struggle for Iraq: Reconstruction," *New York Times*, 4 Sept. 2006, http://select.nytimes.com/search/restricted/article ?res=FA0913FA3B5C0C778CDDA00894DB404482 (accessed 16 Oct. 2006); David H. Petraeus, "Battling for Iraq," *Washington Post*, 26 Sept. 2004, B07, http://www.washingtonpost.com/wp-dyn/articles/A49283–2004Sep25 .html (accessed 6 Sept. 2006); Julian E. Barnes, "An Open Mind for a New

Army," 31 Oct. 2005, USNews.com, http://www.usnews.com/usnews/news/articles/051031/31petraeus.htm (accessed 6 Sept. 2006). While speaking with General Petraeus about his dissertation, he said that he considers himself a pragmatic-absolutist. See Petraeus, "American Military and the Lessons of Vietnam."

40. Petraeus, "American Military and the Lessons of Vietnam," 6.

41. Ibid., 241, 257. Petraeus wrote: "In fact, in the wake of Vietnam a number of senior officers have argued that U.S. troops should not be committed to combat unless certain conditions obtain. Clear military objectives must be established, public backing should be relatively assured, and commanders should be given the freedom and forces necessary to accomplish their mission before the public tires of American involvement. When it comes to the use of force, contemporary military thinking holds, the United States should either bite the bullet or duck, but not nibble" "American Military and the Lessons of Vietnam," 34. He did not cite supporting documents for these thoughts, obviously feeling that they were common enough not to warrant corroboration.

42. Ibid., 34, 42, 257–58. Petraeus provides additional insight on the "Never Again" club: "It is interesting to note that few—if any—Army leaders acknowledged their 'membership' in the Never Again Club. As Richard Betts found, each of the five former Army leaders from that period whom he interviewed 'rejected the designation of the Never Again Club, which was thrust upon them by journalists in the 1950s and 1960s, but under questioning four revealed the same views popularly associated with that designation.' Betts, *Soldiers, Statesmen, and Cold War Crises*, p. 290, note 9." Petraeus, "American Military and the Lessons of Vietnam," 42n24. Betts does not specify who he interviewed other than to say he spoke to "five former army leaders."

43. Petraeus, "American Military and the Lessons of Vietnam," 43. Petraeus described the factors that undermined the legacy of the Korean War and used that to speculate on how long the "conventional wisdom on Vietnam" would "continue to influence military thinking on the use of force."

44. Kitfield, *Prodigal Soldiers*, 149–51.

45. For an excellent article on this topic, see Allan Nairn, "Endgame," *Report of the Americas* (May/June 1984): 19–55.

Chapter 3

1. The last time a government in Latin America had been overthrown by an armed revolution was in 1959, when Fidel Castro seized power from Fulgencio Batista.

2. This sentiment is clearly expressed in a 1997 CNN interview with Dan-

iel Ortega for its *Cold War* series. Ortega was one of the leading commanders of the Sandinista forces that overthrew Somoza in 1979, becoming head of the ruling junta and elected president in November 1984. Throughout the remainder to the 1980s, he led the Sandinistas in their civil war against US-backed Contra rebels. In 1990 Ortega was defeated by Violeta Chamorro and left office in April 1991. Cable News Network, "Episode 18: Backyard, Interviews, Daniel Ortega, Sandinista Leader, Nicaraguan President," *CNN Cold War*, http://www.cnn.com/SPECIALS/cold.war/episodes/18/interviews/ortega/ (accessed 20 Aug. 2007; content discontinued; print copy in author's possession).

3. Kagan, *Twilight Struggle*, 105–108.

4. For a discussion about the calculus the Carter administration used to decide whether or not to intervene, see Pastor, *Condemned to Repetition*, 193–95.

5. For another discussion of the two views regarding revolutionary forces in the Third World that were prevalent in the 1970s and 1980s, see Moreno, *U.S. Policy in Central America*, 3.

6. In addition to President Carter and key leaders in his administration, this group was made up of liberal leaders in Congress and progressives in the State Department. Viron Vaky, assistant secretary of state, who fell into this group of thinkers, stated: "The real issue facing American foreign policy . . . is not how to preserve stability in the face of revolution, but how to create stability out of revolution." Bermann, *Under the Big Stick*, 276.

7. They believed that Castro's slide toward communism was largely a result of the US challenges to his decisions to gain control of Cuba's government and economy. For the lessons the Carter and Reagan administrations drew from the Cuban revolution, see Pastor, *Condemned to Repetition*, 192, 231.

8. The best single source to see these themes is President Carter's speech presented at Notre Dame in May 1977. See Jimmy Carter, "University of Notre Dame—Address at Commencement Exercises at the University," 22 May 1977, American Presidency Project, http://www.presidency.ucsb.edu/ws/index.php?pid=7552 (accessed 2 Jan. 2011).

9. Carter committed a large amount of political capital at the beginning of his administration fighting for ratification of the treaties. For his view on this struggle and the political cost it imposed on him and his supporters, see Carter, *Keeping Faith*, 152–85. Under the treaties, the United States and Panama would operate the canal jointly, with the United States as the senior partner, until the end of the twentieth century, when US military forces were to be withdrawn, though with the right to return to defend the canal's neutrality.

10. Somoza had imposed martial law in December 1974 following a San-

dinista raid on a farewell party held for US Ambassador Turner Shelton. The Sandinistas had taken hostages, and to get them released, Somoza had agreed to free fourteen Sandinistas who were in prison, one of whom was Daniel Ortega; to provide the rebels $1 million in cash; and to publish a communiqué that denounced Somoza and US imperialism and called for the people to rise up and overthrow the regime.

11. Ironically, the Sandinistas saw Somoza's reforms as a threat to their revolution, wanting him to remain in power until after they had defeated the National Guard. They learned from the Chilean and Guatemalan coups that the success of a revolution lay with the ability to destroy the old army and replace it with a new force willing to follow the new leadership and its programs. Kagan, *Twilight Struggle*, 104–105; Pastor, *Condemned to Repetition*, 37. The Carter administration had begun trying to convince Somoza to step aside as early as September 1978 in hopes that power could be transferred to "moderate" elements while the National Guard was still intact and capable of holding the Sandinistas in check. This effort was not successful, and the National Guard disintegrated within twenty-four hours of Somoza's departure. Kornbluh, "Nicaragua," *the Price of Intervention*, 15–16, 18.

12. Jimmy Carter, "The President's News Conference," 25 July 1979, American Presidency Project, http://www.presidency.ucsb.edu/ws/index .php?pid=32653 (accessed 17 Aug. 2007).

13. The administration gave the new regime $15 million in emergency reconstruction aid and a $75 million economic-assistance package. Nevertheless, officials covertly began setting the stage for a counterrevolution. On 19 July 1979, the same day the Sandinistas marched into Managua unchallenged, US operatives began evacuating leaders of the Nicaraguan National Guard (and their families) to Miami, where they were to be reorganized to return to fight the Sandinistas. Dickey, *With the Contras*, 51–55. Additionally, in late 1980 Carter authorized the CIA to fund anti-Sandinista labor, press, and political organizations in an effort to destabilize the regime. Kornbluh, "Nicaragua," *the Price of Intervention*, 19. One account estimates Carter had allocated approximately $1 million for covert anti-Sandinista aid. Burns, *At War in Nicaragua*, 22.

14. This group was based primarily in the Pentagon and the CIA. It also included Democratic neoconservatives and State Department liberals who agreed with John F. Kennedy's vision and style for promoting progress in the Third World.

15. Roosevelt quoted at Thinkexist.com, http://thinkexist.com/quotes/ with/keyword/somoza/ (accessed 22 Feb. 2008).

16. Kirkpatrick, "Dictatorship & Double Standards." Kirkpatrick's thesis was that the United States was undermining its strategic position in the world by forcing friendly autocratic governments, such as the shah's in Iran and Somoza's in Nicaragua, to implement democratic reforms that ultimately would lead to their downfall. Making matters worse, the governments that would succeed the autocrats were no more democratic and were hostile to the United States. She argued that "there was no instance of a revolutionary 'socialist' or Communist society being democratized," however, there were instances of right-wing autocracies evolving into democracies "given time, propitious economic, social, and political circumstances, talented leaders, and a strong indigenous demand for representative government." Kirkpatrick questioned why the Carter administration had selectively applied its principles of self-determination and nonintervention to "nations ruled by 'right-wing' dictators or white oligarchies" while accepting the status quo in communist nations.

17. Pastor, *Condemned to Repetition*, 231.

18. Cuba was viewed as a proxy of the Soviet Union, so in the minds of many US policymakers, the conflicts in Central America were by implication fueled by the Soviet Union. See, for example, Cable News Network, "Episode 18: Backyard, Interviews, John Negroponte, U.S. Diplomat," in *CNN Cold War*, http://www.cnn.com/SPECIALS/cold.war/episodes/18/interviews/negroponte/ (accessed 20 Aug. 2007; content discontinued; print copy in author's possession). Negroponte, the US ambassador to Honduras from 1981 to 1985 who in that role became heavily involved in the US-Contra war against the Sandinistas, said: "I certainly think [the Soviets] must have enjoyed our discomfort. Whether they micromanaged this or not, I just don't know. I'd be reluctant to say. My working hypothesis was that they sort of let Cuba have the lead on this, and basically said to them: 'Have at it boys, and see what you can accomplish.' . . . I don't think there was any doubt of Cuban involvement." Evidence suggests that the Soviets did not become very active with the Sandinistas until after they had overthrown Somoza and were in need of weapons to defend their gains.

19. See Dugger, *On Reagan*, 518. Dugger's work has an appendix that contains excerpts from Reagan's 1975, 1978, and 1979 radio broadcasts.

20. Department of State Paper on Interagency Options for El Salvador, 23 Feb. 1981, folder "NSC 00004, 27 Feb 1981, [Poland, Caribbean Basin, F-15, El Salvador]," box 91282, Executive Secretariat: Meeting File, Papers of Ronald Reagan Presidential Administration, Ronald Reagan Library, 7.

21. Ibid., 8. For an excellent discussion of US security interests in Central America, see Gonzalez, *U.S. Policy for Central America*.

22. Woodward, *Veil*, 39.

23. See Weinberger Papers, I:572, Transition Papers, folder "Foreign Policy Advisory Group," item "Members of the Interim Foreign Policy Advisory Board." Some of the other members were Sens. Howard Baker, Henry Jackson, Richard Stone, and John Tower; Dr. Henry Kissinger; Gen. (Ret.) Alexander M. Haig Jr., USA; Donald Rumsfeld; Richard V. Allen; Jeane J. Kirkpatrick; John J. McCloy; Eugene Rostow; George Shultz; and Caspar Weinberger.

24. Woodward, *Veil*, 38–39. Casey's group was not the only one to argue Central America's strategic importance. The Council of Inter-American Security published a 1980 report entitled *A New Inter-American Policy for the Eighties*. Popularly known as the "Santa Fe Document," the report argued that Soviet surrogates were attacking an important source of US power in the Western Hemisphere and urged the United States to take initiative in Central America both strategically and diplomatically. See Committee of Santa Fe, *New Inter-American Policy*, ii, 4, 3, 52. The members of the Committee of Santa Fe were L. Francis Bouchey, Roger W. Fontaine, David C. Jordan, Gordon Sumner, and Lewis Tambs. Specifically, the report called for "revitalizing the Rio Treaty and the Organization of American States; reproclaiming the Monroe Doctrine; tightening ties with key countries; and, aiding independent nations to survive subversion." Ibid., 52. Several of the men who worked on the report were later assigned positions in the Reagan administration. Fontaine sat on the NSC as a Latin American specialist; Tambs was a consultant to the NSC, then ambassador to Columbia and later to Costa Rica; and Sumner was assigned as a special consultant to the State Department's Bureau of Inter-American Affairs.

25. Daniel Ortega, head of the ruling junta, said the Sandinistas turned to these countries for arms in the early 1980s because the Cubans were very limited in what they could provide. He reported receiving promises of MiG-21s from the Soviet Union, Mirages from France, and smaller planes from Libya. The Libyan aircraft got as far as Brazil, where they were intercepted and sent back; Ortega did not specify who intercepted them. The Soviet MiGs and French Mirages never materialized due to pressure from the United States, he claimed. Cable News Network, "Episode 18: Backyard, Interviews, Daniel Ortega, Sandinista Leader, Nicaraguan President."

26. On 15 October 1979, a coalition of Salvadorian military officers and civilian leaders had overthrown the military dictatorship of Gen. Carlos Humberto Romero. The junta included Guillermo Ungo, head of the Social-Democratic Party, who favored allowing leftists an opportunity to participate politically. But such accommodations with the Left proved unpopular not only with the group's conservative military leaders but also with Carter-administration offi-

cials, who feared a repeat of Nicaragua. In December Christian Democrat José Napoleon Duarte took over as the president of the junta and, backed by the Carter administration, proposed a two-pronged strategy designed to enfeeble the Left. The first prong was to pull support away politically by implementing agrarian reforms and nationalizing the banks and export trade. The second was to appease the Right by eliminating any remaining rebellion with military force. Thus, by early January 1981, the more leftist-oriented members of the government, such as Ungo, had resigned, leaving Duarte's Christian Democratic Party as the civilian component of the regime. On 11 January, Marxist guerrillas launched a "final offensive," which was intended to hand Reagan a "fait accompli"—a revolutionary government in place that could not be dislodged—when he entered office on the twentieth. Duarte and his government survived the offensive, however, largely because the Salvadoran people did not rally around the rebels. Instead of supporting the Marxist guerrillas by rising up and conducting strikes, civilians went to work and largely ignored the rebels' calls for revolution. The Reagan administration read the Salvadoran's response as support for Duarte's revolutionary civilian-military regime. Thus, eager to promote liberal-democratic progress in the Third World, the administration supported Duarte and his government.

27. See Moreno, *U.S. Policy in Central America*, 80–81; and Nairn, "Endgame," 25. Carter invoked emergency executive powers and sent El Salvador $10 million, four helicopters and nineteen military advisors. Aid had been suspended in December 1980 pending the investigation of the murder of four US churchwomen. Lethal aid had been withheld from El Salvador since 1977 on human-rights grounds, though in June 1980 the administration had sent $5 million in military supplies and training funds. These decisions suggest that Carter had begun to see events there in the context of the East-West dispute. As it turned out, the Salvadoran armed forces put down the guerrilla offensive before any US aid arrived. This fact was often used by those who argued against Reagan's calls to send additional aid to El Salvador over the coming months and years.

28. Minutes, NSC Meeting, 6 Feb. 1981, folder "NSC 00002, 11 Feb 81," box 91282, Executive Secretariat: Meeting File, Ronald Reagan Library. Also see Minutes, NSC Meeting, 10 Feb. 1982, folder "NSC 00040, 10 Feb 1982 [the Caribbean Basin]," box 91282, Executive Secretariat, NSC: NSC Meeting File, ibid.; Paper for NSC Feb 11 MTG, folder "NSC 00002, 11 Feb 1981," box 91282, Executive Secretariat: Meeting File, ibid.; Minutes of NSC Meeting (#19085), ibid.; and Paper in Richard Allen's Briefing Book for 6 Feb.

1981 NSC Meeting, folder "NSC 00001, 6 Feb 1981 [Caribbean Basin and Poland]," ibid.

29. Minutes, NSC Meeting, 6 Feb. 1981, 4.

30. Bernard Gwertzman, "El Salvador: A Test Issue," *New York Times*, 14 Feb. 1981 (online archive, accessed 4 May 2007).

31. Haig, "Interview on the *MacNeil/Lehrer Report*," 1, 2. During that interview, conducted on 13 March 1981 while the administration was trying to shift public attention from El Salvador, Haig argued: "After all we didn't trigger El Salvador, I see some press people suggest that we triggered El Salvador and a big draw-the-line operation. The problem with El Salvador was that we inherited massive evidence which had not been collated and had not been drawn together, and we did that in the first 2 weeks of the Administration—really in the first week—and it constituted irrefutable evidence of massive Cuban, Eastern, and Soviet involvement. This isn't a case of manipulating the news or focus or anything else. It [collating and presenting the new intelligence data] was an effort to lay out the facts as we saw them and to get a reasonable degree of support for the actions we felt had to be taken." Also see Haig, "Interviews at Breakfast Meetings," 10.

32. Haig, *Caveat*, 127.

33. See Weinberger Papers, I:645, National Security Council, folder 1, item 14, X12905, "18 Feb 81—Memorandum from Richard Allen, Subject: National Security Council Meeting—18 Feb 81." One of the few papers to be declassified, it also relates the importance the administration placed upon having public and congressional support:

> The full panoply of concerned activist and church groups (with the Roman Catholic hierarchy in the forefront) is beginning efforts to mobilize public opinion to demand an end to U.S. support for the Salvadoran government. This campaign can be expected to have growing effect—particularly in Congress—unless our intelligence on international communist intervention orchestrated by Moscow and Havana convinces the American public that the East-West factor and El Salvador's proximity to the U.S. have assumed overwhelming importance in determining U.S. interest. Sustained U.S. support for El Salvador will obviously require the cooperation of the Congress. For the present, careful adherence to the applicable laws . . . and extensive briefing and consultations should be sufficient to gain necessary support. For the longer term, however, (e.g., FY 82 and beyond), if

there has not been substantial improvement in the situation, Congressional support is likely to erode. This risk can be diminished by an intensive effort, beginning now, to build a broad bipartisan base of support for administration policy objectives through involving the Congress directly in deciding how the U.S. should respond to this communist challenge close to the United States.

While still classified, the following documents examined in the Weinberger Papers are supportive of the narrative presented on Central America: container I:645, National Security Council, folder 1, item 8, X12774, "10 February 1981, Memorandum for Distribution from Richard Allen; Subject: Paper for NSC Meeting on Feb 11, 1981, and Minutes from NSC Meeting on 6 February 1981"; I:630, Cuba, folder 1, item 4, X13244, "11 Mar 81, Memo for SecDef from Richard Stilwell, Subject: State/DoD/CIA Working Group on Cuba Strategy" (General Stilwell worked in the Office of the Undersecretary of Defense); I:630, Cuba, folder 2, item 11, X14665, "6 Jun 81—Memo for SecDef from Richard Allen, Subject: Presidential Decisions on U.S. Policy toward Cuba"; I:630, Cuba, folder 1, item 6, X[no number], "23 May 81—Memo for DepSecDef from Fred Ikle, Subject: SIG [Senior Interdepartmental Group] Meeting on Cuba: Attached Paper—An Initial Approach for Dealing with Cuba" (Ikle worked in the Office of the Undersecretary of Defense); I:630, Cuba, folder 1, item 7, X[no number], "26 May 81—Talking Paper for SecDef from J-5, Subject: Cuba—NSC Meeting on 4 June 1981"; I:630, Cuba, folder 1, item 8, X14515, "27 May 1981—Memo for SecDef from Fred Ikle, Subject: Results of the SIG on Policy toward Cuba"; I:630, Cuba, folder 2, item 9, X14546, "29 May 81—Memo for SecDef from L. Paul Bremer, Subject: Discussion Paper for NSC Meeting—Initial Approach for Dealing with Cuba"; I:630, Cuba, folder 2, item 10, X[no number], "5 Jun 81—DoD Position Paper for SecDef from Francis West, Subject: NSC on Cuba—Tighten Screws on Cuba"; I:630, Cuba, folder 2, item 11, X14665, "6 Jun 81—Memo for SecDef from Richard Allen, Subject: Presidential Decisions on U.S. Policy toward Cuba"; I:630, Cuba, folder 2, item 19, X16237, "17 Sep 81—Memo for SecDef from LTG James Dalton, Subject: Military Readiness Measures"; I:630, Cuba, folder 2, item 21, X[no number], "13 Oct 81—DepSecDef's Briefing Book, Subject: NSC Meeting on Cuba"; I:651, Nicaragua, item 2, X[no number], "3 Mar 81—Memo for Record from M/Gen Decamp, Subject: Nicaragua IG"; I:651, Nicaragua, item 5, X13543, "26 Mar 81—Memo for SecDef from Richard Allen, Subject: Decisions at NSC Meeting, March 26, 1981"; and I:651, Nicaragua, item 15, X[no number], "19 Oct 81—Background Paper for

SecDef, Subject: SecState Haig's Argument at NSC Meeting on Covert Action against Nicaragua." The fact that this is only a partial list of the materials in the Weinberger Papers is indicative that the topic was taken seriously by the administration and not simply an attempt at propaganda or bluster.

34. A talking-points paper for a Joint Chiefs of Staff meeting held in early March 1981 describes what the administration was up against in selling this storyline. The paper made the following three points: (1) "the Government of El Salvador is not a model the American people identify with"; (2) "the overall issue has the public confused"; and (3) "despite DoD's wishes, the Vietnam analogy will not go away." Weinberger Papers, I:628, Central America, folder 1, item 3, X13080, "3 Mar 81—Talking Points for JCS Mtg from Francis West; Subject: Military Training and Central America."

35. Document 01347, "El Salvador Overview," in National Security Archives, *El Salvador*, 4.

36. Bernard Gwertzman, "More Salvador Aid Backed in Congress," *New York Times*, 18 Feb. 1981 (online archive, accessed 4 May 2007).

37. Department of State, "Communist Interference in El Salvador," 1–7. The key details of the "white paper" were put out in a special to *The New York Times* on 20 February 1981, three days before the report's official release.

38. "Text of State Department Report on Communist Support of Salvadoran Rebels," *New York Times*, 24 Feb. 1981 (online archive, accessed 4 May 2007). Despite the presented evidence, not everyone was convinced. In his memoir, Haig quoted one such skeptic: "The White Paper fails to provide a convincing case. . . . Its evidence is flimsy, circumstantial, or nonexistent; the reasoning and logic is slipshod and internally inconsistent; it assumes what needs to be proven; and, finally, what facts are presented refute the very case the State Department is attempting to demonstrate." Haig attributed this response to what he called the "will to disbelieve," which had been unleashed by Vietnam and Watergate, noting: "The White Paper was combed for errors and traces of conspiracy. Were the captured documents quoted in the White Paper forgeries? Were the photographs of captured weapons genuine? The White Paper was subjected to the sort of burning scrutiny that only a heretical document can provoke. Mistranslations and other small errors, which should not have occurred but in no way affected the authenticity of the other information cited, were discovered. These were used to discredit the entire document." *Caveat*, 140.

39. Document 01338, "Department of State Telegram; Subject: Special Briefings on El Salvador," in National Security Archives, *El Salvador*, 2.

40. Congress did not get briefed until 18 February, when Haig held a

closed-door session with members of the Senate Foreign Relations Committee. In addition to sending Eagleburger to Europe, Reagan dispatched retired Lt. Gen. Vernon A. Walters to Brazil, Mexico, Argentina, and Chile to share the message of the threat to El Salvador. See Juan De Onis, "U.S. Seeks Allies' Backing on Salvador," *New York Times*, 14 Feb. 1981 (online archive, accessed 4 May 2007). The administration referred to these briefing teams as "truth squads."

41. "Winning Hearts and Minds," 30. These American weapons probably came from Sandinista sympathizers in the United States. Ortega later noted in an interview: "We also got some weapons from the United States, because some of our comrades worked in the solidarity [movement] in the United States and had connections there, so they found a way of buying weapons in the United States and bringing them to Nicaragua via Mexico." Cable News Network, "Episode 18: Backyard, Interviews, Daniel Ortega, Sandinista Leader, Nicaraguan President."

42. Document 01338, "Department of State Telegram; Subject: Special Briefings on El Salvador," 4. This telegram also stated: "In each capital, teams would appreciate an early, opportunity to brief and be briefed by interested embassy personnel on means of continuing private and public diplomacy efforts in this area, and would appreciate embassy assessments of key audiences and factors contributing to current public opinion climate. . . . The teams' primary mission, however, will be to background opinion shapers and political forces now or potentially active on El Salvador." Ibid., 5.

43. These measures, when considered in light of Haig's proposal for Cuba (which will be discussed later in the chapter) were very moderate. The administration did not like to use the term "advisors" because it conjured up associations with Vietnam. One finds in congressional testimony, recorded interviews, and speeches that the president and his key leaders insisted that the military men sent to El Salvador be referred to as "trainers." Reagan discussed this issue: "You could say they are advisers in that they're training, but when it's used as adviser that means military men who go in and accompany the forces into combat, advise on strategy and tactics. We have no one of that kind. We're sending and have sent teams down there [to El Salvador] to train. They do not accompany them into combat. They train recruits in the garrison area. And as a matter of fact, we have such training teams in more than 30 countries today, and we've always done that." Reagan, "Interview with Walter Cronkite," 8. Also see "Document 675, the Essential Problem in El Salvador," in US Department of State, *American Foreign Policy Current Documents 1981*, 1274 (hereafter abbreviated as *Current Documents 1981*). This document contains extracts from

a press briefing by Secretary of State Haig on 27 February 1981 in which he described the difference between trainers and advisors in the same way Reagan did during his 3 March interview. In addition to not wanting to evoke the Vietnam War, their other motivation in making this distinction was to forestall congressional demands to begin reporting under the War Powers Resolution or the Arms Export Control Act.

44. Haig, *Caveat*, 130.

45. Don Oberdorfer, "More U.S. Effort Yields Less Result," *Washington Post*, 4 Mar. 1982. The administration made this announcement on 2 March 1981. The funding would provide the GOES with additional helicopters, vehicles, radars, and surveillance equipment; equip its new quick-reaction forces; and provide needed spare parts and ammunition. Four five-man training teams were also to be sent to instruct the Salvadorans in communications, intelligence, logistics, and skills used in interdicting infiltrations and responding to terrorists. "Document 676, Additional Security Assistance to El Salvador," in *Current Documents 1981*, 12/6.

46. Judith Miller, "House Panel, 8–7, Votes $5 Million in Extra Military Aid to El Salvador," *New York Times*, 25 Mar. 1981 (online archive, accessed 4 May 2007).

47. Ibid.

48. Representative Conte, ranking minority member of the full House Appropriations Committee, exercised special voting privileges afforded to him from his rank on the full committee to participate in the Foreign Operations Subcommittee vote; Rep. Jamie Whitten (D-Miss.) did the same. Their support allowed the measure to be passed. Arnson, *Crossroads*, 68.

49. Judith Miller, "Congress Mail Heavy on El Salvador Issue," *New York Times*, 26 Mar. 1981 (online archive, accessed 4 May 2007).

50. "Reagan Mail Opposes Involvement," *New York Times*, 29 Mar. 1981 (online archive, accessed 4 May 2007). The White House opened 7,224 pieces of mail on El Salvador: 6,939 were against US involvement, with only 285 for it.

51. Raymond Bonner, "Protests on Salvador Are Staged across U.S.," *New York Times*, 25 Mar. 1981 (online archive, accessed 4 May 2007). Also see "Playing for High Stakes," 10. Not all protestors had come out to register their unhappiness that the United States might be stepping into another quagmire. Instead, some opposed the decision to help the government of El Salvador, which was known to have a poor human-rights record. Others were unhappy that the Reagan administration would send more aid before there was resolution regarding who had assassinated three American nuns at the end of 1980;

the Carter administration had cut off aid in 1980 pending the investigation but reinstated it when the guerrillas began their "final offensive" in January 1981. The Senate Foreign Relations Committee heard testimony on 18 March and 9 April at which the above concerns were considered. See Senate Committee on Foreign Relations, *Situation in El Salvador*. The House Subcommittee on Inter-American Affairs heard similar testimony on 5 and 11 March 1981. See House Subcommittee on Inter-American Affairs, *U.S. Policy toward El Salvador*.

52. See Document 01435, "Presidential Decision to Increase the Number of U.S. Military Advisors in El Salvador," in National Security Archives, *El Salvador*. Twelve days after Zablocki's request, Secretary of State Haig appeared before the House Foreign Affairs Committee and asked its members to develop legislation to allow the administration more flexibility in the conduct of the nation's foreign policy.

53. Senate Committee on Foreign Relations, *Situation in El Salvador*, 31.

54. Even after this revocation, service members in El Salvador continued to receive hostile-fire pay. Arnson, *Crossroads*, 66.

55. Public Law 97–113 demanded the president "certify" that the government of El Salvador was making progress in six areas—human-rights conditions, controlling the misdeeds of security forces, promoting economic reforms, holding elections, negotiating a political settlement, and investigating the murders of six US citizens—before sending aid.

56. Many of the above concerns were considered by the Senate on 18 March and 9 April 1981. See Senate Committee on Foreign Relations, *Situation in El Salvador*. The House Subcommittee on Inter-American Affairs heard similar testimony on 5 and 11 March 1981. See House Subcommittee on Inter-American Affairs, *U.S. Policy toward El Salvador*. For additional discussions about the legislative-executive debate over these issues, see Arnson, *Crossroads*, 69–71; and Moreno, *U.S. Policy in Central America*, 113–20.

57. Weinberger, "Dangerous Constraints on the President's War Powers," 101, 97.

58. The administration had already resorted to using a presidential determination so that it could send funds and defense articles to the government of El Salvador. The determination noted: "an unforeseen emergency exists which requires immediate military assistance to El Salvador; and the aforementioned emergency requirement cannot be met under the authority of the Arms Export Control Act or any other law except section 506(a) of the Act. The president was allowed to publish the determination pursuant to the authority vested by section 506 (1) of the Foreign Assistance Act of 1961, as amended." Weinberger

Papers, I:635, El Salvador, folder 3, item 26, W38137, "5 Mar 81 — Presidential Determination No. 81–4, Subject: Determination to Authorize the Furnishing of Immediate Military Assistance to El Salvador." The Clark Amendment modified the Arms Export Control Act, prohibiting military and covert aid to private groups engaged in paramilitary operations in Angola.

59. House Committee on Foreign Affairs, *Foreign Assistance Legislation for Fiscal Year 1982*, 187. Congress repealed the Clark Amendment in 1985.

60. See Judith Miller, "Once Again, Power Pendulum Swings toward the Executive Branch," *New York Times*, 22 Mar. 1981 (online archive, accessed 4 May 2007). Also see House Committee on Foreign Affairs, *Foreign Assistance Legislation for Fiscal Year 1982*, 155–95.

61. Haig, *Inner Circles*, 166, 127.

62. Haig, *Caveat*, 122.

63. Haig argued: "There could not be the slightest doubt that Cuba was at once the source of supply and the catechist of the Salvadoran insurgency. Cuba, in turn, could not act on the scale of the rebellion in El Salvador without the approval and the material support of the U.S.S.R. I believed that our policy should carry the consequences of this relationship directly to Moscow and Havana, and through the application of a full range of economic, political, and security measures, convince them to put an end to Havana's bloody activities in the hemisphere and elsewhere in the world." He also advocated supporting El Salvador with higher levels of US aid and with "reasonable numbers of military advisors." Ibid., 122, 124.

64. Robert McFarlane, a State Department counselor who Haig instructed to develop a plan to isolate and roll back Marxist control of Cuba, later said that the secretary believed that "during the President's political honeymoon, he should use his great popularity to push forward a tough policy in the Western Hemisphere, where the most immediate problems required the most difficult and most politically unpopular actions." Kagan, *Twilight Struggle*, 174. This is Kagan's paraphrase of McFarlane's remarks made in their 23 January 1991 interview. Also see Haig, *Caveat*, 131.

65. Haig, *Caveat*, 131. At one NSC meeting held on 10 November 1981, Haig noted: "The Soviet threshhold [*sic*] on Cuba meanwhile is very clear: it is the 1962 accords, the promise not to invade is the line. Invasion is the trigger for a serious Soviet response. Up to that point there is a free play area." See Strategy toward Cuba and Central America, folder "NSC 00024, 10 Nov 1981, [Strategy toward Cuba and Central America]," Executive Secretariat, NSC: NSC Meeting File, Ronald Reagan Library.

66. This contradiction has been noted by others. See Sklar, *Washington's*

War on Nicaragua, 72; and Allan Nairn, "The Pieces on the Board," *Report on the Americas* (May/June 1984), 32.

67. Haig, *Caveat*, 96.

68. As Major General Almond's aide, one of Haig's jobs was to keep the situation map used by MacArthur and his subordinate commanders up to date. He was also asked to listen in on the conversations MacArthur and Almond had with the Eighth Army commander, Lt. Gen. Walton H. "Johnny" Walker, and to take notes. Additionally, he was frequently in the communications room when MacArthur reported on the military situation to the Joint Chiefs of Staff and the president. Therefore, he was privy to many of the discussions held at the highest levels. For these stories, see Haig, *Inner Circles*, 12, 21, 27, 23.

69. Ibid., 35–37.

70. Other terms used to capture the same concept are "gradualism" and "incremental-gradualist approach."

71. Haig, *Inner Circles*, 97. Haig's opposition to incrementalism was also developed from a study he conducted while a student at the Army War College the year prior to deploying to Vietnam. He was chairman of Committee Eight, a group of students tasked with conducting a study on the "use of force." Through its historical research and analysis, which did not include Vietnam, the committee concluded "that the lesson of history was that gradual, as opposed to the overwhelming, application of military power, tended to produce the very outcome it was designed to avoid." Its members found that in "nearly every instance, . . . incrementalism had presented the enemy with opportunities to meet or exceed the measure of force applied, leading to localized military defeats, prolonged conflict, and a greater expense in lives and money than had been forecast by those who had made the policy." The group concluded that "senior military officers had a duty to point out these military realities to civilian policymakers." Ibid., 155–56.

72. Ibid., 127.

73. Haig, *Caveat*, 129.

74. Ibid., 124.

75. See Haig, *Inner Circles*, 23, 98, 132, 153; and Haig, *Caveat*, 127, 129, 130.

76. Haig, *Caveat*, 125.

77. Additionally, Haig recognized that using American ground troops in such a capacity was unrealistic given the domestic and foreign political realities the nation faced: "I never envisaged the landing of Marines in Central America. This was not necessary; there was no popular consensus to support such an act, and in any case, it was not possible under the War Power Act without the

consent of Congress. Every realistic being knew that such consent would only be given in case of catastrophe. It risked inflaming the xenophobia of neighboring states and all the consequences this implied." Ibid., 124.

78. See Kagan, *Twilight Struggle*, 175. Also see U.S. Policy in Central America and the Caribbean, folder "NSC00006, 26 Mar 1981, [Poland, Nicaragua, Central American, Southern Africa, Military Operations]," box 91282, Executive Secretariat: Meeting File, Ronald Reagan Library. The latter is a top-secret strategy paper prepared by Robert McFarlane and other members of the State Department for the NSC. The intent of the paper was to gain "NSC approval of a multifaceted and comprehensive long-term U.S. strategy for restoring stability in Central American and the Caribbean." It noted that specific measures vis-à-vis Cuba would be looked at in a separate study.

79. In 1983 Reagan appointed Henry Kissinger to serve as the chairman of the National Bipartisan Commission on Central America. That group was charged to provide advice for a long-term US policy to respond to the challenges presented to the security and stability of each Central American nation from internal and external threats. It concluded that the United States ought to consider "a significantly larger program of military assistance, as well as greatly expanded support for economic growth and social reform." Essentially, the commission proposed a Marshall Plan for Central America. Its recommendations were very similar to those proposed by McFarlane's group in 1981. See National Bipartisan Commission on Central America, *Report*.

80. Don Oberdorfer, "The White House Charts Its Course from Crisis to Crisis: Blockade of Cuba Was Rejected," *Washington Post*, 23 Nov. 1983.

81. Weinberger, *Fighting for Peace*, 31–32. Of course, Haig denied ever considering such an action. *Caveat*, 129. With the exception of that note in Weinberger's memoir, there are no other indications that Haig ever intended a military invasion of Cuba. Nevertheless, his plan did call for a very aggressive stance in the region.

82. Weinberger, *Fighting for Peace*, 31.

83. Senior officials in the Pentagon had concerns with the Haig plan. Specifically, they were troubled about the commitment of significant numbers of ships and aircraft to the Caribbean. The Joint Chiefs worried that the Soviets might take the opportunity to exploit an area of weakness elsewhere in the world, perhaps even attack an American ally. Pentagon leaders were also afraid the plan would damage the prospect of rebuilding the nation's military strength. See Weinberger Papers, I:630, Cuba, folder 2, item 10, X[no number], "5 June 81—DoD Position Paper for SecDef from Francis West, Subject: NSC on Cuba—Tighten Screws on Cuba." The Defense Department opposed

using US ships to shadow Cuban freighters because it was costly and could be mocked. Defense also opposed the transfer of US air squadrons to Florida because officials believed it would be very costly and accomplish very little. Also see Kagan, *Twilight Struggle*, 174–75; Haig, *Caveat*, 124, 127–28; Woodward, *Veil*, 171; and Oberdorfer, "White House Charts Its Course," A10.

84. Journalist Allan Nairn made similar observations about the constraints caused by domestic political realities. See "Pieces on the Board." Also see Sklar, *Washington's War on Nicaragua*, 72. Sklar argued: "Reagan's advisers were divided into two camps: Haig's high-intensity/go-to-the-source minority vs. the incrementalist majority."

85. Oberdorfer, "More U.S. Effort Yields Less Result," *Washington Post*, 4 Mar. 1982.

86. This comes out clearly in many sources. See, for example, Haig, *Caveat*, 144, 127, 129–30; Woodward, *Veil*, 117, 171–72; and Meese, *With Reagan*, 229.

87. Martin Schram, "White House Revamps Top Policy Roles," *Washington Post*, 22 Mar. 1981, A2. Also see Haig, *Caveat*, 81, 92–94, 144. In the end, the troika's concerns seemingly carried the day. On 13 March, John A. Bushnell, the deputy assistant secretary of state for inter-American affairs, provided a background briefing to reporters in which he "charged that news organizations were exaggerating the situation in El Salvador and that this was deflecting attention from other key foreign policy issues." He reportedly said: "'This story has been running five times as big as it is, . . . and we figured, if we talked to you about it, you might not make this thing such a big deal.'" "High Official Now Plays Down El Salvador," *New York Times*, 13 Mar. 1981 (online archive, accessed 4 May 2007). The next day Haig offered that he "wouldn't suggest that it's not that big a deal," however, he cautioned that there were "many equally important issues" such as Afghanistan and Poland and "other vital issues—East-West relations at large, arms control, and a host of other matters of equal importance." See Haig, "Interview on the *MacNeil/Lehrer Report*," 1; and "Salvador Becomes a Smaller Big Deal," *New York Times*, 15 Mar. 1981 (online archive, accessed 4 May 2007). These statements from Bushnell and Haig were in sharp contrast to all that had preceded them. The administration had devoted its first month of political energy and capital to its message regarding the Soviet bloc's involvement in the El Salvadoran insurgency.

88. Weinberger had an opportunity to make these same points in opposition to Haig's successor, George P. Shultz. Like Haig, Shultz believed that the president must be free to commit US military forces without the advance

support of the public or their leaders in Congress. He explained: "There is no such thing as guaranteed public support in advance. Grenada shows that a president who has the courage to lead will win public support if he acts wisely and effectively. And Vietnam show that public support can be frittered away if we do not act wisely and effectively." George P. Shultz, "The Ethics of Power," in Lefever, *Ethics and American Power,* 15. Weinberger clearly enunciated his views on the topic in his annual report to Congress in 1986:

> No aspect of the [Weinberger] doctrine I have enunciated for the use of force has received more comment and criticism than the requirement that we have reasonable assurance of the support of the American people. There can be no assurance, the critics say. A government forced to wait for the people will be paralyzed in international politics. . . . My purpose is not to wish away the frustrations of leadership in a democracy. Perhaps if President Roosevelt had been willing to act on his own authority in 1939, 1940, or 1941, the enormous losses of World War II could have been reduced. But perhaps, only by waiting until the full force of American public opinion was clearly mobilized behind the necessity of winning an all-out war was President Roosevelt able, with our allies, to secure the unconditional surrender of both the Nazis and the Japanese. It is not necessary for me to argue that the considered judgment of the American people is always correct. My thesis is more modest, but more important. It is that American democracy is constructed on the principle not that the American people will always be right, but that there exists no better guide to wise policy. Our government, therefore, constructs a process that forces the President and the Congress to lead and argue, to seek and win the support of the American people in order to sustain a course of action. The inherent assumption here is that this will, in the long run, produce wiser choices than any other mechanism yet discovered.

Caspar W. Weinberger, *Annual Report to the Congress, Fiscal Year 1987* ([Washington, D.C.], 1986), 80. Haig later recalled: "In the NSC and in private meetings with me over breakfast, Cap Weinberger insistently raised the specter of Vietnam." *Caveat,* 128.

89. Weinberger, *Fighting for Peace,* 31. As a vocal secretary of state, Haig had many opportunities to make the American public aware of his plan to "go after the source," and as Weinberger predicted, Americans never warmed to

the idea. The administration was never able to garner public or congressional support for taking decisive action to obtain its policy objectives enunciated for Central America.

90. Senate Committee on Armed Services, *Nomination of Caspar W. Weinberger*, 38.

91. Col. Charles D. Corbett, "Inter-American Security and U.S. Military Policy" (Strategic Studies Institute, U.S. Army War College, 24 June 1977), quoted in Nairn, "Endgame," 22.

92. Three Big Pine exercises were conducted with the Hondurans between 1983 and 1985. The General Accounting Office found that some of the military construction of bases and airstrips that were part of these exercises was intended to benefit the CIA's Contra operations. Big Pine II, which began on 3 August 1983, was the largest and involved over 12,000 US troops and two battleship groups.

93. See Binns, *United States in Honduras*, 12; and Gutman, *Banana Diplomacy*, 45–46. Interestingly, Schweitzer chose Lt. Col. Oliver North to serve on Reagan's NSC staff. See Timberg, *Nightingale's Song*, 281.

94. In April 1981, the leader of the Honduran army, Col. Gustavo Álvarez Martínez, in a meeting with CIA Director Casey offered for his nation to serve as a base for anti-Sandinista insurgents. See Gutman, *Banana Diplomacy*, 16.

95. As late as August 1981, Haig was still trying to make his case to Reagan in regards to taking firm action against Cuba. In a memorandum to the president, the secretary of state wrote: "*Action to put Cuba*—the ultimate source of support for the insurgency—*on the defensive is also necessary.* We are nearing the completion on the package of limited actions you authorized in June—Radio Free Cuba, protecting against a new Mariel boatlift, various limited military preparedness measures, public exposure of Cuba's covert war in the Hemisphere, and tightening the economic sanctions. *Clearly we will have to do more early on—depending on the response I get when I take Gromyko on about Cuba September* [Haig's emphasis]." Memorandum, "The Risk of Losing in El Salvador, and What Can Be Done about It," folder "NSC 00020, 17 Aug 1981, [East-West Trade, Central America, Strategic Forces]," box 91282, Executive Secretariat: Meeting File, Ronald Reagan Library.

96. Federation of American Scientists, "NSDD-17: Cuba and Central America," "NSDD—National Security Decision Directives: Reagan Administration," Intelligence Resource Program, http://www.fas.org/irp/offdocs/nsdd/nsdd-017.htm (accessed 7 Jan. 2008).

97. Ibid.

98. The public did not find out about the covert operations against Nica-

ragua until November 1982, when *Newsweek* broke the story. See "America's Secret War: Target: Nicaragua."

99. The Hughes-Ryan Amendment, passed in 1974, applied to the Foreign Assistance Act of 1961. The amendment prohibited the use of appropriated funds for the use of CIA or Department of Defense covert operations until the president issued an official "finding" that the operation was important to national security. Due to their nature, most presidential findings are classified and presented to the intelligence oversight committees within Congress. The intent of the law was to ensure that the responsibility for such actions was attributable to the president and that Congress was notified.

100. See Don Oberdorfer and Patrick E. Tyler, "Political, Paramilitary Steps Included," *Washington Post*, 14 Feb. 1982; Oberdorfer, "More U.S. Effort Yields Less Result," *Washington Post*, 4 Mar. 1982; Patrick E. Tyler and Bob Woodward, "U.S. Approves Covert Plan in Nicaragua," *Washington Post*, 10 Mar. 1982; Leslie H. Gelb, "U.S. Said to Plan Covert Actions in Latin Region," *New York Times*, 14 Mar. 1982 (online archive, accessed 14 May 2007); and "America's Secret War: Target, Nicaragua," 42–55.

101. Gutman, *Banana Diplomacy*, 85. Gutman's source was a staff member on the Senate Select Intelligence Committee.

102. Ibid. Gutman notes that the decisions Reagan reached in November to sign NSDD-17 and on 1 December 1981 to sign his second finding did not change the direction of policy. Instead, those decisions "ratified a process that had begun months earlier."

103. See Don Oberdorfer and Patrick E. Tyler, "U.S.-Backed Nicaraguan Rebel Army Swells to 7,000 Men," *Washington Post*, 8 May 1983; and Peter Kornbluh, "Covert War," in Walker, *Reagan Versus the Sandinistas*, 23–24. Writers are divided on where they mark the beginning of the covert war against Nicaragua. Some see this first presidential finding as the start. See Sklar, *Washington's War on Nicaragua*, 71; and Kornbluh, "*Nicaragua," the Price of Intervention*, 19. Others record the start as 16 November, when Reagan approved NSDD-17, or 1 December, when he signed a finding authorizing covert paramilitary operations against Nicaragua. See Kagan, *Twilight Struggle*, 204; and Dickey, *With the Contras*, 99–101. For the most neutral explanation, see Gutman, *Banana Diplomacy*, 85.

104. Kagan, *Twilight Struggle*, 200.

105. Gutman, *Banana Diplomacy*, 82–83.

106. See Moreno, *U.S. Policy in Central America*, 101–103.

107. Evidence that the administration did not simply decide to use the Contras as a last resort is the fact that Reagan's first presidential finding, signed

in early March 1981, provided the funding that laid the groundwork for the insurgents' activity.

Chapter 4

1. Like the Somozas in Nicaragua, the Pahlavis had led Iran since the early 1920s. The shah's father, Reza Khan, had commanded the Persian Cossack Division, and his forces had ended the rule of the Qajar dynasty in 1921. After Shi'a religious leaders blocked his plans for a republic, Reza Khan crowned himself as Reza Shah Pahlavi on 12 December 1925. In 1941 British and Soviet troops invaded Iran to secure its oil fields and open additional supply lines to Russia. The Allies sent Reza Shah into exile and placed his son Muhammad Reza Shah on the Peacock Throne. Like the younger Somoza, the younger Pahlavi was a supporter of the United States in its fight against communism. Rubin, *Paved with Good Intentions*, 13, 18.

2. American planners recognized that the Saudis did not have the population or the infrastructure necessary for a large military buildup and that such a rapid growth in the Saudi armed forces might lead it to challenge the royal family.

3. Sick, *All Fall Down*, 13.

4. See Kupchan, *Persian Gulf and the West*, 35–36; Teicher and Teicher, *Twin Pillars to Desert Storm*, 29, 35; and Chadda, *Paradox of Power*, 38–41. Chadda never refers to the "twin pillar" policy and credits the shah rather than Nixon with the idea of using Iran as a "policeman in the Persian Gulf." *Paradox of Power*, 38–39. Kupchan noted that the formulation of the twin-pillar policy can be found in National Security Study Memorandum (NSSM) 66, published on 12 July 1969. The memorandum recommended an increase in arms sales to Iran and Saudi Arabia to help them deter Soviet moves into and to maintain stability throughout the region. *Persian Gulf and the West*, 35. For a discussion of specific actions the shah took in his capacity as a surrogate to the United States, see Chadda, *Paradox of Power*, 40–42.

5. Kupchan, *Persian Gulf and the West*, 28–29.

6. For discussion of superpower activity in the Middle East, see Teicher and Teicher, *Twin Pillars to Desert Storm*, 22–23. Kupchan noted: "Before 1967, arms sales were offered primarily as a means of securing political influence and access to bases. After the war, however, transfers were directed more at building up the regional military capabilities of the Soviet-backed Arabs and the American-supported Israelis." *Persian Gulf and the West*, 29.

7. See Kuniholm, "Retrospect and Prospects," 9–16. Kuniholm elsewhere explained: "The Eisenhower Doctrine extended the containment policy from

the Northern Tier states [Iraq, Turkey, Pakistan, and Iran] to the Middle East in general, and Congress subsequently authorized [the] use of armed force to assist non-Communist Middle Eastern nations threatened by armed aggression from any country controlled by international communism." *Persian Gulf and United States Policy*, 20.

8. See, for example, Kupchan, *Persian Gulf and the West*, 34; Teicher and Teicher, *Twin Pillars to Desert Storm*, 23; and Chadda, *Paradox of Power*, 35.

9. The author has not found anyone else highlighting this distinction between the Nixon Doctrine and the twin-pillar policy. Others have noted that Iran and Saudi Arabia were expected to support US interests, however, they do not emphasize the difference between providing a country with the means to defend itself from internal or external threats and providing a country with means and then asking it to serve as a proxy for American forces. One, Gary Sick, wrote: "This policy [twin-pillar] was perhaps the clearest translation of the Nixon Doctrine into concrete practice anywhere in the world." "The Evolution of U.S. Strategy toward the Indian Ocean and Persian Gulf Regions," in Rubinstein, *Great Game*, 58.

10. See Noyes, *Clouded Lens*, 54.

11. Spiegel, *The Other Arab-Israeli Conflict*, 172–73.

12. Informing these paragraphs on the 1973 Arab-Israeli war were Kupchan, *Persian Gulf and the West*, 45–51, 53–64; and Chadda, *Paradox of Power*, 49–51. For discussions on US plans for military action, see Kupchan, *Persian Gulf and the West*, 47; and Chadda, *Paradox of Power*, 50–51.

13. One senior Carter official explained that the administration continued to follow the policy because it had become largely institutionalized in the bureaucracy since its adoption five years earlier by President Nixon. See Sick, *All Fall Down*, 18, 21. Gary Sick was the principal White House aide for Iran during the Iranian revolution and the hostage crisis and served on the NSC staff under Presidents Ford, Carter, and Reagan. He also noted that Kissinger and Nixon had taken measures to ensure this policy was institutionalized quickly. The Department of Defense had studied the situation in Iran and concluded that introducing complex equipment based upon high technology would be counterproductive. Sick recommended instead that the shah concentrate on educating and professionalizing his force and purchasing weapons that would better match the capabilities of his soldiers and officers. Kissinger found a way around that bureaucratic friction. In July he had the president sign a memorandum directing that all purchasing decisions be left up to the Iranian government. This was universally accepted as a presidential order and allowed the shah to have whatever he desired in the US arsenal save nuclear weapons. See ibid., 14–16.

14. Federation of American Scientists, "PD-18: US National Strategy," "Presidential Directives (PD): Carter Administration, 1977–81" Intelligence Resource Program, http://www.fas.org/irp/offdocs/pd/pd18.pdf (accessed 26 Sept. 2007). PD-18 was signed on 26 August 1977. The policy was a result of a February 1977 presidential-review memorandum (PRM-10) that directed an examination of the overall US national strategy and capabilities. See Federation of American Scientists, "PRM-10: Comprehensive Net Assessment and Military Force Posture Review," "Presidential Review Memorandums (PRM): Carter Administration, 1977–81" Intelligence Resource Program, http://www.fas.org/irp/offdocs/prm/prm10.pdf (accessed 27 Sept. 2007).

15. See Federation of American Scientists, "PD-18: US National Strategy."

16. One historian has emphasized that "the fall of the Shah was a major turning point in the evolution of the rapid deployment concept. It needs to be stressed that it was the Iranian revolution, and not the Soviet invasion of Afghanistan, which provided the decisive impetus for the realization of the deployment force conceived in PD-18." Acharya, *US Military Strategy in the Gulf*, 53.

17. See Brzezinski, *Power and Principle*, 455–56; Kupchan, *Persian Gulf and the West*, 55–56; and Acharya, *US Military Strategy in the Gulf*, 53.

18. Sick, *All Fall Down*, 18.

19. John C. Campbell, "The Gulf Region in the Global Setting," in Amirsadeghi, *Security of the Persian Gulf*, 8.

20. The Soviet loss of influence can be traced back to the beginning of 1971, when Egypt's new president, Anwar al-Sadat, launched his corrective revolution, purging government leaders who were considered pro-Soviet. In July 1972, Sadat also expelled Soviet military advisors. Despite these activities Egypt received support from the Soviet Union during the 1973 war. But US influence in the region increased following that conflict. One reason was that American armaments proved yet again to be superior to those of the Russians. Another was that the United States demonstrated that, of the two superpowers, it was the only one that could successfully negotiate with and on behalf of both sides of the Arab-Israeli conflict. This fact was brought home to the Arab nations when US diplomatic pressure convinced Israel to stop short of destroying the Egyptian Third Army as it was trapped in the Sinai. Kupchan, *Persian Gulf and the West*, 48, 51; Chadda, *Paradox of Power*, 42–46.

21. Kupchan explained that the Carter administration was concerned about how to publicize the RDF concept: "Should the RDF be presented as part of a global strategy, a regional strategy, or a reaction to vulnerability in a specific theater?" *Persian Gulf and the West*, 127.

22. Jimmy Carter, "The State of the Union Address Delivered before a Joint Session of the Congress," 23 Jan. 1980, American Presidency Project, http://www.presidency.ucsb.edu/ws/?pid=33079 (accessed 26 Sept. 2007).

23. The RDF was initially subordinate to the Readiness Command. But on 1 October 1981 it was made into a separate joint task force that was to report directly to the National Command Authority through the Joint Chiefs of Staff. At that time it was also tasked to make its primary focus Southwest Asia. On 1 January 1983, the RDF was transformed again into US Central Command and given geographic responsibility over Southwest Asia. For the evolution of the RDF command organization, see Acharya, *US Military Strategy in the Gulf,* 66.

24. Weinberger Papers, I:645, National Security Council, folder 1, item 3, X17590, "27 Jan 81   Memo for SecDef from Mr. Kramer, Subject: NSC Topics." Some of the issues addressed were peacetime presence, en-route access, exercises, Sinai airbases, allied contributions, and basing requirements.

25. The Lebanese request on 2 July 1982 was informal. It was made formal on 18 August. "Document 389, Lebanese Proposal for a U.S. Contribution to a Temporary Multinational Force in Beirut," in US Department of State, *American Foreign Policy Current Documents 1982,* 835 (hereafter cited as *Current Documents 1982*).

26. While still classified, the following documents examined in the Weinberger Papers are supportive of the narrative presented on Lebanon: container I:687, Lebanon, folder 1, item 5, X19260, "10 Apr 82—Ltr to Col Stanford from Paul Bremer, Subject: Contingency Planning for Israeli Attack on Lebanon"; I:687, Lebanon, folder 1, item 7, X19296, "Memo for Paul Bremmer from Col Stanford, Subject: Contingency Planning for Israeli Attack on Lebanon"; I:688, Lebanon, folder 4, item 16, X[no number], "13 Jun 82—Memo for President from DCI, Subject: Next Steps in Lebanon"; I:688, Lebanon, folder 4, item 18, X[no number], "15 Jun 82—Memo from SecDef from ISA, Subject: Invasion of Lebanon—Next Moves—Info. Memo"; I:688, Lebanon, folder 4, item 23, X20320, "19 Jun 82—Memo for SecDef from Gen. Vessey, Subject: Lebanon"; I:688, Lebanon, folder 4, item 25, X[no number], "23 Jun 82—Memo for SecDef from Noel Koch, Subject: Reply to Crown Prince Hassan Letter Concerning Crisis in Lebanon"; I:688, Lebanon, folder 4, item 33, X20519, "1 Jul 82—Memo for President from Mr. Haig, Subject: Lebanon Crisis: Status Report as of Mid-day June 30"; I:688, Lebanon, folder 4, item 35, X20562, "2 Jul 82—Memo for President from Walter Stoessel, State, Subject: Habib Mission: An International Force for Beirut"; I:688, Lebanon, folder 4, item 37, X20617, "8 Jul 82—Memo for SecDef from Fred Ikle, Subject: Let-

ter to President Reagan from Brezhnev"; I:688, Lebanon, folder 5, item 50, X21154, "5 Aug 82— Msg for SecDef, Subject: Habib Mission: Participation of U.S. Forces in Beirut Peacekeeping"; I:688, Lebanon, folder 5, item 51, X21214, "7 Aug 82—Memo for SecDef from Fred Ikle, Subject: Status of Habib's Negotiations"; I:688, Lebanon, folder 5, item 53, X21320, "13 Aug 82—Memo for SecDef from Francis West, Subject: U.S. Participation in the Beirut Multinational Force: Exchange of Diplomatic Notes and Public Affairs Treatment"; I:688, Lebanon, folder 5, item 59, X21392, "18 Aug 82—Memo for SecDef from Francis West, Subject: CPPG Meeting on Lebanon August 18"; I:688, Lebanon, folder 5, item 65, X[no number], "24 Aug 82—Msg to AMEMBASSY Beirut from SecDef, Subject: Habib Mission: U.S. Troop Disposition"; "I: 688, Lebanon, folder 5, item 70, X21608, "1 Sep 82—Msg to AMEMB TEL AVIV from JCS, Subject: US Participation in Operations in the Middle East"; I:688, Lebanon, folder 5, item 71, X21607, "1 Sep 82—Msg to White House & SecDef from USDAO Tel Aviv, Subject: Message to the President"; I:688, Lebanon, folder 5, item 73, X21634, "3 Sept 82, Memo for Col Stanford from Paul Bremer, Subject: Habib Mission: US Marine Departure from Beirut"; and I:688, Lebanon, folder 5, item 74, X[no number], "3 Sep 82—Msg to SecDef from AMEMBASSY Beirut, Subject: SecDef Visit to Lebanon on 1 Sept."

27. Jordan had served as the Palestinians' major base for operations against Israel, but Jordanian military and political elites decided that their nation would be better served without the presence of the PLO and expelled them. Thus, many of the refugees Lebanon received in 1971 were top leaders and activists in the Palestinian fight against Israel. See Rabinovich, *War for Lebanon*, 40; and Evron, *War and Intervention in Lebanon*, 8.

28. The Arab Deterrent Force consisted of approximately 30,000 soldiers who were mostly Syrian. The command was funded by the oil-producing states but under the authority of the Lebanese president. It was not asked to depart the country until 1982. Information for the Palestinian and Lebanese problems with sovereignty came from the following sources: Rabinovich, *War for Lebanon*, 40–41, 54–56; Evron, *War and Intervention in Lebanon*, 7–9, 13–16; and Gilmour, *Lebanon*, 86–96, 129–42.

29. This Christian militia group served as a proxy force in Lebanon for the Israelis and was led by Saad Haddad.

30. Gilmour, *Lebanon*, 143, 146, 150–51.

31. The PLO used the period following the ceasefire to build up its artillery, rocket, and other heavy-arms supplies, while the Israelis made plans to attack and destroy PLO forces in southern Lebanon. In October 1981, Begin

told Secretary of State Haig about Israeli plans to move into Lebanon. Haig recalled: "In the months ahead the subject would arise again and again." *Caveat*, 326–27, 332.

32. Administration leaders did not agree with the Israeli interpretation that an attack on an Israeli anywhere in the world constituted a violation of the ceasefire agreement. See Weinberger, *Fighting for Peace*, 140–41; Haig, *Caveat*, 335; and Reagan, "Monday, June 21," *Reagan Diaries*, 89. Haig told the Israelis that the United States would consider an attack justified "only in a strictly proportional response to 'an internationally recognized provocation.'" Weinberger wrote that "the PLO['s compliance] with the cease-fire greatly vexed Israeli Defense Minister Ariel Sharon, who needed a pretext to deliver a knockout blow." Indeed, Sharon told the *Jerusalem Post* that he had started planning the Lebanon operation when he took office in July 1981 and even made a reconnaissance trip to Beirut in January 1982. See Jansen, *Battle of Beirut*, 124. For the internal and external factors that drove the Israeli decision to attack the PLO in 1982, see Davis, *40Km into Lebanon*, 61–71.

33. On 25 February, Moshe Arens, the Israeli ambassador, told US reporters that an invasion of Lebanon was "a matter of time." *Current Documents 1982*, 7n, 801. Earlier that month, Gen. Yahoshua Sagay, director of Israeli military intelligence, had called on Haig and told him of Israel's plans to attack the PLO in Lebanon. One of the administration's memorandums on this subject has been declassified and thus allows this meeting to be discussed with further candor. According to the memorandum, "Secretary Haig warned the Israeli emissary, General Sagi [*sic*], the Chief of Intelligence, that such an attack would have 'grave implications' for US-Israeli relations." It went on to state: "The United States has nothing to gain and much to lose should Israel again invade Lebanon. We must alert Arabs (Saudis, Jordanians, Syrians, and others) to the dangers and enlist their support for PLO restraint. Our goal must be to dissuade Israel, and should that fail, to keep Israel's response in some reasonable proportion to a provocation." One can see from this document and others that are still classified that the administration was very opposed to the prospect of an Israeli invasion. Weinberger Papers, I:687, Lebanon, folder 1, item 1, X18317, "1 Feb 82—Memo for DepSecDef from Noel Koch, Subject: Lebanon—Information Memorandum." In May 1982, Defense Minister Sharon visited Washington and sketched out two possible military campaigns to a room of State Department officials. Haig, *Caveat*, 332, 335. For specific information on Israelis war plans, see Gabriel, *Operation Peace for Galilee*, 60–61; and "Document 350, U.S. Reaction to the Attempted Assassination of Israel's Ambassador to the United Kingdom," and "Document 351, Appeal for

a Cease-Fire in Lebanon," in *Current Documents 1982*, 803–804. The impotence of the UNIFIL was demonstrated when Israeli forces rolled right through its positions.

34. "Document 353, Efforts to Limit the War in Lebanon," in *Current Documents 1982*, 804.

35. See Davis, *40Km into Lebanon*, 92. It is still unknown why the Israeli actions did not match their words. Haig argued that the attacks were extended due to military concerns. *Caveat*, 338. Others have seen the extension as representative of a battle between Begin and Sharon over what ends Israel ought to be pursuing. See, for example, Davis, *40Km into Lebanon*, 77. Still others argue that the Israelis' intent from the start was duplicitous. See, for example, Gilmour, *Lebanon*, 143, 146, 161.

36. Evron, *War and Intervention in Lebanon*, 138.

37. Weinberger Papers, I:687, Lebanon, folder 4, item 22, X20284, "17 June 82—Memo for SecDef from Francis West, Subject: U.S. Policy in Lebanon."

38. Ibid. UN Resolution 242 was adopted by the Security Council on 22 November 1967 and called for a withdrawal of Israeli armed forces from territories (Sinai Peninsula, Gaza Strip, West Bank, eastern Jerusalem, and the Golan Heights) occupied during the 1967 Arab-Israeli war. Weinberger believed that such a demand would divide the PLO and allow the United States to work with its moderate elements. He also recommended that the administration announce that it intended to put forward American proposals for full Palestinian autonomy as envisioned at Camp David. Following twelve days of secret negotiations at Camp David, President Sadat and Prime Minister Begin signed two agreements, the second of which led directly to the Israel-Egypt Peace Treaty signed in March 1979. That agreement made plans for the Israelis to withdrawal from the Sinai.

39. Ibid. Weinberger ended: "While this program both preserves our interests and buttresses Israel's security over the long-term, it probably will provoke outrage from Begin and Sharon because it brings in the PLO and forces a compromise short of the Israeli goal of eventual annexation of the West Bank. Many Israelis would welcome the above initiatives from us, as would broad sections of Congress and the U.S. public. Such a policy also would secure our standing in the Arab world and among our alarmed allies."

40. Shultz, *Turmoil and Triumph*, 46. Also see Weinberger, *Fighting for Peace*, 144n3.

41. Bernard Gwertzman, "Key Lawmakers Express Doubts about Plan," *New York Times*, 7 July 1982 (online archive, accessed 14 Sept. 2007). This

article also reported that Yasser Arafat did not have an objection to the United States being involved in an international force charged with guaranteeing the Palestinian departure from Beirut.

42. "U.S. Warships Ordered to Stand by off Lebanon," *Washington Times*, 7 July 1982.

43. Mary McGrory, "Playing Rodney Dangerfield in the Mideast Has Its Hazards," *Washington Post*, 8 July 1982. In general, Weinberger was very sympathetic to the Palestinian cause and frustrated by Israeli unilateralism. In June he recommended that the administration support a UN resolution condemning Israel for its invasion and threaten the state with sanctions. By August the secretary was so frustrated with the Israelis over their tough tactics that Shultz wrote, "he [Weinberger] seemed almost ready to sever relations." See Weinberger, *Fighting for Peace*, 140–46; Haig, *Caveat*, 343–44; and Shultz, *Turmoil and Triumph*, 60.

44. "U.S. Warships Ordered to Stand By."

45. See Hallenbeck, *Military Force as an Instrument*, 14. Hallenbeck cited many of the same newspaper articles used as sources here but reached very different conclusions. He argued that Weinberger and Vessey were concerned about employing US Marines in Lebanon because it "entailed risks similar to those that had accompanied the initial introduction of U.S. units into Vietnam," not noting Weinberger's concerns regarding how the deployment might interfere with US relations with the Arab states. In his memoir, Weinberger provided more-specific concerns regarding the second MNF deployment that were closely related to the worries of becoming involved in another Vietnam-type situation. This author does not believe those concerns were as strong with Weinberger on the first deployment because he and Vessey were able to get the administration to agree to have the forces deployed for only thirty days and made plans for restricting their mission. This will be discussed in greater detail later in this chapter. Also see McFarlane, *Special Trust*, 211. Regarding the push to get the marines out quickly after the PLO fighters were evacuated, McFarlane wrote: "Weinberger, with his pro-Arab convictions, had no doubt acted out of concern that the Marines could be identified as tilting toward Israel, and that they could become involved, even if only coincidentally, in violence against Arabs that would damage our position *vis-à-vis* the Arab states." This statement seems to back the argument posited above that many of Weinberger's concerns stemmed from strategic considerations.

46. "Document 366, Policy Goals in Lebanon," in *Current Documents 1982*, 817.

47. Shultz, *Turmoil and Triumph*, 47; Haig, *Caveat*, 349.

48. On 25 June 1982, Reagan gave Haig a note: "Dear Al, It is with the most profound regret that I accept your letter of resignation." This caused Haig to hurry back to his office to write his letter of resignation. For details about the events leading to this, see Haig, *Caveat*, 310–16, 350–51.

49. Gwertzman, "Key Lawmakers Express Doubts about Plan." This *Times* article reported: "Mr. Reagan's decision to allow up to 1,000 American troops to participate in keeping the peace in Beirut . . . was made in utmost secrecy last Friday night [2 July], according to the White House." Also see "Document 369, Agreement in Principle to Contribute U.S. Personnel for Peacekeeping in Beirut," in *Current Documents 1982*, 820. The United States formally accepted the proposal to be involved in the MNF on 20 August 1982. See "Document 390, The U.S. Acceptance of Lebanon's Proposal for a Temporary Multinational Force," in ibid., 836–37.

50. White House announcement quoted in Don Oberdorfer, "Plan to Send in the Marines Caught Up in Controversy," *Washington Post*, 11 July 1982.

51. Don Oberdorfer and John M. Goshko, "U.S. Set to Send Troops to Lebanon: Peace-Keeping Force," *Washington Post*, 7 July 1982; Gwertzman, "Key Lawmakers Express Doubts about Plan." Members of Congress were not brought in on the discussion until the matter of using US troops was announced by the Israeli press. In response Reagan made a formal announcement on 6 July that he had agreed in principle to contribute to a peacekeeping force in Lebanon. In an effort at damage control, senior White House and State Department officials quickly placed calls to Capitol Hill.

52. Gwertzman, "Key Lawmakers Express Doubts about Plan."

53. They were Lee Hamilton (D-Ind.) of the House Foreign Affairs Subcommittee on Europe and the Middle East and Joseph P. Addabbo (D-N.Y.), chairman of the House Defense Appropriations Subcommittee. See Michael Getler, "Israel Approves Most of U.S. Plan for PLO Pullout," *Washington Post*, 8 July 1982. For an explanation as to why it is common to see congressional leaders crossing party lines in the formulation of positions concerning Israel, see Novik, *United States and Israel*, 39.

54. "2 Senators Split on Use of Troops," *New York Times*, 10 July 1982 (online archive, accessed 14 Sept. 2007).

55. The author examined numerous articles from the period, and the only reference to Vietnam came from Sen. Charles Percy (R-Ill.). The senator was very critical of Israel's decision to invade Lebanon and noted that the situation could turn out to be "Israel's Vietnam." See William Branigin, "Fighting in Beirut Mounts with Talks Still at an Impasse," *Washington Post*, 12 July 1982.

56. Paul Taylor, "Conditions for Use of Troops in Beirut Unmet, Reagan Says," *Washington Post*, 14 July 1982.

57. "War Powers Resolution of 1973: Public Law 93–148, 93rd Congress, H. J. Res. 542," 7 Nov. 1973, Almanac of Policy Issues, http://www.policyalmanac .org/world/archive/war_powers_resolution.shtml (accessed 9 Oct. 2007).

58. See Hendrick Smith, "Reagan Is Undecided on Sending Marines to Beirut," *New York Times*, 14 July 1982 (online archive, accessed 14 Sept. 2007); Taylor, "Conditions for Use of Troops in Beirut Unmet, Reagan Says"; Hall, *Reagan Wars*, 156–57.

59. Bernard Gwertzman, "Shultz on the Hill: Not Your Usual 'Consultations,'" *New York Times*, 19 Aug. 1982 (online archive, accessed 14 Sept. 2007).

60. What is difficult to ascertain, but what must be mentioned, is the power of the pro-Israel lobby, the American-Israel Public Affairs Committee (AIPAC), over congressional leaders and their decisions. AIPAC began its operations in 1951 and by the late 1980s could boast of a forty-person staff representing a broad range of expertise on the US political process, particularly the workings of Congress. A study on information sources in foreign policy conducted by the Congressional Research Service for the House Foreign Affairs Committee stated that AIPAC is "widely regarded today as the most effective ethnic/foreign policy lobby on Capitol Hill." The report said that AIPAC and the Conference of Presidents of Major American Jewish Organizations "have been most effective in insuring a relatively uninterrupted flow of military and economic aid to Israel, especially since 1967." Nevertheless, it is difficult to know just how much influence they had over the decisions made by congressional leaders. See Leopold Yehuda Laufer, "U.S. Aid to Israel: Problems and Perspectives," in Sheffer, *Dynamics of Dependence*, 146–47. Laufer noted that AIPAC's support for Israeli government policy should not "be taken for granted," adding: "Evidence of this became public when in September 1982, the Israeli government abruptly rejected the Reagan peace plan, while Tom Dine, Director of AIPAC, saw in it 'great worth' despite some negative elements." For more discussion on how AIPAC shapes US foreign policy, see Mearsheimer and Walt, *Israel Lobby and U.S. Foreign Policy*; and Findley, *They Dare to Speak Out*.

61. Eytan Gilboa, "Trends in American Attitudes toward Israel," in Sheffer, *Dynamics of Dependence*, 67.

62. Ibid., 37. In 1982 the Jewish population in the United States was estimated to be 5.725 million, or 2.5 percent of the overall American population. Mandell L. Berman Institute, "North American Jewish Data Bank," http://www.jewishdatabank.org/AJYB/AJY-1983.pdf (accessed 18 Mar. 2008).

Mearsheimer and Walt contended that US support to Israel cannot be explained either on strategic or moral grounds. Instead, it is gained because of the activities of the Israeli lobby, which the authors described as "a loose coalition of individuals and organizations that actively works to move U.S. foreign policy in a pro-Israel direction." *Israel Lobby and U.S. Foreign Policy* 5.

63. See Novik, *United States and Israel*, 21.

64. Ibid., 155n39.

65. For a contradictory argument to this claim, see Rubenberg, *Israel and the American National Interest*, 285. Rubenberg argued: "Haig announced on June 10 after a meeting between President Reagan and Saudi foreign minister Prince Saud al-Faisal that Saudi Arabia had given no indication of any possible interruption in the flow of oil to the West in spite of Arab 'anger' over the invasion. Thus the United States was assured at an early date that it had nothing to fear from the Arab oil-producers for its support of Israel's actions in Lebanon."

66. Like his predecessor, Reagan also considered the Persian Gulf region a vital interest to the United States and its allies. Likewise, he was committed to defending the nation's interests there with military force.

67. Shultz, *Turmoil and Triumph*, 61; Edward Walsh, "Israeli Guns Pour Shells on W. Beirut in 14-Hour Attack," *Washington Post*, 2 Aug. 1982.

68. Oberdorfer and Goshko, "U.S. Set to Send Troops to Lebanon." Also see Thomas L. Friedman, "Food Is Becoming the Critical Problem in Lebanon," *New York Times*, 18 July 1982 (online archive, accessed 4 Oct. 2007); and Shawn G. Kennedy, "Arab-Americans Seeking to Bring Children to U.S.," *New York Times*, 12 Aug. 1982 (online archive, accessed 4 Oct. 2007). A *Washington Post*/ABC poll conducted on 17 August 1982 found an 8-percent increase in sympathies for the Arab nations since a similar poll was conducted in June 1982. See Gilboa, "Trends in American Attitudes toward Israel," 66 (table 2.10), 67–72. During the summer of 1982, the American media was accused of being pro-PLO and anti-Israel. For a thorough discussion of this issue, see Chomsky, *Fateful Triangle*, 280–89.

69. "Document 381, 'The Bloodshed Must Stop,'" in *Current Documents 1982*, 830.

70. Minutes of NSC Meeting on Lebanon Situation, 4 Aug. 1982, folder "NSC 00057, 04 Aug 1982 [Lebanon Situation]," box 91284, Executive Secretariat, NSC: Records NSC Meeting Files, Ronald Reagan Library.

71. In late June 1982, despite such reporting, 79 percent of Americans still labeled Israel as either "a close ally" or "friend" of the United States. That represented a 4-percent increase since January 1982. See Novik, *United States and Israel*, 155–56n43.

72. Hallenbeck, *Military Force as an Instrument*, 14.

73. In his memoir, Weinberger did not provide a specific explanation for why he and General Vessey were against US troops participating in the first MNF operation. Thus, the explanation provided for his concerns regarding the mission relies on evidence from the memoirs of other leaders, newspapers, and secondary sources. See Haig, *Caveat*, 343; "U.S. Warships Ordered to Stand by off Lebanon"; Don Oberdorfer, "Plan to Send in the Marines Caught Up in Controversy," *Washington Post*, 11 July 1982; McGrory, "Playing Rodney Dangerfield in the Mideast Has Its Hazards"; and Hallenbeck, *Military Force as an Instrument*, 14.

74. Weinberger Papers, I:688, Lebanon 1982, folder 4, item 48, X21012, "29 Jul 82—Memo for SecDef from Gen. Vessey, Subject: Rebuilding the Lebanese Armed Forces."

75. Ibid.

76. Oberdorfer and Goshko, "U.S. Set to Send Troops to Lebanon," A12; Getler, "Israel Approves Most of U.S. Plan for PLO Pullout."

77. See "U.S. Warships Ordered to Stand by off Lebanon"; McGrory, "Playing Rodney Dangerfield in the Mideast Has Its Hazards"; Getler, "Israel Approves Most of U.S. Plan for PLO Pullout"; and Branigin, "Fighting in Beirut Mounts with Talks Still at an Impasse." Weinberger's points mirror Senator Levin's argument for very similar conditions before deploying forces.

78. Branigin, "Fighting in Beirut Mounts with Talks Still at an Impasse."

79. "Document 392, Announcement of an Agreement for the Withdrawal of the PLO from Beirut," in *Current Documents 1982*, 839–40.

80. "Document 389, Lebanese Proposal for a U.S. Contribution to a Temporary Multinational Force in Beirut," ibid., 835–36; "Document 390, The U.S. Acceptance of Lebanon's Proposal for a Temporary Multinational Force," ibid., 836.

81. "Document 395, Notification to Congress Regarding the U.S. Role in the Multinational Force," ibid., 855.

82. Hall, *Reagan Wars*, 157.

83. Frank, *U.S. Marines in Lebanon*, 12.

84. "Document 394, Deployment of U.S. Marines in Beirut," in *Current Documents, 1982*, 849, 852.

85. Ibid., 846. Also see Richard Halloran, "Pentagon See 'Pacific' Role for U.S. Troops in Lebanon," *New York Times*, 21 Aug. 1982 (online archive, accessed 4 Sept. 2007).

86. "Document 394, Deployment of U.S. Marines in Beirut," 852.

87. Shultz, *Turmoil and Triumph*, 80, 103.

88. Ibid., 80.

89. Weinberger, *Fighting for Peace*, 150.

90. Roy Gutman, "Division at the Top Meant Half-Measures, Mistakes," *Long Island Newsday*, 8 Apr. 1984, Chairman of Joint Chiefs of Staff Clippings, binder 84, Vessey Papers, National Defense University Library, Washington DC. Robert McFarlane later claimed that Weinberger sent the order for the withdrawal without consulting the secretary of state or the president and was "criminally irresponsible." *Special Trust*, 211. This argument is not supported elsewhere. Hallenbeck noted that on 1 September Reagan announced that the marines would be withdrawn from Lebanon within two weeks. *Military Force as an Instrument*, 16. Shultz later wrote: "I had misgivings about such a quick withdrawal, but under the circumstances, I realized that the marines would in fact leave as soon as possible after the PLO departure." *Turmoil and Triumph*, 103.

91. Arafat's intermediary during the negotiations, Saeb Salem, a leader of West Beirut's dominant Sunni Muslim community, told the press that it had been his understanding that the MNF would stay in Beirut for a brief period after the PLO left while the Israelis withdrew from the capital and the international airport. Beirut's Muslims also wanted the MNF to remain to shield them from the Israelis. See Jay Ross and Loren Jenkins, "Marines Expected to Quit Beirut Soon," *Washington Post*, 2 Sept. 1982. Concerns about Palestinian safety had been expressed to Weinberger as well. On 12 July, Henry E. Catto Jr., who worked in the Office of the Assistant Secretary of Defense, was called by Ambassador Ghorbal of Egypt, a friend of his, and passed a message. Catto characterized that communication as "clearly along foreign policy lines." He wrote to Weinberger that the Egyptian ambassador had expressed that the United States "should not go into Lebanon with the sole purpose of evacuating the PLO. He pointed out that, after the PLO leaves, there will still be thousands of Palestinians left behind and subjected to the tender mercies of the Israelis: 'An international force could protect these Palestinians from Israeli excess. The Israelis say arbitrarily this one is a terrorist, this is not. If you are going to remove their armed forces but leave the civilians exposed, the result might be a rebellion of Muslims as the Israelis mix in Lebanese politics. You can't say to hell with the rest "after the PLO is out." Don't clean the living room and leave the rest of the house dirty.'" Ghorbal recommended that the force sent include troops from Muslim countries as well as France so that it would look better to the Arab world. Weinberger Papers, I:688, Lebanon, folder 4, item 40, 14862, "12 July 82—Memo for SecDef from Henry Catto, PA, Subject: A Message from Ambassador Ghorbal of Egypt." Defense Department leaders were not

callous to the plight of the Palestinian refugees. A memorandum drafted on 19 July recommended that the United States consider accepting responsibility for the Palestinian civilians. Ibid., item 44, X21077, "19 Jul 82—Memo for DepSecDef from Noel Koch, Subject: Disposition of Palestinian Refugees" (Koch was the principal deputy assistant secretary for international security affairs).

92. Shultz, *Turmoil and Triumph*, 103.

93. Weinberger, *Fighting for Peace*, 144, 150.

94. See "Document 404, Mission of the Second Multinational Force," in *Current Documents 1982*, 865. Not everyone saw the US mission in the narrow form accepted by Weinberger and Shultz. Robert McFarlane described Weinberger's order to remove the marines as "fateful" and "treacherous." *Special Trust*, 209.

95. Shultz, *Turmoil and Triumph*, 103.

Chapter 5

1. While still classified, the following documents examined in the Weinberger Papers support the narrative on Lebanon: container I:688, Lebanon, folder 6, item 83, X[no number], "20 Sep 82—Msg to AMEMBASSY Amman from SecState; Subject: Beirut Situation: U.S. Initiative"; I:688, Lebanon, folder 6, item 87, X21923, "20 Sep 82—Memo for Record from Francis West, Subject: Middle East Status Report—20 Sep 82"; I:688, Lebanon, folder 6, item 89, X[no number], "23 Sep 82—Msg to AMEMBASSY Beirut from SecState; Subject: Draper Mission: Exchange of Notes on Participation of US Forces in Second Beirut MNF"; I:688, Lebanon, folder 6, item 91, X22012, "24 Sep 82—Memo for Record from Francis West, Subject: 24 Sep Crisis Planning Group Secure Phone Discussion of Beirut Planning"; I:688, Lebanon, folder 6, item 95, X22041, "27 Sep 82—Memo for Record from Francis West, Subject: MNF for Beirut: Secure Conference Call, 27 Sep 82"; I:688, Lebanon, folder 8, item 108, X22288, "12 Oct 82—Msg to SecDef from AMEMBASSY Beirut, Subject: Security Assistance for Lebanon"; I:688, Lebanon, folder 10, item 116, X22395, "18 Oct 82—Memo for Secretary of Army from DepSecDef, Subject: Security Assistance for Lebanon"; I:688, Lebanon, folder 10, item 122, X22489, "22 Oct 82—Memo for Secretary Shultz from William Clark, Subject: Presidential Decision on Lebanon Plan"; I:689, Lebanon, folder 11, item 129, X22582, "27 Oct 82—Memo for SecDef from Mr. McFarlane, NSA, Subject: Next Steps in Lebanon"; I:689, Lebanon, folder 11, item 132, X22626, "29 Oct 82—Ltr to President Gemayel from DepSecDef, Subject: Lebanese Army Modernization Plan"; I:689, Lebanon, folder 11, item 133, X22627, "29 Oct 82—Memo

for President from DepSecDef, Subject: Immediate Training for Lebanese
Forces"; I:689, Lebanon, folder 11, item 134, X22664, "1 Nov 82—Memo for
William Clark from DepSecDef, Subject: Next Steps in Lebanon—Notional
Force Packages"; I:689, Lebanon, folder 12, item 137, X22668, "1 Nov 82—
Memo for President from Secretary Shultz, Subject: Diplomatic Strategy for
Lebanon"; I:689, Lebanon, folder 12, item 138, X22636, "2 Nov 82—Memo
for Distribution from DepSecDef, Subject: Coordination and Policy towards
Lebanon"; I:689, Lebanon, folder 12, item 139, X[no number], "3 Nov 82—
Memo for President from Secretary Shultz and Secretary Weinberger, Sub-
ject: Next Steps in Lebanon"; I:689, Lebanon, folder 12, item 142, X22738,
"4 Nov 82—Memo for Secretary of Army from DepSecDef, Subject: Support
for Lebanon"; I:689, Lebanon, folder 12, item X22732, "4 Nov 82—Memo for
William Clark from Paul Bremer, Subject: Diplomatic Strategy—Approximate
Timetable"; I:689, Lebanon, folder 12, item 144, X22737, "5 Nov 82—Msg
to AMEMBASSY Beirut from SecState, Subject: Expanded MNF—Low Key Approach"; I:689, Lebanon, folder 13, item 150, X23046, "22 Nov 82—Memo
for SecDef from Francis West, Subject: Lebanese Army Modernization Plan
(LAMP)"; I:689, Lebanon, folder 13, item 152, X23122, "26 Nov 82—Memo
for SecDef from Secretary Marsh, Subject: Security Assistance—Lebanon";
I:689, Lebanon, folder 13, item 153, X23123, "26 Nov 82—Memo for SecDef
from Secretary Marsh, Subject: Security Assistance—Lebanon"; I:689, Lebanon, folder 13, item 155, X[no number], "30 Nov 82—Memo for Record from
Francis West, Subject: Lebanon and the President's Peace Initiative"; I:689,
Lebanon, folder 13, item 160, X[no number], "8 Dec 82—Memo for SecDef
from Francis West, Subject: Habib Comprehensive Withdrawal Plan"; I:689,
Lebanon, folder 13, item 161, X23791, "8 Dec 82—Memo for President from
Acting Secretary/State, Subject: Withdrawal of External Forces from Lebanon"; I:689, Lebanon, folder 13, item 162, X[no number], "Memo for Sec-
retary Shultz from Mr. Veliotes/State, Subject. Middle East Options Paper";
I:728, Lebanon, folder 1, item 11, X[no number], "27 Jan 83—Background Paper for SecDef, Subject: Status of U.S.-Israeli-Lebanese Negotiations"; I:728,
Lebanon, folder 2, item 24, X[no number], "3 Feb 83—Memorandum for
the Record from LTG Paul Gorman, Subject: 'Best Offer'"; I:728, Lebanon,
folder 2, item 26, X[no number], "4 Feb 83—To SecDef from William P. Clark,
Subject: National Security Council Planning Group Decisions"; I:728, Lebanon, folder 2, item 27, X[no number], "4 Feb 83—To DepSecDef from Francis J. West, Jr., Subject: Current Situation in Lebanon: Background for NSPG
Meeting"; I:728, Lebanon, folder 4, item 122, X25206, "22 Apr 83—To SecDef
from William P. Clark, Subject: National Security Planning Group Meeting

to Review Middle East Policy"; I:728, Lebanon, folder 4, item 132, X25284, "27 Apr 83—To SecState/SecDef from William Clark, Subject: NSDD-92: Accelerating the Withdrawal of Foreign Forces from Lebanon"; I:729, Lebanon, folder 6, item 181, X[no number], "25 Aug 83—To the President from SecState and SecDef, Subject: International Military Presence in Lebanon"; I:729, Lebanon, folder 6, item 182, X26887, "26 Aug 83—To Charles Hill from Robert M. Kimmitt, Subject: International Military Presence in Lebanon"; I:729, Lebanon, folder 6, item 184, X26888, "27 Aug 83—To Menachem from the President, Subject: Movement of Israeli Troops from the Shuf"; I:729, Lebanon, folder 6, item 198, X26944, "1 Sep 83—To Charles Hill from Robert Kimmitt, Subject: Special Situation Group (SSG) Meeting—31 Aug"; I:729, Lebanon, folder 6, item 201, X26995, "3 Sep 83—To Charles Hill from Bob Kimmitt, Subject: Talking Points for President Reagan's Meeting with Congressional Leadership"; I:729, Lebanon, folder 6, item 202, X[no number], "3 Sep 83—To SecState from Ambassador Dillon, Subject: McFarlane/Fairbanks Mission: September 3 Meeting with President Gemayel"; I:729, Lebanon, folder 6, item 203, X[no number], "3 Sep 83—To NPIC from CIA, Subject: LAF Decision Not to Deploy into Shuf and Alayh Districts after Israeli Redeployments"; I:729, Lebanon, folder 6, item 204, X27015, "7 Sep 83—To SecDef (while in Panama) from Capt., Subject: Gemayel Talks of Resignation"; I:729, Lebanon, folder 7, item 206, X27060, "8 Sep 83—To SecDef from William H. Taft, Subject: Legislative Strategy Group Meeting Scheduled for 10:00 A.M., Friday, September 9, on Lebanon and the Congress"; I:729, Lebanon, folder 7, item 207, X[no number], "9 Sep 83—To SecDef from Policy, Subject: Situation Update"; I:729, Lebanon, folder 7, item 208, X27079, "9 Sep 83—To SecDef from Policy, Subject: Staff Papers on Lebanon"; I:729, Lebanon, folder 7, item 209, X[no number], "9 Sep 83—Memorandum from Conversation, Subject: Phone Call between President Gemayel of Lebanon and Vice President George Bush"; I:729, Lebanon, folder 7, item 210, X27083, "11 Sep 83—To V/Admiral Moreau from John M. Poindexter, Subject: Addendum to National Security Decision Directive—Strategy for Lebanon"; I:729, Lebanon, folder 7, item 213, X27082, "12 Sep 83—To Donald Gregg from Robert M. Kimmitt, Subject: NSDD on Lebanon"; I:729, Lebanon, folder 7, item 214, X27099, "12 Sep 83—To Assistant to the President for National Security Affairs from SecDef, Subject: Response to 10 September 1983 NSDD, Strategy for Lebanon"; I:729, Lebanon, folder 7, item 217, X[no number], "17 [sic, 15] Sep 83—To JCS from USCINCEUR, Subject: Tactical Air Strikes in Lebanon"; I:729, Lebanon, folder 7, item 221, X27209, "19 Sep 83—To SecDef from L/Gen Philip Gast, Subject: Expedited Deliveries for Lebanon";

I:729, Lebanon, folder 7, item 225, "22 Sep 83—National Military Command Center Significant Event Report, Subject: Naval Gunfire Support for Suq al-Gharb." Other sources particularly helpful to constructing the narrative were Hallenbeck, *Military Force as an Instrument*; Dupuy and Martell, *Flawed Victory*; Rabinovich, *War for Lebanon*; Gilmour, *Lebanon*; Bavly and Salpeter, *Fire in Beirut*; Nathan A. Pelcovits, "What Went Wrong?" in McDermott and Skjelsbaek, *Multinational Force in Beirut*, 37–79; Shultz, *Turmoil and Triumph*; Weinberger, *Fighting for Peace*; and McFarlane, *Special Trust*.

2. "Document 399, Call for Israeli Withdrawal from West Beirut," in *Current Documents 1982*, 859; "Document 400, U.N. Resolution 520, Demand for Israeli Withdrawal from West Beirut," ibid.

3. See Dupuy and Martell, *Flawed Victory*, 181–94, Abba Eban, "Introduction," in Commission of Inquiry, *Beirut Massacre*, xiii; and Shultz, *Turmoil and Triumph*, 106. The Kahan Commission was charged with conducting an inquiry into the massacres. In February 1983, Israeli defense minister Ariel Sharon stepped down after the commission found him negligent in the tragedy.

4. Shultz, *Turmoil and Triumph*, 104.

5. Robert McFarlane recalled a conference call that was held on Saturday, 18 September, with Edwin Meese, William Clark, George Shultz, Casper Weinberger, William Casey, and John Vessey. "With the exception of Weinberger," he wrote, "all the participants expressed guilt at the massacres and a sense that the United States should offer to do something to ease the situation in Beirut." McFarlane largely blamed the tragedy on what he referred to as "Weinberger's irresponsible removal of our Marine protection from these hapless innocents." *Special Trust*, 211.

6. "Document 869, The U.S. Effort to Establish Security for Lebanon and Israel," in *Current Documents 1982*, 869.

7. Reuters, "Arabs Blame U.S. in Beirut Deaths," *New York Times*, 22 Sept. 1982 (online archive, accessed 10 Oct. 2007).

8. McFarlane, *Special Trust*, 211. In an interview conducted over fifteen years after the attack, Vessey explained: "After the massacre we [Weinberger and the Joint Chiefs] didn't want to go back in, but there wasn't any good argument for not going back in." Strober and Strober, *Reagan Presidency*, 213.

9. Shultz, *Turmoil and Triumph*, 106. Shultz wrote, "Everyone knew that President Reagan was ready to send the marines back to Beirut, so the Pentagon had at least to appear to be responsive." Ibid., 107.

10. McFarlane, *Special Trust*, 212.

11. Gutman, "Division at the Top Meant Half-Measures, Mistakes."

12. The NSC also met on 20 September to discuss Lebanon. See NSC

Meeting Announcement, folder "NSC 00060, 20 Sept. 1982 [Lebanon]," box 91284, Executive Secretariat, NSC: Records NSC Meeting Files, Ronald Reagan Library.

13. Reagan, "Sunday, September 19," *Reagan Diaries*, 101. Clearly, the administration's sense of guilt over the massacres did not preclude it from wanting to achieve broader aims. This argument was made also in Pelcovits, "What Went Wrong?," 41.

14. "Document 403, Announcement of a New Multinational Force Deployment in Beirut," in *Current Documents 1982*, 863.

15. An Israeli departure from Beirut was a prerequisite for the return of the marines and is not listed here as a US objective. Note that these three objectives were the same goals the administration had outlined in June 1982, shortly after the initial Israeli invasion. See "Document 366, Policy Goals in Lebanon," in *Current Documents, 1982*, 817.

16. Congress was generally supportive of the president's decision so long as he followed the terms of the War Powers Resolution. The favorable political climate could be attributed primarily to two matters. First, the Israelis initially had decided not to conduct an inquiry into the events surrounding the massacres at the Palestinian refugee camps. Congressional leaders were reportedly surprised by the news, which left them disapproving and disenchanted. Hedrick Smith, "Congress Shocked at Refusal of Israel to Have an Inquiry," *New York Times*, 22 Sept. 1982 (online archive, accessed 10 Oct. 2007). Second, many legislative leaders believed that the situation was too precarious to be ignored. Senate Majority Leader Baker, who had opposed the first deployment, said: "I don't believe you can leave that situation, dangerous as it is, unattended." Bernard Gwertzman, "U.S. Plans to Send Marines Back to Beirut," *New York Times*, 21 Sept. 1982 (online archive, accessed 10 Oct. 2007).

17. Chamoun appealed for help under the Eisenhower Doctrine and received it. His opposition came from Pan-Arabists backed by Egypt's Gamal Abdel Nasser and the politically disadvantaged Muslim community.

18. McFarlane, *Special Trust*, 212.

19. Halloran, "Reagan as Military Commander," 25. Halloran wrote: "Back in September 1982, General Vessey and the four service chiefs had argued against sending American forces into Lebanon for fear that the United States would become entangled in a conflict that might turn into a quagmire like the war in Vietnam."

20. Shultz, *Turmoil and Triumph*, 106–109; McFarlane, *Special Trust*, 211.

21. Hallenbeck, *Military Force as an Instrument*, 29. Hallenbeck served in US European Command as the chief of current operations in the Directorate

of Operations and Plans. In that role, he was involved in planning the deployment of US forces to Lebanon.

22. Shultz wrote that he conceptualized the mission in two phases: "Phase I, namely, an MNF presence in Beirut, and a Phase II, dealing with the larger issues of Lebanon." Presumably, by "larger issues," Shultz meant getting all foreign forces to depart Lebanon. *Turmoil and Triumph*, 108.

23. McFarlane, *Special Trust*, 212. Following Bashir Gemayel's assassination, his brother, Amin Gemayel, became president of Lebanon.

24. Pelcovits, "What Went Wrong?," 39. See also Shultz, *Turmoil and Triumph*, 108–110.

25. Shultz, *Turmoil and Triumph*, 108. Curiously, Weinberger did not discuss this in his memoir. Thus, one is left to rely on Shultz.

26. Weinberger, *Fighting for Peace*, 151–53. Similar to the first MNF, Ambassador Habib had received assurances from the Lebanese government that the armed militias would not interfere. The Druze and other principal Muslim parties wanted the MNF to serve as a counterweight to the Phalangist militia. Pelcovits, "What Went Wrong?," 42. Weinberger believed that the threat from the Phalangists alone might require that the United States deploy a division (16,000 to 20,000 men) to be prepared to deal militarily with that force. Shultz, *Turmoil and Triumph*, 108. The assurances held up until March 1983, when members of the MNF began to come under attack from various factional militias. DoD Commission on Beirut International Airport, *Report*, 39–41 (hereafter *Long Commission Report*). Yet it was not until August 1983 that marine positions began receiving sustained rocket and mortar attacks from Muslim militias.

27. Shultz, *Turmoil and Triumph*, 108.

28. From the perspective of the Arab nations, which were critical to American security interests in the Persian Gulf region, Israeli actions were controlled by the United States. But that was more perception than reality. The Reagan administration did try to influence Israel, but as discussed earlier, those efforts were largely ineffective. See chap. 4, n. 33. Instead, Israeli actions in Lebanon were ultimately curbed by realities on the ground and at home. Any further gains would require urban fighting and result in casualties that the small nation could not afford. Additionally, Israeli domestic support for the war had begun to crumble following the Sabra and Shatila massacres.

29. "Document 408, Lebanese Request for a U.S. Contingent in the Second Multinational Force," in *Current Documents 1982*, 869 (emphasis added).

30. *Long Commission Report*, 35 (emphasis added).

31. The marines would have been on the ground three days earlier, but the Israelis were delayed in their departure. Beirut International Airport was selected for US forces because it was considered one of the least dangerous sectors assigned to the MNF. The French took up positions in downtown Beirut, while the Italians were to oversee three major Palestinian refugee camps. Hoffman, *Decisive Force*, 43. Also see Hallenbeck, *Military Force as an Instrument*, 177nn10, 29. Hallenbeck explained: "The initial mission and force size decisions were accomplished by cribbing from policy statements that had been issued in coordination with the PLO evacuation. . . . The work was accomplished within the Joint Staff, in conjunction with HQ USEUCOM. The number 1,200, for example, originated as a staff officer's best guess of the size of the Marine unit then deployed with the U.S. Sixth Fleet in the Mediterranean." He also noted: "Whereas President Reagan's decision to reintroduce U.S. forces meant committing U.S. forces for largely politico-diplomatic purposes, the diplomats had neither asked for nor been assigned a responsibility to determine the size, composition, or employment of the military force."

32. Hallenbeck, *Military Force as an Instrument*, 31–33.

33. Shultz, *Turmoil and Triumph*, 108. Note that these are McFarlane's views as described by Shultz. McFarlane had wanted to send in a large force to convince the Syrians and Israelis to depart Lebanon. But when that option was not accepted, he supported the marines serving in a symbolic role of US interest and resolve.

34. "Document 410, The U.S. Effort to Establish Security for Lebanon and Israel," in *Current Documents 1982*, 870.

35. Charles Mohr, "U.S. Says 1,200 Marines May Join Beirut Force," *New York Times*, 28 Sept. 1982 (online archive, accessed 10 Oct. 2007). State Department and White House officials were reportedly not as optimistic as the president and issued clarifications about what Reagan really meant. A spokesman from the Pentagon said troops would remain as long as necessary, while the State Department said that the withdrawal of foreign troops was a goal, not a criterion for the withdrawal of US troops. See Sanction, "Once More into the Breach," 28.

36. Evron, *War and Intervention in Lebanon*, 138; Gilmour, *Lebanon*, 182–83; Rabinovich, *War for Lebanon*, 122. After Bashir Gemayel was assassinated, the militia force he had commanded conducted the massacres in the Palestinian refugee camps. Israel provided more than $100 million in support to Bashir's militia between 1976 and 1982. See Hallenbeck, *Military Force as an Instrument*, 4.

37. Weinberger, *Fighting for Peace*, 116. Of the idea, Weinberger wrote: "To

me, Gemayel's plan was little more than a wild idea. Here was a small country torn by civil war, without strategically important resources, whose main claim to American attention was its ability to serve as a breeding ground for trouble in a very volatile region of the world. Lacking any real leverage, Bashir Gemayel put forth the political equivalent of a 'blank check'—saying, in effect, 'Do anything you want with Lebanon—just save us.' I, of course, reported Gemayel's idea fully to the President and to State, and discussed it with my Defense staff. No one reached a conclusion different from mine." Ibid., 147.

38. Shultz, *Turmoil and Triumph*, 99.

39. Bavly and Salpeter, *Fire in Beirut*, 192. The authors placed Begin's confrontation of Gemayel in Nahariya, where the prime minister was vacationing, and described the event as having occurred on 8 September rather than 2 September. This author believes that the 2 September date related in Shultz's memoir is more accurate given the fact that the impetus for the encounter was likely the announcement of the Reagan administration's Middle East peace initiative.

40. For the full text of the speech, see Ronald Reagan, "Address to the Nation on United States Policy for Peace in the Middle East," 1 Sept. 1982, American Presidency Project, http://www.presidency.ucsb.edu/ws/?pid=42911 (accessed 30 Jan. 2008).

41. Ibid.

42. The administration began working on its peace plan on 17 July 1982. When Reagan entered office in January 1981, he was committed to follow the broad guidelines laid down by the Carter administration regarding the peace process between Israel and its Arab neighbors. That broad outline was to follow the Camp David accord framework, which made the Egyptian-Israeli peace treaty a first priority and autonomy talks for the Palestinians the second step. The first step was completed in April 1982, when the Egyptians returned to the Sinai, while the second step was preempted when the Israelis invaded Lebanon. With his 1 September speech, Reagan announced to the nation and the world at large his intention to link the situation in Lebanon to the wider negotiations for peace in the Middle East. This decision made the administration's dealings with Israel over Lebanon that much more challenging. Israel wanted to turn Lebanon into a pro-Western nation and sign a peace treaty with it before cooperating on any larger peace issues. When Ambassador Arens learned that Reagan was trying to revitalize the peace process, he said: "We have wiped the PLO from the scene. Don't you Americans now pick the PLO up, dust it off, and give it artificial respiration." Shultz, *Turmoil and Triumph*, 91.

43. Ibid., 98.

44. Ibid.

45. Bavly and Salpeter, *Fire in Beirut*, 195.

46. Ralph Hallenbeck has provided a very good description of the LAF: "In 1982, the Lebanese Armed Forces (LAF) were at best a ragtag excuse for a national guard. Although approximately 20,000 men strong, . . . the LAF was poorly equipped (lacking even complete uniforms), very poorly led, untrained, and riddled with corruption, factional loyalties, and political intrigue. Since the Army's disintegration during the 1975–76 Lebanese Civil War it had seen no combat (the LAF had remained in its garrisons even during the June Israeli invasion). As a result, LAF units were no match for any of the factional militias, all of which had been seasoned by recent fighting." *Military Force as an Instrument*, 37.

47. Ibid., 38–39. What is unclear is how truly devoted Gemayel was to the concept of rebuilding a government that included all parties, Druze, Muslim, and Christian alike.

48. Smith, "Looking to Washington," 45.

49. "Document 413, Visit of President Amin Gemayel of Lebanon," in *Current Documents 1982*, 872.

50. Hallenbeck, *Military Force as an Instrument*, 37.

51. Many of the documents informing NSDD-64 are unclassified and available for research at the Ronald Reagan Library. See folder "NSDD-64(1) [Next Steps in Lebanon]," box 91286, Executive Secretariat, NSC: Records NSDD; and folder "NSDD-64(2) [Next Steps in Lebanon]," Ronald Reagan Library.

52. "Document 414, 'We Had a Very Good Visit with Amin Gemayel,'" in *Current Documents 1982*, 874.

53. Smith, "Looking to Washington," 46.

54. Memorandum, Clark to Shultz, Weinberger re: NSDD-64, folder "NSDD-64(2) [Next Steps in Lebanon]," box 91286, Executive Secretariat, NSC: Records NSDD, Ronald Reagan Library.

55. NSDD-64, ibid.

56. Weinberger Papers, I:689, Lebanon, folder 12, item 139, X[no number], "3 Nov 82—Memo for President from Secretary Shultz and Secretary Weinberger." The header information for this memorandum does not include Secretary Weinberger, however, it was from both cabinet officers.

57. See Frank, *U.S. Marines in Lebanon*, 36–39; and Hallenbeck, *Military Force as an Instrument*, 41.

58. Hallenbeck, *Military Force as an Instrument*, 41–42.

59. Ibid., 40.

60. "Document 415, The Extent and Duration of U.S. Military Assistance to Lebanon," in *Current Documents 1982*, 874–76.

61. Shultz later wrote: "Our most important missed opportunity came in September and early October 1982—a time when the situation was most fluid, when Syria was in a weakened position, and when the Lebanese could have best responded to a strong U.S. initiative." *Turmoil and Triumph*, 232. Ralph Hallenbeck characterized matters this way: "If the situation was not rosy, neither was it bleak." *Military Force as an Instrument*, 39.

62. Hallenbeck, *Military Force as an Instrument*, 39.

63. Ibid., 39–40.

64. Ibid., 40.

65. Shultz, *Turmoil and Triumph*, 232–33.

66. Memorandum, Clark to Acting Sec. of State, et al. re: NSPG meeting, folder "NSPG 0051, 4 Feb 1983, [Lebanon]," box 91306, Executive Secretariat, NSC: Records NSPG, Ronald Reagan Library. The memorandum stated: "In the event that the proposals in the current plan for the security zone in southern Lebanon are unacceptable to Israel, Habib is authorized to say that the United States is prepared to deploy additional units of its contingent of the MNF into the southern zone temporarily until Lebanese and/or other non-Israeli forces are capable of securing the area." Also see Hallenbeck, *Military Force as an Instrument*, 49.

67. Hallenbeck, *Military Force as an Instrument*, 49.

68. Ibid., 52–53. Hallenbeck noted: "Available intelligence pointed to Iranian responsibility and Syrian complicity." Ibid., 53.

69. Memo, George Shultz to Ronald Reagan, 21 Apr. 1983, folder "NSPG 0062, 22 Apr 83," box 91306, Executive Secretariat, NSC: Records NSPG, Ronald Reagan Library.

70. NSDD-92, folder "NSDD92," box 91290, ibid.

71. Weinberger described the situation as one in which the Syrians now exercised "veto power over any withdrawal and thus over Israel's ability to establish better relations with a key Arab neighbor, Lebanon." *Fighting for Peace*, 156. Robert McFarlane later declared, "It [the 17 May agreement] was a dead letter the day it was signed." *Special Trust*, 240.

72. Over time, the marines had come to be seen as pro-Israel, pro-Christian, and anti-Muslim. *Long Commission Report*, 41. For details regarding when and how the marines came to lose their neutral status in Lebanon, see Hallenbeck, *Military Force as an Instrument*; Hoffman, "Babes in Beirut," in *Decisive Force*, 39–59; Frank, *U.S. Marines in Lebanon*; *Long Commission Report*; and Sloyan, "Lebanon: Anatomy of a Foreign Policy Failure."

73. Gilmour, *Lebanon*, 194; Hallenbeck, *Military Force as an Instrument*, 68; Shultz, *Turmoil and Triumph*, 220–21.

74. Gilmour, *Lebanon*, 192–94.

75. See folder "NSPG0064," box 91306, Executive Secretariat, NSC: Records, Ronald Reagan Library; folder "NSPG0065," ibid.; and folder "NSPG0066," ibid.

76. Talking points for the President, folder "NSPG0065," ibid.

77. Talking points for the President, folder "NSPG0066," ibid.

78. Hallenbeck, *Military Force as an Instrument*, 70–71.

79. See folder "NSPG0068 & 0068A (1) 3 Sep 1983," box 91306, Executive Secretariat, NSC: Records NSPG, Ronald Reagan Library.

80. Talking points re: phone call to P.M. Begin, folder "NSPG0068 & 0068A (1), 3 Sep 1983," ibid.

81. See Reagan, "Saturday, September 3," *Reagan Diaries*, 176. On 28 August, Begin had surprised the world by announcing his resignation. When Reagan called him on 3 September, Begin had the president talk to Moshe Arens, now defense minister.

82. The House vote was 253–156 in favor of authorizing an additional eighteen months, while the Senate vote was 54–46.

83. "Document 369, The Death of Two U.S. Marines," in US Department of State, *American Foreign Policy Current Documents 1983*, 772 (hereafter *Current Documents 1983*). Reagan himself did not specify that his report was consistent with Section 4 (a) (1), imminent hostilities.

84. "Document 374, Executive-Congressional Compromise on Lebanon and Restatement of U.S. Objective," in *Current Documents 1983*, 782.

85. On 12 October 1983, Congress passed Public Law 98–119, "The Multi-National Force in Lebanon Resolution," which authorized forces to remain in Lebanon for eighteen months. "Document 377, The Multinational Force in Lebanon Resolution," in *Current Documents 1983*, 785–87. Reagan signed the law but with reservations. He did not agree with the congressional determination that section 4 (a) (1) of the War Powers Resolution became operational on 29 August, when the marines suffered casualties, arguing: "I would note that the initiation of isolated or infrequent acts of violence against the United States Armed Forces does not necessarily constitute actual or imminent involvement in hostilities, even if casualties to those forces result." "Document 376, Signing into Law, though with Reservations, the Multinational Force in Lebanon Resolution," ibid., 784.

86. "Document 376," ibid., 781.

87. See Reagan, "Saturday, September 3," *Reagan Diaries*, 176.

88. See folder "NSC 00087 6 Sep 1983," box 91285, Executive Secretariat, NSC: NSC Meeting Files, Ronald Reagan Library.

89. Reagan, "Wednesday, September 7," *Reagan Diaries*, 177.

90. The meeting was held Saturday, 3 September 1983, in the White House Situation Room from 11:15 A.M. to 1:00 P.M. President Reagan, Vice Pres. George H. W. Bush, Secretary Shultz, Secretary Weinberger, Ambassador McFarlane, General Vessey, William Clark, Edwin Meese, and James Baker were all in attendance. Thus, Reagan was afforded perspective on the situation in Lebanon from the State Department, the Defense Department, and his political team. The purpose of the meeting was to make decisions on the administration's diplomatic and military strategy for Lebanon over the coming weeks. The briefing memorandum presented to participants noted that officials needed to be "especially sensitive to the legislative and public affairs dimension of any decisions we take." Folder "NSPG 0068 & 0068A (1), 3 Sep 1983," box 91306, Executive Secretariat, NSC: Records NSPG, Ronald Reagan Library. The administration held meetings with congressional leaders the following day, Sunday, 4 September, to discuss the situation in Lebanon.

91. Folder "NSC 0088 10 Sep 1983 (1)," box 91285, Executive Secretariat, NSC: Records NSC Meeting Files, ibid. In this cable, McFarlane recapped the points he made during the 3 September NSPG meeting. He noted that while the administration wanted Syria to leave Lebanon, it was willing to accept the political reality that any Lebanese reconciliation government would include figures beholden to Syria. Also see McFarlane, *Special Trust*, 248–50. In his memoir, McFarlane wrote: "On more than one occasion, after formal meetings, key Arab advisors would take me aside and say something like, 'Bud, the United States has wasted eight months out here. Hafez al-Assad respects power, and unless you are prepared to use it against him, he will not yield. None of the Arab states are going to deliver anything of consequence to put pressure on Syria.'" Ibid., 246–47. He also noted: "Early in my sessions with Assad, it became clear that he felt no pressure to make any concessions, and that I had no leverage to coerce them. Even the prospect of U.S. assistance in promoting an Israeli pullout was not a convincing instrument. After a year of struggle and combat losses, the Israeli body politic was becoming less and less supportive of the war and had begun to call for the withdrawal of Israeli troops. From Assad's point of view, if the Israeli withdrawal was inevitable, there was no need for him to give anything up to achieve it. Indeed, he could seize the opportunity of an Israeli withdrawal to solidify his own position inside Lebanon." Ibid., 247.

92. Weinberger Papers, I:729, Lebanon, folder 6, item 195, X[no number],

"31 Aug 83—To SecDef from Joint Chiefs of Staff, Subject: U.S. Initiatives in Lebanon."

93. Ibid.

94. Ibid. The memorandum suggested a number of actions that were available to the United States: (1) remind the Syrians that confrontation will have long-term negative effects; (2) emphasize that the United States remains the only avenue available to assist in return of the Golan Heights to Syrian control; (3) point out that Syrian failure to cooperate could lead to indefinite Israeli occupation of southern Lebanon; (4) direct the US ambassador to protest immediately each instance of artillery or mortar fire originating in Syrian-controlled areas into Beirut; and, (5) inform the Damascus that fire from Syrian-controlled areas at MNF forces could lead to a direct Syrian-US confrontation. The discussion paper prepared for the 3 September NSPG made the following assumptions: (1) Syria is unlikely to be persuaded to change its present course through persuasion, and the implicit threat of Israeli military reaction is now a less-credible deterrent; (2) Syria will make serious efforts to prevent the LAF from peacefully extending its authority into the Shuf following Israeli redeployment; and (3) Gemayel's attempts to form a government of national unity are likely to be opposed by Syria unless the influence and power of the Phalange is significantly reduced and the government abandons any potential Lebanese-Israeli agreement. See folder "NSPG 0068 & 0068A (1), 3 Sep 1983," box 91306, Executive Secretariat, NSC: Records NSPG, Ronald Reagan Library.

95. Congress would not approve an additional eighteen-month deployment until 21 September.

96. One of Reagan's talking points for the 3 September NSPG meeting was: "I need your [cabinet officers'] advice on how to handle the Congressional leaders tomorrow [4 September]. What themes do you think I should stress? I don't think they will be interested in the details of confessional problems of Lebanon. Isn't it the bigger picture we have to worry about? And how do we bring Israel into the equation? I presume the Israeli lobby can be helpful on the hill." Folder "NSPG 0068 & 0068A (1), 3 Sep 1983," box 91306, Executive Secretariat, NSC: Records NSPG, Ronald Reagan Library.

97. On 10 September, Reagan met with the NSC to discuss the START negotiations with the Soviets. Lebanon was added to the agenda and given fifteen minutes of the one-hour session. President Reagan, Vice President Bush, Secretary Shultz, Secretary Weinberger, General Vessey, William Clark, and Edwin Meese were all in attendance. See folder "NSC0088, 10 Sep 1983 (1)," box 91285, Executive Secretariat, NSC: Records NSC Meeting Files, ibid.

For the text of NSDD-103, see folder "NSDD-103 (1)," box 91291, Executive Secretariat, NSC: Records NSDD, ibid.; or Federation of American Scientists, "NSDD-103: Strategy for Lebanon," "NSDD—National Security Decision Directives: Reagan Administration," Intelligence Resource Program, http://www.fas.org/irp/offdocs/nsdd/nsdd-103.htm (accessed 2 Feb. 2008).

98. Folder "NSDD-103 (1)."

99. Folder "NSC0088, 10 Sep 1983 (1)," box 91285, Executive Secretariat, NSC: Records NSC Meeting Files, Ronald Reagan Library. See also Memorandum for the Honorable George P. Shultz, the Honorable Caspar W. Weinberger, the Honorable William Casey, and General John W. Vessey, Subject: Staff Papers on Lebanon from William P. Clark, ibid.

100. McFarlane, *Special Trust*, 250–51.

101. Reagan, "Sunday, September 11," *Reagan Diaries*, 178–79.

102. Simpson, *National Security Directives*, 326.

103. Reagan, "Sunday, September 11," *Reagan Diaries*, 179.

104. Hallenbeck, *Military Force as an Instrument*, 82–83.

105. Weinberger, *Fighting for Peace*, 154. Although the rules of engagement were changed, as Shultz and McFarlane desired, the final decision to call for fire support was given to the commander on the ground and not to the diplomats. That made it very difficult for such strikes to be used as leverage in talks with Syria since the commanding officer was told that three specific conditions must be met before calling in fire support from the Sixth Fleet. First, Suq al-Gharb had to be in danger of falling. Second, the enemy threatening Suq al-Gharb had to be non-Lebanese. Third, the support had to be requested by the Lebanese government. Hallenbeck, *Military Force as an Instrument*, 82. It would be a week before the United States fired on the forces opposing the LAF. The marine commander who called for this support was reportedly hesitant due to the retaliatory attacks his forces would probably face. The officer, under pressure from one of McFarlane's associates, yelled. "We'll pay the price. . . . We'll get slaughtered down here." See Hammel, *The Root*, 220.

106. Hallenbeck, *Military Force as an Instrument*, 90–91.

107. On 27 September 1983, Reagan wrote letters to Thomas P. O'Neill Jr., Speaker of the House; Senate Majority Leader Baker; Sen. Charles Percy, chairman, Committee on Foreign Relations; and Rep. Clement Zablocki, chairman, Committee on Foreign Affairs. In those letters, he stated: "I know you were as gratified as I with Sunday's announcement of a cease fire in Lebanon. While there were many things that contributed to the cease fire, it is my belief that your agreement to advance the compromise resolution on war powers . . . were particularly important. At a crucial point, your agreement and

the supporting committee actions expressed a commitment to bipartisanship in U.S. foreign policy. Please accept my thanks." Weinberger Papers, I:729, folder 7, item 227, W05567, "27 Sep 83—To Donald P. Gregg from Robert Kimmitt, Subject: Presidential Letters on War Power."

108. Hallenbeck, *Military Force as an Instrument*, 88.

109. See Weinberger, *Fighting for Peace*, 160n7. Weinberger proposed that the marines be kept on navy ships 400 to 500 yards offshore. There they would be safer but still available to support Gemayel if necessary. For more discussion on the military's attempts to get the marines out of Beirut before the barracks bombing, see Gutman, "Division at the Top Meant Half-Measures, Mistakes"; Halloran, "Reagan as Military Commander"; and Sloyan, "Lebanon: Anatomy of a Foreign Policy Failure."

110. On 28 September, Syrian Foreign Minister Khaddam delivered a speech at the UN which warned that the MNF should be immediately withdrawn. His speech made it politically difficult for the Reagan administration to immediately adjust the disposition of the marines. Additionally, though the administration had received approval from Congress to maintain the Lebanon deployment, officials were constrained as to how US forces could be disposed. See Hallenbeck, *Military Force as an Instrument*, 91–92.

Chapter 6

1. K. T. McFarland, Secretary of Defense Weinberger's speechwriter, interview with author, 9 Aug. 2010.

2. In addition to the memoirs of Reagan's cabinet officers, the following sources were useful on Grenada: Burrowes, *Revolution and Rescue in Grenada*; Schoenhals and Melanson, *Revolution and Intervention in Grenada*; and Lewis, *Grenada*. For information about the media and Grenada, see Hertsgaard, "Grenada High," in *On Bended Knee*, 205–37; and George H. Quester, "Grenada in the News Media," in Dunn and Watson, *American Intervention in Grenada*, 109–28. For general background information about Grenada and more-specific information about the congressional response, see Hall, "Grenada, 1983," in *Reagan Wars*, 167–210; and Raymond, "Collision or Collusion?," 395–516.

3. The strategic significance of Grenada is that it sits astride the southern Caribbean sealanes. For a war in Europe, Africa, or Asia, approximately 85 percent of the material support would be shipped through either the Straits of Florida or the Yucatan Channel. While Cuba threatened the straits, Grenada, with Soviet support, could threaten the channel. See Hall, *Reagan Wars*, 167.

4. Ronald Reagan, "Address to the Nation on Defense and National Secu-

rity," 23 Mar. 1983, American Presidency Project, http://www.presidency.ucsb .edu/ws/index.php?pid–41093&st=&stl= (accessed 10 Oct. 2010).

5. Weinberger, *Fighting for Peace*, 106.

6. Shultz, *Turmoil and Triumph*, 329.

7. The directive stated: "The Secretary of Defense and the Chairman of the Joint Chiefs of Staff, in coordination with the Secretary of State and the Director of Central Intelligence, will land U.S. and allied Caribbean military forces in order to take control of Grenada, no later than dawn Tuesday, October 2, 1983. . . . This operation has a three-fold objective: Assuring the safety of American citizens on Grenada; In conjunction with other OECS/ friendly government participants, the restoration of democratic government on Grenada; The elimination of current, and the prevention of further, Cuban intervention in Grenada." Federation of American Scientists, "NSDD-110A: Response to Caribbean Governments' Request to Restore Democracy on Grenada," "NSDD—National Security Decision Directives: Reagan Administration," Intelligence Resource Program, http://www.fas.org/irp/offdocs/nsdd/ 23-2171t.gif (accessed 9 Feb. 2008).

8. Supporting documents noted that Pentagon leaders would have preferred to have had more time to plan the operation. Nevertheless, with this exception, defense officials were supportive of the mission.

9. Richard Halloran, "Joint Chiefs Supported U.S. Action as Feasible," *New York Times*, 27 Oct. 1983 (online archive, accessed 12 Feb. 2008). The article contrasted the Grenada operation with the Lebanon mission and noted that the Joint Chiefs had been reluctant to support the latter operation because the objective there was seen as political rather than military.

10. Weinberger, *Fighting for Peace*, 114.

11. Shultz, *Turmoil and Triumph*, 329.

12. Weinberger, *Fighting for Peace*, 111, 111n3. It is clear from reading his memoirs that Weinberger's thinking was also greatly influenced by the manner in which the nation conducted the Vietnam War: "The war in Vietnam, with our 'limited objectives' and yet unlimited willingness to commit troops, reinforced my belief, which I expressed many times when I was the Secretary of Defense, that it was a very terrible mistake for a government to commit soldiers to battle without any intention of supporting them sufficiently to enable them to win, and indeed without any intention to win." Ibid., 8–9.

13. Ibid.

14. Weinberger, *In the Arena*, 297. Also see Weinberger, *Fighting for Peace*, 31, 180–81, 398.

15. Lewis, *Grenada*, 101.

16. Reagan asked one question: "Is there any military reason for not going ahead with the operation?" The chiefs said no, and the president signed the official authorization for the operation to proceed. Quoted in Meese, *With Reagan*, 218.

17. Raymond, "Collision or Collusion?," 427–31, 437.

18. See McFarlane, *Special Trust*, 264; and Steven Roberts, "Capitol Hill Is Sharply Split over the Wisdom of Invading," *New York Times*, 26 Oct. 1983 (online archive, accessed 12 Feb. 2008).

19. Roberts, "Capitol Hill Is Sharply Split"; Raymond, "Collision or Collusion?," 439; Schoenhals and Melanson, *Revolution and Intervention in Grenada*, 153–55.

20. Raymond, "Collision or Collusion?," 442–43.

21. On 28 October, the Senate approved a rider, 64–20, to an unrelated bill that invoked the War Powers Resolution. That bill never passed the Senate. Thus, the Congress as a whole never invoked the resolution. See Hall, *Reagan Wars*, 199. Also see Schoenhals and Melanson, *Revolution and Intervention in Grenada*, 155.

22. Steven Roberts, "Democrats to Move on War Powers Act," *New York Times*, 27 Oct. 1983 (online archive, accessed 12 Feb. 2008).

23. President Reagan had notified Prime Minister Margaret Thatcher before the invasion took place, but she was vehemently opposed to the idea. His phone conversation with the British leader is recounted in the memoirs of those present. Apparently, Reagan, who was known to have very poor hearing, had to hold the phone away from his ear because Thatcher was expressing her dismay very vigorously. See Weinberger, *Fighting for Peace*, 119–20; and McFarlane, *Special Trust*, 265.

24. Richard Bernstein, "U.S. Vetoes U.N. Resolution 'Deploring' Grenada Invasion," *New York Times*, 29 Oct. 1983 (online archive, accessed 12 Feb. 2008). Also see Burrowes, *Revolution and Rescue in Grenada*, 94.

25. Hertsgaard, *On Bended Knee*, 211–21. Also see Quester, "Grenada in the News Media," 109–28. Interestingly, the press did not report on the censorship until 28 October, and polls showed that a majority of Americans supported the administration's decision.

26. Ronald Reagan, "Address to the Nation on Events in Lebanon and Grenada," 27 Oct. 1983, American Presidency Project, http://www.presidency .ucsb.edu/ws/index.php?pid=40696&st=&st1= (accessed 10 Oct. 2010). Also see Schoenhals and Melanson, *Revolution and Intervention in Grenada*, 139–41, 147–53.

27. David Shribman, "Poll Shows Support for Presence of U.S. Troops in

Lebanon and Grenada," *New York Times*, 29 Oct. 1983 (online archive, accessed 12 Feb. 2008).

28. Shultz, *Turmoil and Triumph*, 339.

29. Robert McFadden, "From Rescued Students, Gratitude and Praise," *New York Times*, 28 Oct. 1983 (online archive, accessed 12 Feb. 2008).

30. The majority of women did not approve of the operation. Only 41 percent of them approved; 43 percent did not. Shribman, "Poll Shows Support for Presence of U.S. Troops in Lebanon and Grenada."

31. Schoenhals and Melanson, *Revolution and Intervention in Grenada*, 153.

32. Ibid., 153–54.

33. For instance, a *New York Times*/CBS News poll taken on 26 and 27 October indicated that only 22 percent of Americans believed that the United States should help overthrow the government of Nicaragua. Shribman, "Poll Shows Support for Presence of U.S. Troops in Lebanon and Grenada."

34. Strober and Strober, *Reagan Presidency*, 250.

35. Shultz, *Turmoil and Triumph*, 345.

36. Weinberger, *Fighting of Peace*, 126.

37. *Long Commission Report*, 2. Of the decision to convene the commission, Weinberger wrote: "Given the magnitude of the Beirut barracks disaster, with 241 American servicemen killed and United States policy in Lebanon reeling from the effects of a bomb laden truck driven by a suicidal driver against U.S. forces that I did not think should have been there in the first place, I believed that an independent inquiry into what had happened was absolutely necessary." *Fighting for Peace*, 162. The commission was chaired by Adm. (Ret.) Robert L. J. Long, USN, and assisted by Robert J. Murray; Lt. Gen. (Ret.) Lawrence F. Snowden, USMC; Lt. Gen. (Ret.) Eugene F. Tighe Jr., USAF; and Lt. Gen. Joseph T. Palastra Jr., USA. While still classified, the following documents examined in the Weinberger Papers were supportive of the narrative presented in this chapter: container I:729, Lebanon, folder 11, item 393, X28829, "6 Dec 83—To M/Gen Powell from Richard Armitage, Subject: Mr. Armitage's Opinion on the Next Steps in Lebanon—*Not Policy Statement*"; I:729, Lebanon, folder 11, item 416, X28489, "12 Dec 83—To SecDef from Richard L. Armitage, Subject: Congressional Briefings on Lebanon"; I:730, Lebanon, folder 13, item 430, X28571, "22 Dec 83—To SecDef from Gen John Vessey, Subject: Report of DoD Commission on the Beirut International Airport Terrorist Attack"; I:730, Lebanon, folder 13, item 434, X28633, "27 Dec 83—To SecDef from Richard Armitage, Subject: Lebanon Non-Paper—Next Steps in Lebanon"; I:778, Lebanon, folder 1, item 4,

X28804, "6 Jan 84—Memo for SecDef from Richard Armitage, Subject: President Gemayel's Proposed New MNF Deployments"; I:778, Lebanon, folder 2, item 13, X28833, "10 Jan 84—Memo for SecDef from William Casey, Subject: Saudi Views of U.S. Policy in Lebanon and the Impact of that Policy on the Overall Middle East Equation"; I:778, Lebanon, folder 2, item 26, X28884, "12 Jan 84—Memo for SecDef from Richard Armitage, Subject: JCS Analysis and Recommendations on Lebanese Armed Forces"; I:779, Lebanon, folder 4, item 37, X29169, "17 Jan 84—Memo for Mr. Armitage from Arnold Raphel, Subject: MNF Deployment Options Paper"; I:779, Lebanon, folder 4, item 45, X29280, "23 Jan 84—Memo for SecDef from Gen Rogers, Subject: The Long Commission Report: Setting the Record Straight"; I:779, Lebanon, folder 6, item 90, X[no number], "16 Feb 84—Status Report, Subject: Plan for Redeployment of the U.S. MNF Contingent", I:779, Lebanon, folder 7, item 95, X[no number], "18 Feb 84—Msg to USCINCEUR from JSC, Subject: Execute Order—USMNF Redeployment"; I:779, Lebanon, folder 7, item 116, X29794, "8 Mar 84 Note to SecDef from Rich, Subject: Memorandum to the President on Disbanding the MNF"; I:779, Lebanon, folder 7, item 117, X29811, "9 Mar 84—Memo for SecDef from Gen John Vessey, Subject: Future of the MNF"; I:779, Lebanon, folder 8, item 122, X30052, "26 Mar 84—Memo for SecDef from Noel Koch, Subject: U.S. Military Presence in Lebanon."

38. *Long Commission Report*, 4.

39. Shultz addressed these issues in *Turmoil and Triumph*, 646.

40. Ibid. Also see "Document 1, Power and Diplomacy Always Go Together," in US Department of State, *American Foreign Policy Current Documents 1984*, 3 (hereafter *Current Documents 1984*).

41. Shultz, *Turmoil and Triumph*, 646.

42. "Document 1, Power and Diplomacy Always Go Together," 3.

43. For still-classified archival materials that support this contention, see note 37.

44. For more details about the congressional role in funding the Contras, see William M. LeoGrande, "The Contras and Congress," in Walker, *Reagan Versus the Sandinistas*, 202–227; and Kagan, "The Boland Amendment," in *Twilight Struggle*, 238–47. LeoGrande explained that the language of the "Classified Annex to the Fiscal Year (FY) 1983 Intelligence Authorization" (Pub. L. 97–269), which prohibited US aid to paramilitary groups "'for the purpose of overthrowing the Government of Nicaragua or provoking a military exchange between Nicaragua and Honduras,'" was "not designed to bring the covert operation to a halt; on the contrary, it was intentionally crafted to register the com-

mittees' growing uneasiness without interfering in the operation. The Reagan administration was able to interpret the law as allowing support for the contras so long as the purpose of the United States was not one of those proscribed." He further explained that the language used by Rep. Edward Boland (D-Mass.) "merely reaffirmed existing law, the Boland amendment was another warning to the administration that it had not assuaged congressional concerns."

45. Shultz, *Turmoil and Triumph*, 285.

46. Ibid., 285–86.

47. Federation of American Scientists, "NSDD-77: Management of Public Diplomacy Relative to National Security," "NSDD—National Security Decision Directives: Reagan Administration," Intelligence Resource Program, http://www.fas.org/irp/offdocs/nsdd/nsdd-077.htm (accessed 13 Oct. 2009).

48. Ibid. These were the Public Affairs Committee, International Information Committee, International Political Committee, and the International Broadcasting Committee.

49. Ibid.

50. All four speeches are available in *Current Documents 1984*: "Document 1, Power and Diplomacy Always Go Together," 1–6; "Document 2, American Leadership Is Back," 6–14; "Document 16, The Uses of Military Power," 65–70; and "Document 17, The Ethics of Power," 70–74. Other speeches covered some, but not all, of the four themes. For example, see Secretary Shultz to the National Convention of the Veterans of Foreign Wars, 20 Aug. 1984, "Document 14, Diplomacy and Strength," 60–63; and Secretary Shultz to the Los Angeles World Affairs Council, 19 Oct. 1984, "Document 3, Let Us Reforge a National Consensus on Foreign Policy," 14–22.

51. Weinberger, *Fighting for Peace*, 436.

52. Ibid., 435.

53. See Caspar W. Weinberger, *Annual Report to the Congress, Fiscal Year 1987* ([Washington, DC: GPO], 1986), 81–82.

54. When he revisited the six tests in a speech given in September 1999, Weinberger emphasized this point first. "Aerospace Power and the Use of Force," Air Force Association Policy Forum, http://www.afa.org/media/scripts/wein999.asp (accessed 28 Dec. 2006). For his clearest enunciation of these points, see Weinberger, *Annual Report to the Congress, Fiscal Year 1987*, 77–82.

55. For further discussion on the rationalist approach, see Palmer, "The Rationalist Approach in American Defense Policy," in *McNamara Strategy*, 1–18.

56. The other instruments of national power typically discussed are diplomatic, informational, and economic.

57. Weinberger, *Annual Report to the Congress, Fiscal Year 1987*, 80.

58. Clausewitz, *On War*, 87.

59. See Twining, "Vietnam and the Six Criteria," 10–18. Twining wrote: "The resort to military force by a democracy, particularly its American variant, is not just a deliberate, rational decision, but a moral one as well." Ibid., 15. He argued that Weinberger's six criteria recognized that "the responsible use of military force is a moral issue." Ibid., 10. Also see Hawkins, *Power vs. Force*, 132–33, 68–69. Hawkins presents a conceptualization of the difference between power and force.

60. As Jane Mayer and Doyle McManus described: "The battle over the proper response to terrorism drove the two cabinet officers out into the nation's pulpits like feuding medieval theologians debating a point of doctrine." *Landslide*, 53. David C. Martin and John Walcott, whose work was strictly focused on the US war against terrorism, conceptualized the debate in a broader fashion, noting that Shultz and Weinberger were grappling with a strategic question of how to relate power to diplomacy. *Best Laid Plans*, 155. Shultz offered his insight into the situation by explaining that this debate "over the proper use of force to combat terrorism" was part of "the larger debate over the proper relationship of power and diplomacy." *Turmoil and Triumph*, 649.

61. Shultz, *Turmoil and Triumph*, 650.

62. Weinberger, *Fighting for Peace*, 188.

63. Shultz, *Turmoil and Triumph*, 647. For more details on the dispute between Weinberger and Shultz regarding terrorism, see ibid., 643–88.

64. The following articles highlighted the differences between Shultz and Weinberger and overlooked their larger message that the nation needed to be prepared to routinely use military force as a tool of statecraft: Richard Halloran, "Shultz and Weinberger: Disputing Use of Force," *New York Times*, 30 Nov. 1984 (online archive, accessed 4 Sept. 2007); "U.S. Must be Ready to Use Its Power, Shultz Declares," *New York Times*, 10 Dec. 1984; Tom Burgess, "SecDef Says Use Troops O'seas as 'Last Resort,'" *Army Times*, 10 Dec. 1984; and Hedrick Smith, "Shultz-Weinberger Discord Seen in Nearly All Foreign Policy Issues," *New York Times*, 11 Dec. 1984.

65. J. William Fulbright and Seth P. Tillman, "Shultz, Weinberger Non-differences," *New York Times*, 9 Dec. 1984 (online archive, accessed 8 Nov. 2007).

66. Weinberger, *Fighting for Peace*, 435–36. Also see Richard Halloran, "U.S. Will Not Drift into a Latin War Weinberger Says," *New York Times*, 29 Nov. 1984. Pentagon officials stated that Weinberger had the War Powers Resolution in mind when he spoke.

67. "Document 17, The Ethics of Power," in *Current Documents 1984*, 73.

68. Weinberger, *Fighting for Peace*, 433, 435.

69. William Safire, "Only the 'Fun' Wars," *New York Times*, 25 Feb. 1983 (online archive, accessed 3 Aug. 2006).

70. In an essay written for *Foreign Affairs* in 1986, Weinberger explained that the six tests came from the administration's reading of the post–World War II period. "Despite our best efforts to deter or prevent such developments, situations will arise in which it may be appropriate to commit U.S. military forces to combat. From our reading of the postwar period, this Administration derives several lessons that can be stated as tests to be applied in facing such choices. These tests cannot be applied mechanically or deductively. Weighing the evidence in specific cases will always require judgment. But applying these tests to the evidence will make it clear that while there are situations in which U.S. troops are required, there are even more situations in which U.S. combat forces should *not* be used." Weinberger, "U.S. Defense Strategy," 190.

71. McFarland, interview. McFarland noted that to write the speech, she researched the US experience in Vietnam and consulted the military-service chiefs along with several brigadier generals who were Vietnam veterans.

72. Adm. (Ret.) John Poindexter, interview with author, 17 Sept. 2010.

73. See Remarks by Secretary Weinberger to the National Press Club, 28 Nov. 1984, FG013 281190, WHORM Subject File, Ronald Reagan Library.

74. Weinberger, *In the Arena*, 307. This note is taken from Weinberger's calendar. The "re" in this instance is shorthand for "reference."

75. Remarks by Secretary Weinberger to the National Press Club, 28 Nov. 1984. The WHORM Subject File contains 101 pages and includes the original draft of Weinberger's speech, a copy of the changes recommended when staffed at the NSC level, and one additional copy of the delivered speech. The NSC received the draft on 27 November, so the members who saw the text did not have long to comment.

76. Ibid.

77. Poindexter, interview.

BIBLIOGRAPHY

Archives

Casey, William J. Public speeches, 1981–84. Received through FOIA request from the Central Intelligence Agency, Washington, DC.

Papers of Ronald Reagan Presidential Administration. Ronald Reagan Presidential Library, Simi Valley, CA.

Papers of the Joint Chiefs of Staff. Records, Research, and Content Branch, Pentagon, Washington, DC.

Vessey, Gen. John W., USA (Ret.). Papers. National Defense University Library, Washington, DC.

Weinberger, Caspar W. Papers. Library of Congress, Washington, DC.

Primary Sources

The American Presidency Project. http://www.presidency.ucsb.edu (accessed June 2006–October 2010).

Binns, Jack R. *The United States in Honduras, 1980–1981: An Ambassador's Memoir.* Jefferson, NC: McFarland, 2000.

Brzezinski, Zbigniew. *Power and Principle: Memoirs of the National Security Advisor, 1977–1981.* New York: Farrar, Straus, Giroux, 1983.

Buckingham, William A., ed. *Defense Planning for the 1990s and the Changing International Environment: Based on the Tenth National Security Affairs Conference, October 7–8, 1983.* Washington, DC: National Defense University Press, 1984.

Cable News Network. "Episode 18: Backyard, Interviews, Fidel Castro, Cuban President." *CNN Cold War.* http://www.cnn.com/SPECIALS/cold.war/episodes/18/interviews/castro/ (accessed 20 Aug. 2007; content discontinued; print copy in author's possession).

———. "Episode 18: Backyard, Interviews, John Negroponte, U.S. Diplomat." *CNN Cold War.* http://www.cnn.com/SPECIALS/cold.war/episodes/18/interviews/negroponte/ (accessed 20 Aug. 2007; content discontinued; print copy in author's possession).

———. "Episode 18: Backyard, Interviews, Daniel Ortega, Sandinista Leader, Nicaraguan President." *CNN Cold War.* http://www.cnn.com/SPECIALS/

cold.war/episodes/18/interviews/ortega/ (accessed 20 Aug. 2007; content discontinued; print copy in author's possession).

———. "Episode 18: Backyard, Interviews, Oscar Manuel Sobalvarro, Chief of Staff, 'Contra' Rebel Army, Nicaragua." *CNN Cold War.* http://www.cnn .com/SPECIALS/cold.war/episodes/18/interviews/sobalvarro/ (accessed 20 Aug. 2007; content discontinued; print copy in author's possession).

Carter, Jimmy. *Keeping Faith: Memoirs of a President.* Toronto: Bantam Books, 1982.

Casey, William J. "CIA: Confronting 'Undeclared War.'" *American Legion,* June 1984.

Chamorro, Edgar. "I Was a 'Contra' for the CIA." *New Republic,* August 5, 1985.

Commission of Inquiry into the Events at the Refugee Camps in Beirut. *The Beirut Massacre: The Complete Kahan Commission Report.* Princeton, NJ: Karz-Cohl, 1983.

Committee of Santa Fe. *A New Inter-American Policy for the Eighties.* Washington, DC: Council for Inter-American Security, 1980.

Cushman, John H. *Command and Control of Theater Forces: Adequacy.* Cambridge, MA: Harvard University, Center for Information Policy Research, Program on Information Resources Policy, 1983.

Damm, Helene von. *Sincerely, Ronald Reagan.* Ottawa, IL: Green Hill, 1976.

Deaver, Michael K. *Behind the Scenes: In which the Author Talks about Ronald and Nancy Reagan . . . and Himself.* With Mickey Herskowitz. New York: Morrow, 1987.

———. *A Different Drummer: My Thirty Years with Ronald Reagan.* New York: Harper Collins, 2001.

Dickey, Christopher. *With the Contras: A Reporter in the Wilds of Nicaragua.* New York: Simon and Schuster, 1985.

Dobrynin, Anatoly Fedorovich. *In Confidence: Moscow's Ambassador to America's Six Cold War Presidents (1962–1986).* New York: Random House, 1995.

DoD Commission on Beirut International Airport Terrorist Act. *Report of the DoD Commission on Beirut International Airport Terrorist Act, October 23, 1983.* Washington, DC: By the commission, 1983.

E. C. Meyer, General, United States Army, Chief of Staff, June 1979–June 1983. Washington, DC: Headquarters, Dept. of the Army, 1983.

Federation of American Scientists. "NSDD—National Security Decision Directives: Reagan Administration." Intelligence Resource Program. http://

www.fas.org/irp/offdocs/nsdd/index.html (accessed June 2006–October 2010).

———. "PD—Presidential Directives: Carter Administration." Intelligence Resource Program. http://www.fas.org/irp/offdocs/pd/index.html (accessed June 2006–March 2008).

———. "PRM—Presidential Review Memorandums: Carter Administration." Intelligence Resource Program. http://www.fas.org/irp/offdocs/prm/index .html (accessed June 2006–March 2008).

Gates, Robert M. *From the Shadows: The Ultimate Insider's Story of Five Presidents and How They Won the Cold War*. New York: Simon and Schuster, 1996.

Gavin, James M. *War and Peace in the Space Age*. New York: Harper, 1958.

Greene, James R., and Brent Scowcroft. *Western Interests and U.S. Policy Options in the Caribbean Basin: Report of the Atlantic Council's Working Group on the Caribbean Basin*. Boston, MA: Oelgeschlager, Gunn, and Hain, 1984.

Habib, Philip C. *Diplomacy and the Search for Peace in the Middle East*. Washington, DC: Institute for the Study of Diplomacy, School of Foreign Service, Georgetown University, 1985.

Haig, Alexander Meigs. *Caveat: Realism, Reagan, and Foreign Policy*. New York: Macmillan, 1984.

———. "The Democratic Revolution and Its Future." *Vital Speeches of the Day* 48, no. 3 (November 1981): 66–68.

———. "Foreign Policy and the American Spirit." *Department of State Bulletin* 81, no. 2051 (June 1981): 13.

———. *Inner Circles: How America Changed the World: A Memoir*. With Charles McCarry. New York: Warner Books, 1992.

———. "Interview for *Great Decisions*." *Department of State Bulletin* 81, no. 2051(June 1981): 23–26.

———. "Interview for NBC Television." *Department of State Bulletin* 81, no. 2051(June 1981): 26–29.

———. "Interview for Spanish Television." *Department of State Bulletin* 81, no. 2050 (May 1981): 7–9.

———. "Interview on the *MacNeil/Lehrer Report*." *Department of State Bulletin* 81, no. 2050 (May 1981): 1–3.

———. "Interview on *Meet the Press*." *Department of State Bulletin* 81, no. 2050 (May 1981): 4–7.

———. "Interviews at Breakfast Meetings." *Department of State Bulletin* 81, no. 2050 (May 1981): 9–17.

——. "An Interview with Haig: The How and Why behind America's Mandate for Change." *Time*, 16 March 1981.

——. "NATO and the Restoration of American Leadership." *Department of State Bulletin* 81, no. 2051 (June 1981): 11–12.

——. "A New Direction in U.S. Foreign Policy." *Department of State Bulletin* 81, no. 2051 (June 1981): 5–7.

——. "Question-and-Answer Session following Address before ASNE." *Department of State Bulletin* 81, no. 2051 (June 1981): 7–10.

Jones, David C. "Perspectives on Security and Strategy in the 1980s." *Vital Speeches of the Day* 47, no. 12 (1981): 357.

Jordan, Donald. "Emerging Principles for the Use of Force in the Post–Cold War Era." December 1998. Unpublished essay, copy in author's possession.

Jordan, Hamilton. *Crisis: The Last Year of the Carter Presidency.* New York: Putnam, 1982.

Kirkpatrick, Jeane J. "Dictatorship & Double Standards." November 1979. *Commentary.* http://www.commentarymagazine.com/cm/main/viewArticle.aip?id=6189 (accessed 28 March 2007).

Kronenberg, Philip S., ed. *Planning U.S. Security.* Washington, DC: National Defense University Press, 1981.

Krulak, Victor H. *Organization for National Security: A Study.* Washington, DC: US Strategic Institute, 1983.

Lehman, John F. *Command of the Seas.* New York: Scribner's, 1988.

Matlock, Jack F., Jr. *Autopsy on an Empire: The American Ambassador's Account of the Collapse of the Soviet Union.* New York: Random House, 1995.

——. *Reagan and Gorbachev: How the Cold War Ended.* New York: Random House Trade Paperbacks, 2005.

McFarlane, Robert C. *Special Trust.* With Zofia Smardz. New York: Cadell and Davies, 1994.

Meese, Edwin. *With Reagan: The Inside Story.* Washington, DC: Regnery Gateway, 1992.

Menges, Constantine Christopher. *Inside the National Security Council: The True Story of the Making and Unmaking of Reagan's Foreign Policy.* New York: Simon and Schuster, 1988.

National Bipartisan Commission on Central America. *Report of the National Bipartisan Commission on Central America.* Washington, DC, 1984.

National Security Archives. *El Salvador: The Making of U.S. Policy, 1977–1984.* Washington, DC: National Security Archive, 1989. Microfiche.

Noonan, Peggy. *When Character Was King: A Story of Ronald Reagan.* New York: Viking, 2001.

North, Oliver. *Under Fire: An American Story.* With William Novak. New York: Harper Collins, 1991.

Petit, Michael. *Peacekeepers at War: A Marine's Account of the Beirut Catastrophe.* Boston: Faber and Faber, 1986.

Pipes, Richard. *Vixi: Memoirs of a Non-Belonger.* New Haven, CT: Yale University Press, 2003.

Powell, Colin L. *My American Journey.* With Joseph E. Persico. New York: Random House, 1995.

President's Commission for a National Agenda for the Eighties. *A National Agenda for the Eighties.* Washington, DC: GPO, 1980.

President's Commission on Strategic Forces. *Report of the President's Commission on Strategic Forces.* Washington, DC: By the commission, 1983.

Reagan, Ronald. *An American Life.* New York: Simon and Schuster, 1990.

———. *The Creative Society: Some Comments on Problems Facing America.* New York: Devin-Adair, 1968.

———. "Five-Year Economic Program for U.S." *Vital Speeches of the Day* 46, no. 24 (October 1980): 738–44.

———. "Interview with Walter Cronkite." *Department of State Bulletin* 81, no. 2049 (April 1981): 8–11.

———. "News Conference of March 6." *Department of State Bulletin* 81, no. 2049 (April 1981): 11–13.

———. The Public Papers of President Ronald W. Reagan, 1981–1989. Ronald Reagan Presidential Library. http://www.reagan.utexas.edu/archives/speeches/publicpapers.html (accessed February 2007–March 2008).

———. *The Reagan Diaries.* Edited by Douglas Brinkley. New York: Harper-Collins, 2007.

———. "State of the Union Message on Economic Recovery." *Vital Speeches of the Day* 47, no. 11 (March 1981): 322–26.

———. *Where's the Rest of Me?* With Richard Gibson Hubler. New York: Duell, Sloan, and Pearce, 1965.

Record, Jeffrey. *The Rapid Deployment Force and U.S. Military Intervention in the Persian Gulf.* Cambridge, MA: Institute for Foreign Policy Analysis, 1981.

Regan, Donald T. *For the Record: From Wall Street to Washington.* New York: Harcourt Brace Jovanovich, 1988.

Rethinking US Security Policy for the 1980s: Proceedings of the Seventh Annual

National Security Affairs Conference, 21–23 July 1980. Washington, DC: National Defense University Press, 1980.

Sarkesian, Sam Charles, and William L. Scully, eds. *U.S. Policy and Low-Intensity Conflict: Potentials for Military Struggles in the 1980s.* New Brunswick, NJ: Transaction Books, 1981.

Seabury, Paul, and Walter A. McDougall, eds. *The Grenada Papers.* San Francisco, CA: Institute for Contemporary Studies, 1984.

Shultz, George P. "Shaping American Foreign Policy: New Realities and New Ways of Thinking." *Foreign Affairs* 63, no. 4 (Spring 1985): 705–721.

———. *Turmoil and Triumph: My Years as Secretary of State.* New York: Scribner's, 1993.

Simpson, Christopher. *National Security Directives of the Reagan and Bush Administrations: The Declassified History of U.S. Political and Military Policy, 1981–1991.* Boulder, CO: Westview, 1995.

Skinner, Kiron K., Annelise Graebner Anderson, and Martin Anderson, eds. *Reagan, a Life in Letters.* New York: Free Press, 2003.

———, eds. *Reagan, in His Own Hand: The Writings of Ronald Reagan That Reveal His Revolutionary Vision for America.* New York: Simon and Schuster, 2002.

Stockman, David Alan. *The Triumph of Politics: How the Reagan Revolution Failed.* New York: Harper and Row, 1986.

Stoessel, Walter J., Jr. "Review of El Salvador." *Department of State Bulletin* 81, no. 2049 (April 1981): 38–39.

Strober, Deborah H., and Gerald S. Strober. *The Reagan Presidency: An Oral History of the Era.* Rev. 1st ed. Washington, DC: Brassey's, 2003.

Taylor, Maxwell D. *Swords and Plowshares.* New York: W. W. Norton, 1972.

———. *The Uncertain Trumpet.* New York: Harper, 1960.

US Congress. House. Committee on Foreign Affairs. *Foreign Assistance Legislation for Fiscal Year 1982 (Part I).* 97th Cong., 1st sess., 18 March 1981.

———. Committee on Foreign Affairs. *Statutory Authorization under the War Powers Resolution—Lebanon.* 98th Cong., 1st sess., 21–22 September 1983.

———. Subcommittee on Inter-American Affairs, Committee on Foreign Affairs. *U.S. National Interest in Latin America.* 97th Cong., 1st sess., 4 March 1981.

———. Subcommittee on Inter-American Affairs, Committee on Foreign Affairs. *U.S. Policy toward El Salvador.* 97th Cong., 1st sess., 5, 11 March 1981.

US Congress. Senate. Committee on Armed Services. *Defense Organization: The Need for Change: Staff Report to the Committee on Armed Services, United States Senate.* Washington, DC: GPO, 1985.

————. Committee on Armed Services. *Department of Defense Authorization for Appropriations for Fiscal Year 1982: Part I, Posture Statement.* 97th Cong., 1st sess., 28 January, 4 March 1981.

————. Committee on Armed Services. *Nomination of Caspar W. Weinberger to be Secretary of Defense.* 97th Cong., 1st sess., 6 January 1981.

————. Committee on Foreign Relations. *Foreign Assistance Authorization for Fiscal Year 1982.* 97th Cong., 1st sess., 19 March, 4 May 1981.

————. Committee on Foreign Relations. *Nomination of Alexander M. Haig, Jr.* 97th Cong., 1st sess., 9–10, 13–15 January 1981.

————. Committee on Foreign Relations. *The Situation in El Salvador.* 97th Cong., 1st sess., 18 March, 9 April 1981.

————. Committee on Foreign Relations. *War Powers Resolution.* 98th Cong., 1st sess., 21 September 1983.

US Department of Defense. *Report of the Secretary of Defense Caspar W. Weinberger to the Congress, on the FY 1987 Budget, FY 1988 Authorization Request, and FY 1987–1991 Defense Programs.* Washington, DC: GPO, 1986.

————. *Soviet Military Power.* Washington, DC: GPO, 1981.

US Department of State. *American Foreign Policy Current Documents 1981.* Washington, DC: Department of State, 1984.

————. *American Foreign Policy Current Documents 1982.* Washington, DC: Department of State, 1985.

————. *American Foreign Policy Current Documents 1983.* Washington, DC: Department of State, 1985.

————. *American Foreign Policy Current Documents 1984.* Washington, DC: Department of State, 1986.

————. "Communist Interference in El Salvador." *Department of State Bulletin* 81, no. 2048 (March 1981): 1–7.

US National Bipartisan Commission on Central America. *Report of the National Bipartisan Commission on Central America.* Washington, DC: By the commission, 1984.

Vance, Cyrus R. *Hard Choices: Critical Years in America's Foreign Policy.* New York: Simon and Schuster, 1983.

Van Cleave, William R., and W. Scott Thompson, eds. *Strategic Options for the Early Eighties: What Can Be Done?* White Plains, MD: Automated Graphic Systems, 1979.

Weinberger, Caspar W. "Dangerous Constraints on the President's War Powers." In *The Fettered Presidency: Legal Constraints on the Executive Branch*, edited by Gordon L. Crovitz and Jeremy A. Rabkin, 95–101. Washington, DC: American Enterprise Institute for Public Policy Research, 1989.

———. *Fighting for Peace: Seven Critical Years in the Pentagon.* New York: Warner Books, 1990.

———*In the Arena: A Memoir of the 20th Century.* With Gretchen Roberts. Washington, DC: Regnery, 2001.

———. "Keynote Speech: US Military Strategy for the 1980s." In *The 1980s: A Decade of Confrontation: Proceedings of the Eighth Annual National Security Affairs Conference 13–15 July 1981.* Washington, DC: National Defense University Press, 1981.

———. "The Nature of Deterrence." *SAIS Review* 5, no. 4 (Winter–Spring 1985): 37–41.

———. "U.S. Defense Strategy." In *The Reagan Foreign Policy*, edited by William G. Hyland, 180–202. New York: New American Library, 1987.

———. "The Use of Force—The Six Criteria Revisited." Air Force Association Policy Forum. http://www.afa.org/media/scripts/wein999.asp (accessed 28 December 2006).

Periodicals

"America's Secret War: Target: Nicaragua." *Newsweek*, 8 November 1982.

Anderson, Kurt. "Showing the Flag: Not since Viet Nam had the U.S. Flexed so Much Muscle Abroad." *Time*, 22 August 1983.

Bonior, David E. "Reagan and Central America." *SAIS Review* 2 (Summer 1981): 3–11.

Campbell, Kenneth J. "Once Burned, Twice Cautious: Explaining the Weinberger-Powell Doctrine." *Armed Forces & Society* 24, no. 3 (Spring 1998): 357–74.

"Carter Defuses a Crisis: Getting Rid of the Issue, If Not the Soviet Brigade, but at Some Cost." *Time*, 15 October 1979.

"Carter's Great Purge: Out Go Five Cabinet Members in a Shake-Up that Shocks the Country." *Time*, 30 July 1979.

Cohen, Eliot A. "Constraints on America's Conduct of Small Wars." *International Security* 9, no. 2 (Fall 1984): 151–81.

Cordesman, Anthony H. "Measuring the Strategic Balance: Secretary of Defense Brown as an American Oracle." *Comparative Strategy* 3, no. 3 (1982): 187–218.

"A Crisis of the Spirit: Down from Camp David, Carter Seeks to Rally all America." *Time*, 23 July 1979.

Davis, Vincent. "Americans and War." *SAIS Review* 4, no. 2 (Summer–Fall 1984): 25–41.

Eagleburger, Lawrence. "Interview." With Philip Geyelin. *SAIS Review* 4, no. 2 (Summer–Fall 1984): 43–63.

"In a Fiercely Hawkish Mood: TIME Poll Shows Voters Rallying Strongly Round Carter." *Time*, 11 February 1980.

Garn, Jake. "The SALT II Verification Myth." *Strategic Review* 7, no. 3 (Summer 1979): 16–24.

Gray, Colin S. "The Implications of Preemptive and Preventive War Doctrines: A Reconsideration." Strategic Studies Institute. http://www .strategicstudiesinstitute.army.mil/pdffiles/PUB/89.pdf (accessed 27 March 2008).

———. "What RAND Hath Wrought." *Foreign Policy* 4 (Fall 1971): 111–29.

Gutman, Roy. "Battle over Lebanon." *Foreign Service Journal* (June 1984): 29.

Halloran, Richard. "Reagan as Military Commander." *New York Times Magazine*, 15 January 1984.

Harrison, Michael M. "Reagan's World." *Foreign Policy* 43 (Summer 1981): 3–16.

Hudson, Michael. "To Play the Hegemon: 50 Years of US Policy toward the Middle East." *Middle East Journal* 50, no. 3 (Summer 1996): 329–43.

Iklé, Fred Charles. "The Reagan Defense Program: A Focus on the Strategic Imperatives." *Strategic Review* 10, no. 2 (Spring 1982): 11–18.

———. "Strategic Principles of the Reagan Administration." *Strategic Review* 11, no. 4 (Fall 1983): 13–18.

International Institute for Strategic Studies. *Strategic Survey, 1980–1981*. London: Institute for Strategic Studies, 1981.

———. *Strategic Survey, 1981–1982*. London: Institute for Strategic Studies, 1982.

———. *Strategic Survey, 1982–1983*. London: Institute for Strategic Studies, 1983.

———. *Strategic Survey, 1983–1984*. London: Institute for Strategic Studies, 1984.

———. *Strategic Survey, 1984–1985*. London: Institute for Strategic Studies, 1985.

Isaacson, Walter. "America's Incredible Day: When Ronald Reagan Takes Command and the Hostages Are Finally Freed." *Time*, 2 February 1981.

———. "Weighing the Proper Role: Grenada and Lebanon Illustrate the Uses and Limits of Power." *Time*, 7 November 1983.

Jackson, Henry M. "A Post-Detente Strategy for the United States." *Strategic Review* 8, no. 2 (Spring 1980): 11–16.

Krulak, Victor H. "The Rapid Deployment Force: Criteria and Imperatives." *Strategic Review* 8, no. 2 (Spring 1980): 39–43.

Kuniholm, Bruce R. "Retrospect and Prospects: Forty Years of US Middle East Policy." *Middle East Journal* 41, no. 1 (Winter 1987): 7–25.

Lehman, John F. "Rebirth of a U.S. Naval Strategy." *Strategic Review* 9, no. 3 (Summer 1981): 9–15.

LeoGrande, William M. "A Splendid Little War: Drawing the Line in El Salvador." *International Security* 6, no. 1 (Summer 1981): 27–52.

Linville, Ray P. "Assisting the Third World in the 1980s." *Military Review* 56, no. 12 (December 1981): 8–20.

McColm, Bruce R. "Central America and the Caribbean: The Larger Scenario." *Strategic Review* 11, no. 3 (Summer 1983): 28–42.

Menges, Constantine Christopher. "Central America and the United States." *SAIS Review* 2 (Summer 1981): 13–33.

Nairn, Allan. "Endgame." *Report on the Americas* (May/June 1984): 19–55.

The New York Times, July 1979–November 1984.

Nitze, Paul. "SALT II and American Strategic Considerations." *Comparative Strategy* 2, no. 1 (1980): 9–34.

Nuri, Maqsud U. "The Rapid Deployment Force: U.S. Dilemmas for Security in the Gulf." *Strategic Studies* 5, no. 4 (Summer 1982): 26–40.

Pastor, Robert A. "Three Perspectives on El Salvador. *SAIS Review* 2 (Summer 1981): 35–48.

"Playing for High Stakes: Reagan Dispatches More 'Trainers' to El Salvador." *Time*, 16 March 1981.

Powell, Colin L. "U.S. Forces: Challenges Ahead." *Foreign Affairs* (Winter 1992/93). Council on Foreign Relations. http://www.cfr.org/publication/7508/us_forces.html (accessed 4 August 2006).

Powers, Robert C. "Flexible Response and External Force: A Contrast of U.S. and Soviet Strategies." *Strategic Review* 9, no. 1 (Winter 1981): 52–60.

"The Price of Power: Billions and Billions—the Pentagon Wants More and it Has a Strong Case." *Time*, 29 October 1979.

Quester, George. "Consensus Lost." *Foreign Policy* 40 (Fall 1980): 18–32.

Russett, Bruce, and Donald R. Deluca. "'Don't Tread on Me': Public Opinion and Foreign Policy in the Eighties." *Political Science Quarterly* 96, no 3 (Fall 1981): 381–99.

Sanchez, Nestor D. "The Communist Threat." *Foreign Policy* 52 (Fall 1983): 43–50.

Sanction, Thomas A. "Once More into the Breach." *Time*, 11 October 1982.

Shultz, Richard. "The Role of External Forces in Third World Conflicts." *Comparative Strategy* 4, no. 2 (1983): 79–111.

Simes, Dimitri K. "Disciplining Soviet Power." *Foreign Policy* 43 (Summer 1981): 33–52.

Sloyan, Patrick J. "Lebanon: Anatomy of a Foreign Policy Failure: A Special Report." *Newsday*, 8 April 1984.

Smith, William E. "Looking to Washington: Arab Visitors Draw the U.S. further into the Search for Peace." *Time*, 1 November 1982.

Stewart, Blair. "MX and the Counterforce Problem: A Case for Silo Deployment." *Strategic Review* 9, no. 3 (Summer 1981): 16–26.

———. "The Scowcroft Commission and the 'Window of Coercion.'" *Strategic Review* 9, no. 3 (Summer 1983): 21–27.

"The Storm over Cuba: Soviet Troops, Senate Fury, and Suddenly SALT Is Endangered." *Time*, 17 September 1979.

Summers, Harry G., Jr. "A Strategic Perception of the Vietnam War." *Parameters* 13, no. 2 (June 1983): 41–46.

Twining, David T. "Vietnam and the Six Criteria for the Use of Military Force." *Parameters* 15, no. 4 (Winter 1985): 10–18.

Wallop, Malcolm. "U.S. Covert Action: Policy Tool or Policy Hedge?" *Strategic Review* 12, no. 3 (Summer 1984): 9–16.

The Washington Post, January 1981–November 1984.

Watts, William, and Lloyd A. Free. "Nationalism, Not Isolationism." *Foreign Policy* (Fall 1976): 16–19.

"Winning Hearts and Minds: U.S. Officials Launch an Offensive over El Salvador." *Time*, 2 March 1981.

Secondary Sources

Acharya, Amitav. *US Military Strategy in the Gulf.* London: Routledge, 1989.

Amirsadeghi, Hossein, ed. *The Security of the Persian Gulf.* Guildford, London: Croom Helm, 1981.

Arnson, Cynthia J. *Crossroads: Congress, the President, and Central America, 1976–1993.* 2nd ed. University Park, PA: Pennsylvania State University Press, 1993.

Arquilla, John. *The Reagan Imprint: Ideas in American Foreign Policy from the Collapse of Communism to the War on Terror.* Chicago: Ivan R. Dee, 2006.

Association of the US Army. *Strategic Mobility: Can We Get There from Here—in Time.* Arlington, VA: Association of the US Army, 1984.

Bacevich, A. J. *American Military Policy in Small Wars: The Case of El Salvador.* Washington, DC: Pergamon-Brassey's, 1988.

———. *The New American Militarism: How Americans Are Seduced by War.* New York: Oxford University Press, 2005.

Barnett, Frank R., B. Hugh Tovar, and Richard H. Shultz, eds. *Special Operations in US Strategy.* Washington, DC: National Defense University Press, 1984.

Barrett, Laurence I. *Gambling with History: Ronald Reagan in the White House.* Garden City, NJ: Doubleday, 1983.

Baucom, Donald R. *The Origins of SDI, 1944–1983.* Lawrence: University Press of Kansas, 1992.

Bavly, Dan, and Eliahu Salpeter. *Fire in Beirut: Israel's War in Lebanon with the PLO.* New York: Stein and Day, 1984.

Ben-Zvi, Abraham. *The Reagan Presidency and the Palestinian Predicament: An Interim Analysis.* Tel Aviv: Tel Aviv University, 1982.

Berman, Robert P., and John C. Baker. *Soviet Strategic Forces: Requirements and Responses.* Washington, DC: Brookings Institution, 1982.

Bermann, Karl. *Under the Big Stick: Nicaragua and the United States since 1848.* Boston: South End Press, 1986.

Best, Edward. *U.S. Policy and Regional Security in Central America.* New York: St. Martin's Press, 1987.

Betts, Richard K. *Soldiers, Statesmen, and Cold War Crises.* New York: Columbia University Press, 1991.

Bjork, Rebecca. *The Strategic Defense Initiative: Symbolic Containment of the Nuclear Threat.* Albany: SUNY Press, 1992.

Blechman, Barry M., and Stephen S. Kaplan. *Force without War: U.S. Arms Forces as a Political Instrument.* Washington, DC: Brookings Institution, 1978.

Boaz, David, ed. *Assessing the Reagan Years.* Washington, DC: Cato Institute, 1988.

Bodenheimer, Thomas, and Robert Gould. *Rollback!: Right-Wing Power in U.S. Foreign Policy.* Boston: South End, 1989.

Bonner, Raymond. *Weakness and Deceit: U.S. Policy and El Salvador.* New York: Times Books, 1984.

Boot, Max. *The Savage Wars of Peace: Small Wars and the Rise of American Power.* New York: Basic Books, 2002.

Bourne, Peter G. *Jimmy Carter: A Comprehensive Biography from Plains to Post-Presidency.* New York: Scribner, 1997.

Brodie, Bernard. *The Meaning of Limited War.* Santa Monica, CA.: Rand, 1958.

———. *Strategy in the Missile Age.* Princeton, NJ: Princeton University Press, 1965.

———. *War and Politics.* New York: Macmillan, 1973.

Brown, Seyom. *The Faces of Power: Constancy and Change in United States Foreign Policy from Truman to Reagan.* New York: Columbia University Press, 1983.

Brownlee, W. Elliot, and Hugh Davis Graham. *The Reagan Presidency: Pragmatic Conservatism and its Legacies.* Lawrence: University Press of Kansas, 2003.

Burns, E. Bradford. *At War in Nicaragua: The Reagan Doctrine and the Politics of Nostalgia.* New York: Harper and Row, 1987.

Burrowes, Reynold A. *Revolution and Rescue in Grenada: An Account of the U.S.-Caribbean Invasion.* New York: Greenwood, 1988.

Busch, Andrew. *Reagan's Victory: The Presidential Election of 1980 and the Rise of the Right.* Lawrence: University Press of Kansas, 2005.

Caldwell, Dan. *The Dynamics of Domestic Politics and Arms Control: The SALT II Treaty Ratification Debate.* Columbia: University of South Carolina Press, 1991.

Cannon, Lou. *President Reagan: The Role of a Lifetime.* New York: Simon and Schuster, 1991.

———. *Reagan.* New York: Putnam, 1982.

Chadda, Maya. *Paradox of Power: The United States in Southwest Asia, 1973–1984.* Santa Barbara, CA: ABC-Clio, 1986.

Chomsky, Noam. *The Fateful Triangle: The United States, Israel, and the Palestinians.* Boston: South End, 1983.

Clausewitz, Carl von. *On War.* Edited and translated by Michael Eliot Howard and Peter Paret. Princeton, NJ: Princeton University Press, 1976.

Cockburn, Leslie. *Out of Control: The Story of the Reagan Administration's Secret War in Nicaragua, the Illegal Arms Pipeline, and the Contra Drug Connection.* New York: Atlantic Monthly Press, 1987.

Cohen, Eliot A. *Supreme Command: Soldiers, Statesmen, and Leadership in Wartime.* New York: Anchor Books, 2002.

Collins, John M., Elizabeth Ann Severns, and Thomas P. Glakas. *U.S. Defense Planning: A Critique.* Boulder, CO: Westview, 1982.

Cordesman, Anthony H. *The Gulf and the Search for Strategic Stability: Saudi Arabia, the Military Balance in the Gulf, and Trends in the Arab-Israeli Military Balance.* Boulder, CO: Westview, 1984.

Cordier, Sherwood S. *U.S. Military Power and Rapid Deployment Requirements in the 1980s.* Boulder, CO: Westview, 1983.

Cottrell, Alvin J., and Michael Moodie. *The United States and the Persian Gulf: Past Mistakes, Present Needs.* New Brunswick, NJ: National Strategy Information Center, 1984.

Crabb, Cecil Van Meter, and Pat M. Holt. *Invitation to Struggle: Congress, the President, and Foreign Policy.* 4th ed. Washington, DC: CQ Press, 1992.

Davis, M. Thomas. *40Km into Lebanon: Israel's 1982 Invasion.* Washington, DC: National Defense University Press, 1987.

Deitchman, Seymour J. *Limited War and American Defense Policy: Building and Using Military Power in a World at War.* 2nd rev. ed. Cambridge, MA: MIT Press, 1969.

Destler, I. M., Leslie H. Gelb, and Anthony Lake. *Our Own Worst Enemy: The Unmaking of American Foreign Policy.* New York: Simon and Schuster, 1984.

Diggins, John P. *Ronald Reagan: Fate, Freedom, and the Making of History.* New York: W. W. Norton, 2007.

Draper, Theodore. *A Very Thin Line: The Iran-Contra Affairs.* New York: Hill and Wang, 1991.

Dugger, Ronnie. *On Reagan: The Man & His Presidency.* New York: McGraw-Hill, 1983.

Dulles, John Foster. *War, Peace, and Change.* New York: Harper and Brothers, 1939.

Dumbrell, John. *The Carter Presidency: A Reevaluation.* 2nd ed. New York: Manchester University Press, 1995.

Dunn, Peter M., and Bruce W. Watson, eds. *American Intervention in Grenada: The Implications of Operation "Urgent Fury."* Boulder, CO: Westview, 1985.

Dupuy, Trevor Nevitt, and Paul Martell. *Flawed Victory: The Arab-Israeli Conflict and the 1982 War in Lebanon.* Fairfax, VA: Hero Books, 1986.

Ehrman, John. *The Rise of Neoconservatism: Intellectuals and Foreign Affairs, 1945–1994.* New Haven, CT: Yale University Press, 1995.

Emerson, Steven. *Secret Warriors: Inside the Covert Military Operations of the Reagan Era.* New York: Putnam, 1988.

Evron, Yair. *War and Intervention in Lebanon: The Israeli-Syrian Deterrence Dialogue.* Baltimore: Johns Hopkins University Press, 1987.

Feinberg, Richard E. *Central America, International Dimensions of the Crisis.* New York: Holmes and Meier, 1982.

Findley, Paul. *They Dare to Speak Out: People and Institutions Confront Israel's Lobby.* Westport, CT: Lawrence Hill, 1985.

Finer, S. E. *The Man on Horseback: The Role of the Military in Politics.* New York: Praeger, 1962.

Fink, Gary M., and Hugh Davis Graham, eds. *The Carter Presidency: Policy Choices in the Post–New Deal Era.* Lawrence: University Press of Kansas, 1998.

Fischer, Beth A. *The Reagan Reversal: Foreign Policy and the End of the Cold War.* Columbia: University of Missouri Press, 1997.

Fisher, Louis. *Presidential War Power.* 2nd rev. ed. Lawrence: University Press of Kansas, 2004.

FitzGerald, Frances. *Way Out There in the Blue: Reagan, Star Wars, and the End of the Cold War.* New York: Simon and Schuster, 2000.

Frank, Benis M. *U.S. Marines in Lebanon, 1982–1984.* Washington, DC: US Marine Corps, History and Museums Division, 1987.

Gabriel, Richard A. *Operation Peace for Galilee: The Israeli-PLO War in Lebanon.* New York: Hill and Wang, 1984.

Gaddis, John Lewis. *The Cold War: A New History.* New York: Penguin Books, 2005.

———. *Strategies of Containment: A Critical Appraisal of American National Security Policy during the Cold War.* New York: Oxford University Press, 2005.

———. *Strategies of Containment: A Critical Appraisal of Postwar American National Security Policy.* New York: Oxford University Press, 1982.

———. *Surprise, Security, and the American Experience.* Cambridge, MA: Harvard University Press, 2004.

———. *The United States and the End of the Cold War: Implications, Reconsiderations, Provocations.* New York: Oxford University Press, 1992.

Garthoff, Raymond L. *Détente and Confrontation: American-Soviet Relations from Nixon to Reagan.* Washington, DC: Brookings Institution, 1985.

———. *A Journey through the Cold War: A Memoir of Containment and Coexistence.* Washington, DC: Brookings Institution Press, 2001.

Gilmour, David. *Lebanon: The Fractured Country.* New York: St. Martin's, 1983.

Gonzalez, Edward. *U.S. Policy for Central America: A Briefing.* Santa Monica, CA: Rand, 1984.

Graham, Hugh Davis, and W. Elliot Brownlee. *The Reagan Presidency: Prag-

matic Conservatism and its Legacies. Lawrence: University Press of Kansas, 2003.

Grandin, Greg. *Empire's Workshop: Latin America, the United States, and the Rise of the New Imperialism.* New York: Metropolitan Books, 2006.

Green, Stephen. *Taking Sides: America's Secret Relations with a Militant Israel.* New York: W. Morrow, 1984.

Greenstein, Fred I., ed. *The Reagan Presidency: An Early Assessment.* Baltimore: Johns Hopkins University Press, 1983.

Gutman, Roy. *Banana Diplomacy: The Making of American Policy in Nicaragua, 1981–1987.* New York: Simon and Schuster, 1988.

Guttmann, Allen. *Korea: Cold War and Limited War.* 2nd ed. Lexington, MA: Heath, 1972.

Haass, Richard. *Intervention: The Use of American Military Force in the Post–Cold War World.* Washington, DC: Carnegie Endowment for International Peace, 1994.

Hadar, Leon T. *Quagmire: America in the Middle East.* Washington, DC: Cato Institute, 1992.

Haffa, Robert P. *The Half War: Planning U.S. Rapid Deployment Forces to Meet a Limited Contingency, 1960–1983.* Boulder, CO: Westview, 1984.

Haftendorn, Helga, and Jakob Schissler, eds. *The Reagan Administration: A Reconstruction of American Strength?* New York: W. de Gruyter, 1988.

Hall, David Locke. *The Reagan Wars: A Constitutional Perspective on War Powers and the Presidency.* Boulder, CO: Westview, 1991.

Hallenbeck, Ralph A. *Military Force as an Instrument of U.S. Foreign Policy: Intervention in Lebanon, August 1982–February 1984.* New York: Praeger, 1991.

Halloran, Richard. *To Arm a Nation: Rebuilding America's Endangered Defenses.* New York: Macmillan, 1986.

Halperin, Morton H. *Limited War in the Nuclear Age.* Westport, CT: Greenwood, 1978.

Hammel, Eric M. *The Root: The Marines in Beirut, August 1982–February 1984.* San Diego: Harcourt Brace Jovanovich, 1985.

Handel, Michael I. *Masters of War: Classical Strategic Thought.* 3rd rev. and exp. ed. London. F. Cass, 2001.

Hargrove, Erwin C. *Jimmy Carter as President: Leadership and the Politics of the Public Good.* Baton Rouge: Louisiana State University Press, 1988.

Hawkins, David R. *Power vs. Force, Revised Edition: The Hidden Determinants of Human Behavior.* Carlsbad, CA: Hay House, 2002.

Herspring, Dale R. *The Pentagon and the Presidency: Civil-Military Rela-*

tions from FDR to George W. Bush. Lawrence: University Press of Kansas, 2005.

Hertsgaard, Mark. *On Bended Knee: The Press and the Reagan Presidency.* New York: Farrar, Straus, Giroux, 1988.

Hill, Dilys M., Raymond A. Moore, and Phil Williams, eds. *The Reagan Presidency: An Incomplete Revolution?* New York: St. Martin's, 1990.

Hoffman, F. G. *Decisive Force: The New American Way of War.* Westport, CT: Praeger, 1996.

Hogan, Joseph, ed. *The Reagan Years: The Record in Presidential Leadership.* New York: Manchester University Press, 1990.

Hogan, Michael J., ed. *America in the World: The Historiography of American Foreign Relations since 1941.* Cambridge, UK: Cambridge University Press, 1995.

Holsti, Ole R., and James N. Rosenau. *American Leadership in World Affairs: Vietnam and the Breakdown of Consensus.* Boston: Allen and Unwin, 1984.

Howard, Michael. *War and the Liberal Conscience.* New Brunswick, NJ: Rutgers University Press, 1978.

Hunter, Kerry L. *The Reign of Fantasy: The Political Roots of Reagan's Star Wars Policy.* New York: P. Lang, 1992.

Huntington, Samuel P. *The Soldier and the State: The Theory and Politics of Civil-Military Relations.* Cambridge, MA: Belknap Press of Harvard University Press, 1957.

———. "The Soldier and the State in the 1970s." In *Civil-Military Relations,* edited by Andrew Jackson Goodpaster and Samuel P. Huntington, 5–28. Washington, DC: American Enterprise Institute for Public Policy Research, 1977.

———. *The Strategic Imperative: New Policies for American Security.* Cambridge, MA: Ballinger, 1982.

Janowitz, Morris. *The Professional Soldier: A Social and Political Portrait.* New York: Free Press, 1971.

Jansen, Michael E. *The Battle of Beirut: Why Israel Invaded Lebanon.* Boston: South End, 1983.

Johnson, Haynes Bonner. *Sleepwalking through History: America in the Reagan Years.* New York: W. W. Norton, 1991.

Johnson, Nicholas L. *Soviet Military Strategy in Space.* London; New York: Jane's, 1987.

Kagan, Robert. *A Twilight Struggle: American Power and Nicaragua, 1977–1990.* New York: Free Press, 1996.

Katz, Samuel M., Lee E. Russell, and Ron Volstad. *Armies in Lebanon, 1982–1984*. London: Osprey, 1985.

Kaufman, Burton Ira. *The Presidency of James Earl Carter Jr.* Lawrence: University Press of Kansas, 1993.

Kaufmann, William W. *The McNamara Strategy*. New York: Harper and Row, 1964.

Kengor, Paul. *God and Ronald Reagan a Spiritual Life*. New York: HarperCollins, 2004.

Kengor, Paul, and Peter Schweizer, eds. *The Reagan Presidency: Assessing the Man and His Legacy*. Lanham: Rowman and Littlefield, 2005.

Key, V. O., and Milton C. Cummings. *The Responsible Electorate: Rationality in Presidential Voting, 1936–1960*. Cambridge, MA: Belknap Press of Harvard University Press, 1966.

Kissinger, Henry. *Diplomacy*. New York: Simon and Schuster, 1994.

Kitfield, James. *Prodigal Soldiers: How the Generation of Officers Born of Vietnam Revolutionized the American Style of War*. Washington, DC: Brassey's, 1997.

Klare, Michael T., and Peter Kornbluh. *Low Intensity Warfare: Counterinsurgency, Proinsurgency, and Antiterrorism in the Eighties*. New York: Pantheon Books, 1987.

Kolko, Joyce, and Gabriel Kolko. *The Limits of Power: The World and United States Foreign Policy, 1945–1954*. New York: Harper and Row, 1972.

Kornbluh, Peter. *"Nicaragua," the Price of Intervention: Reagan's Wars against the Sandinistas*. Washington, DC: Institute for Policy Studies, 1987.

Krepon, Michael, and Dan Caldwell, eds. *The Politics of Arms Control Treaty Ratification*. New York: St. Martin's, in association with the Henry L. Stimson Center, 1991.

Kuniholm, Bruce Robellet. *The Persian Gulf and United States Policy: A Guide to Issues and References*. Claremont, CA: Regina Books, 1984.

Kupchan, Charles. *The Persian Gulf and the West: Dilemmas of Security*. Boston: Allen and Unwin, 1987.

Kurz, Kenneth Franklin. *The Reagan Years A to Z: An Alphabetical History of Ronald Reagan's Presidency*. Los Angeles: Lowell House, 1997.

Kymlicka, B. B., and Jean V. Matthews, eds. *The Reagan Revolution?* Chicago. Dorsey, 1988.

Kyvig, David E., ed. *Reagan and the World*. New York: Greenwood, 1990.

Lagon, Mark P. *The Reagan Doctrine: Sources of American Conduct in the Cold War's Last Chapter*. Westport, CT: Praeger, 1994.

Laham, Nicholas. *Selling AWACS to Saudi Arabia: The Reagan Administration and the Balancing of America's Competing Interests in the Middle East.* Westport, CT: Praeger, 2002.

Landau, Saul. *The Dangerous Doctrine: National Security and U.S. Foreign Policy.* Boulder, CO: Westview, 1988.

Ledeen, Michael Arthur, and William Hubert Lewis. *Debacle: The American Failure in Iran.* New York: Knopf, 1981.

Lees, John David, and Michael Turner, eds. *Reagan's First Four Years: A New Beginning?* Manchester, UK: Manchester University Press, 1988.

Lesch, David W. *1979: The Year That Shaped the Modern Middle East.* Boulder, CO: Westview, 2001.

Lesser, Ian O., and US Middle East Central Command. *Oil, the Persian Gulf, and Grand Strategy: Contemporary Issues in Historical Perspective.* Santa Monica, CA: Rand, 1991.

Lettow, Paul. *Ronald Reagan and His Quest to Abolish Nuclear Weapons.* New York: Random House Trade Paperbacks, 2006.

Lefever, Ernest W., ed. *Ethics and American Power.* Washington, DC: Ethics and Public Policy Center, 1985.

Leffler, Melvyn P. *A Preponderance of Power: National Security, the Truman Administration, and the Cold War.* Stanford, CA: Stanford University Press, 1992.

Lewis, Gordon K. *Grenada: The Jewel Despoiled.* Baltimore: Johns Hopkins University Press, 1987.

Locher, James R., III. *Victory on the Potomac: The Goldwater-Nichols Act Unifies the Pentagon.* College Station: Texas A&M University Press, 2002.

Lovell, John P., and Philip S. Kronenberg, eds. *New Civil-Military Relations: The Agonies of Adjustment to Post-Vietnam Realities.* New Brunswick, NJ: Transaction Books, 1974.

Lowe, Carl, ed. *Reaganomics: The New Federalism.* New York: H. W. Wilson, 1984.

Lowenthal, Abraham F. *Exporting Democracy: The United States and Latin America.* Baltimore: Johns Hopkins University Press, 1991.

Mann, James. *The Rebellion of Ronald Reagan: A History of the End of the Cold War.* New York: Penguin Books, 2009.

——— *Rise of the Vulcans: The History of Bush's War Cabinet.* New York: Penguin Books, 2004.

Mansūr, Kamīl. *Beyond Alliance: Israel in U.S. Foreign Policy.* New York: Columbia University Press, 1994.

Marquis, Susan L. *Unconventional Warfare: Rebuilding U.S. Special Operations Forces.* Washington, DC: Brookings Institution, 1997.

Martin, David C., and John L. Walcott. *Best Laid Plans: The Inside Story of America's War against Terrorism.* New York: Harper and Row, 1988.

Martin, Lenore G. *Assessing the Impact of U.S.–Israeli Relations on the Arab World.* Carlisle Barracks, PA: Strategic Studies Institute, US Army War College, 2003.

May, Ernest R. *"Lessons" of the Past: The Use and Misuse of History in American Foreign Policy.* New York: Oxford University Press, 1973.

Mayer, Jane, and Doyle McManus. *Landslide: The Unmaking of the President, 1984–1988.* Boston: Houghton Mifflin, 1988.

McClintock, Robert. *The Meaning of Limited War.* Boston: Houghton Mifflin, 1967.

McDermott, Anthony, and Kjell Skjelsbaek, eds. *The Multinational Force in Beirut, 1982–1984.* Miami: Florida International University Press, 1991.

McDougall, Walter A. *Promised Land, Crusader State: The American Encounter with the World since 1776.* Boston: Houghton Mifflin, 1997.

McLellan, David S. *Cyrus Vance.* Totowa, NJ: Rowman and Allanheld, 1985.

McMahan, Jeff. *Reagan and the World: Imperial Policy in the New Cold War.* New York: Monthly Review Press, 1985.

Mead, Walter Russell. *Special Providence: American Foreign Policy and How it Changed the World.* New York: Routledge, 2002.

Mearsheimer, John J., and Stephen M. Walt. *The Israel Lobby and U.S. Foreign Policy.* New York: Farrar, Straus, and Giroux, 2007.

Melanson, Richard A. *Reconstructing Consensus: American Foreign Policy since the Vietnam War.* New York: St. Martin's, 1991.

Menges, Constantine Christopher. *The Twilight Struggle: The United States v. the Soviet Union Today.* Washington, DC: Aei Press, 1990.

Moreno, Dario. *U.S. Policy in Central America: The Endless Debate.* Miami: Florida International University Press, 1990.

Morris, Roger. *Haig, the General's Progress.* New York: Playboy Press, 1982.

Novik, Nimrod. *The United States and Israel: Domestic Determinants of a Changing U.S. Commitment.* Boulder, CO: Westview, 1986.

Noyes, James H. *The Clouded Lens: Persian Gulf Security and U.S. Policy.* Stanford, CA: Hoover Institution Press, 1979.

Nye, Joseph S., Jr., ed. *The Making of America's Soviet Policy.* New Haven, CT: Yale University Press, 1984.

———. *Soft Power: The Means to Success in World Politics.* New York: Public Affairs, 2004.

Olson, William J. *US Strategic Interests in the Gulf Region.* Boulder, CO: Westview, 1987.

Osgood, Robert Endicott. *Limited War: The Challenge to American Strategy.* Chicago: University of Chicago Press, 1957.

Osgood, Robert Endicott, and Robert W. Tucker. *Force, Order, and Justice.* Baltimore: Johns Hopkins Press, 1967.

Oye, Kenneth A., Donald S. Rothchild, Robert J. Lieber, eds. *Eagle Entangled: U.S. Foreign Policy in a Complex World.* New York: Longman, 1979.

Oye, Kenneth A., Robert J. Lieber, and Donald S. Rothchild, eds. *Eagle Defiant: United States Foreign Policy in the 1980s.* Boston: Little, Brown, 1983.

Palmer, Gregory. *The McNamara Strategy and the Vietnam War: Program Budgeting in the Pentagon, 1960–1968.* Westport, CO: Greenwood, 1978.

Parmet, Herbert S. *George Bush: The Life of a Lone Star Yankee.* New York: Scribner, 1997.

Pastor, Robert A. *Condemned to Repetition: The United States and Nicaragua.* Princeton, NJ: Princeton University Press, 1987.

———. *Not Condemned to Repetition: The United States and Nicaragua.* 2nd rev. and updated ed. Boulder, CO: Westview, 2002.

Patterson, James T. *Restless Giant: The United States from Watergate to Bush v. Gore.* New York: Oxford University Press, 2005.

Pearlman, Michael D. *Warmaking and American Democracy: The Struggle over Military Strategy, 1700 to the Present.* Lawrence: University Press of Kansas, 1999.

Perry, Roland. *Hidden Power: The Programming of the President.* New York: Beaufort Books, 1984.

Persico, Joseph E. *Casey: From the OSS to the CIA.* New York: Viking, 1990.

Peterson, John. *Defending Arabia.* New York: St. Martin's, 1986.

Pfaltzgraff, Robert L., Jr., and Jacquelyn K. Davis, eds. *National Security Decisions: The Participants Speak.* Lexington, MA: Lexington Books, 1990.

Podhoretz, Norman. *The Present Danger: "Do We Have the Will to Reverse the Decline of American Power?"* New York: Simon and Schuster, 1980.

Pomper, Marlene Michels, ed. *The Election of 1980: Reports and Interpretations.* Chatham, NJ: Chatham House, 1981.

Prados, John. *Keepers of the Keys: A History of the National Security Council from Truman to Bush.* New York: Morrow, 1991.

Quandt, William B. *Saudi Arabia in the 1980s: Foreign Policy, Security, and Oil.* Washington, DC: Brookings Institution, 1981.

Rabinovich, Itamar. *The War for Lebanon, 1970–1985.* Rev. ed. Ithaca, NY: Cornell University Press, 1985.

Ranney, Austin, ed. *The American Elections of 1980.* Washington, DC: American Enterprise Institute for Public Policy Research, 1981.

Ratnesar, Romesh, *Tear Down This Wall: A City, a President, and the Speech That Ended the Cold War*. New York: Simon and Schuster, 2009.

Record, Jeffrey. *Revising U.S. Military Strategy: Tailoring Means to Ends*. Washington, DC: Pergamon-Brassey's, 1984.

Rees, David. *Korea: The Limited War*. Baltimore: Penguin Books, 1970.

Reveley, W. Taylor. *War Powers of the President and Congress: Who Holds the Arrows and Olive Branch?* Charlottesville: University Press of Virginia, 1981.

Roberts, Paul Craig. *The Supply-Side Revolution: An Insider's Account of Policymaking in Washington*. Cambridge, MA: Harvard University Press, 1984.

Rodman, Peter W. *More Precious than Peace: The Cold War and the Struggle for the Third World*. New York: C. Scribner's Sons, 1994.

Rubenberg, Cheryl A. *Israel and the American National Interest: A Critical Examination*. Urbana: University of Illinois Press, 1986.

Rubin, Barry M. *The Arab States and the Palestine Conflict*. Syracuse, NY: Syracuse University Press, 1981.

———. *Paved with Good Intentions: The American Experience and Iran*. New York: Oxford University Press, 1980.

Rubinstein, Alvin Z., ed. *The Great Game: Rivalry in the Persian Gulf and South Asia*. New York: Praeger, 1983.

Sabrosky, Alan Ned, and Robert L. Sloane, eds. *The Recourse to War: An Appraisal of the "Weinberger Doctrine."* Carlisle Barracks, PA: Strategic Studies Institute, US Army War College, 1988.

Safran, Nadav. *Saudi Arabia: The Ceaseless Quest for Security*. Cambridge, MA: Belknap Press of Harvard University Press, 1985.

Sanders, Jerry Wayne. *Peddlers of Crisis: The Committee on the Present Danger and the Politics of Containment*. Boston: South End, 1983.

Sandoz, Ellis, and Cecil Van Meter Crabb, eds. *A Tide of Discontent: The 1980 Elections and Their Meaning*. Washington, DC: Congressional Quarterly Press, 1981.

Schelling, Thomas C. *The Strategy of Conflict*. Cambridge, MA: Harvard University Press, 1960.

Schlesinger, Arthur M., Jr. *The Vital Center: The Politics of Freedom*. Boston: Houghton Mifflin, 1949.

———. *War and the American Presidency*. New York: W. W. Norton, 2004.

Schmertz, Eric J., Natalie Datlof, and Alexej Ugrinsky, eds. *President Reagan and the World*. Westport, CT: Greenwood, 1997.

Schoenhals, Kai P., and Richard A. Melanson. *Revolution and Intervention in*

Grenada: The New Jewel Movement, the United States, and the Caribbean. Boulder, CO: Westview, 1985.

Schweizer, Peter. *Reagan's War: The Epic Story of His Forty-Year Struggle and Final Triumph over Communism.* New York: Doubleday, 2002.

———. *Victory: The Reagan Administration's Secret Strategy That Hastened the Collapse of the Soviet Union.* New York: Atlantic Monthly Press, 1994.

Scott, Frances. *US Policy in the Middle East: The Struggle for Peace and Prosperity.* Colorado Springs: US Air Force Academy Library, 2000.

Scott, James M. *Deciding to Intervene: The Reagan Doctrine and American Foreign Policy.* Durham, NC: Duke University Press, 1996.

Sheffer, Gabriel, ed. *Dynamics of Dependence: U.S.–Israeli Relations.* Boulder, CO: Westview, 1987.

Sherry, Michael S. *In the Shadow of War: The United States since the 1930s.* New Haven, CT: Yale University Press, 1995.

Short, Frisco W., Richard G. Head, and Robert C. McFarlane. *Crisis Resolution: Presidential Decision Making in the Mayaguez and Korean Confrontations.* Boulder, CO: Westview, 1978.

Sick, Gary. *All Fall Down: America's Tragic Encounter with Iran.* New York: Random House, 1985.

Sirriyeh, Hussein. *Lebanon: Dimensions of Conflict.* London: Brassey's for the International Institute for Strategic Studies, 1989.

Sklar, Holly. *Washington's War on Nicaragua.* Boston: South End, 1988.

Spiegel, Steven L. *The Other Arab-Israeli Conflict: Making America's Middle East Policy, from Truman to Reagan.* Chicago: University of Chicago Press, 1985.

Sterling, Claire. *The Terror Network: The Secret War of International Terrorism.* New York: Holt, Rinehart, and Winston, 1981.

Summers, Harry G. J. *On Strategy: A Critical Analysis of the Vietnam War.* Reprint, New York: Random House, 1995.

Szumski, Bonnie, Terry O'Neill, and Claudia Debner, eds. *Central America, Opposing Viewpoints.* St. Paul, MN: Greenhaven, 1984.

Tarr, David W. *American Strategy in the Nuclear Age.* New York: Macmillan, 1966.

Teicher, Howard, and Gayle Radley Teicher. *Twin Pillars to Desert Storm: America's Flawed Vision in the Middle East from Nixon to Bush.* New York: William Morrow, 1993.

Tillman, Seth P. *The United States in the Middle East: Interests and Obstacles.* Bloomington: Indiana University Press, 1982.

Timberg, Robert. *The Nightingale's Song*. New York: Simon and Schuster, 1995.

Trager, Frank N., and Philip S. Kronenberg. *National Security and American Society: Theory, Process, and Policy*. Lawrence: University Press of Kansas, 1973.

Troy, Gil. *Morning in America: How Ronald Reagan Invented the 1980s*. Princeton, NJ: Princeton University Press, 2005.

Turner, Robert F. *Repealing the War Powers Resolution: Restoring the Rule of Law in U.S. Foreign Policy*. Washington, DC: Brassey's, 1991.

Tyroler, Charles, II, ed. *Alerting America: The Papers of the Committee on the Present Danger*. Washington, DC: Pergamon-Brassey's, 1984.

Ulam, Adam Bruno. *Dangerous Relations: The Soviet Union in World Politics, 1970–1982*. New York: Oxford University Press, 1983.

Valenta, Jiri, and Herbert J. Ellison. *Grenada and Soviet Cuban Policy: Internal Crisis and U.S. OECS Intervention*. Boulder, CO: Westview, 1986.

Vanderlaan, Mary B. *Revolution and Foreign Policy in Nicaragua*. Boulder, CO: Westview, 1986.

Walker, Thomas W., ed. *Reagan Versus the Sandinistas: The Undeclared War on Nicaragua*. Boulder, CO: Westview, 1987.

Weigley, Russell Frank. *The American Way of War: A History of United States Military Strategy and Policy*. New York: Macmillan, 1973.

Woodward, Bob. *Veil: The Secret Wars of the CIA, 1981–1987*. New York: Simon and Schuster, 1987.

Yankelovich, Daniel, and Larry Kaagan. "Assertive America." In *The Reagan Foreign Policy*, edited by William G. Hyland, 1–18. New York: New American Library, 1987.

Yergin, Daniel. *Shattered Peace: The Origins of the Cold War and the National Security State*. Boston: Houghton Mifflin, 1977.

Yergin, Daniel, and Joseph Stanislaw. *The Commanding Heights: The Battle between Government and the Marketplace That Is Remaking the Modern World*. New York: Simon and Schuster, 1998.

Theses and Dissertations

Arnson, Cynthia J. "Congress and Central America: The Search for Consensus." PhD diss., Johns Hopkins University, 1988.

Bahramzadeh, Mohammad Ali. "The U.S. Foreign Policy in the Persian Gulf, 1968–1988: From Regional Surrogate to Direct Military Involvement." PhD diss., University of Arizona, 1993.

Brady, Michael J. "The Army and the Strategic Military Legacy of Vietnam." Master's thesis, Fort Leavenworth, KS, 1990.

Petraeus, David Howell. "The American Military and Lessons of Vietnam: A Study of Military Influence and the Use of Force in the Post-Vietnam Era." PhD diss., Princeton University, 1987.

Raymond, William Montgomery. "Collision or Collusion? The Congress, the President, and the Ambiguity of War Powers." 2 vols. PhD diss., University of Michigan, 1993.

INDEX

Abrams, Creighton, 31–32
"absolutists" *vs.* "pragmatists," 160*n*35
Afghanistan, Soviet invasion of, 15, 65
"age of consensus," 20–23
"aggressive self-defense" *vs.* "presence,"
    108, 109
aid, military/financial
    Clark Amendment, 28
    as diplomacy, 130–31
    to El Salvador, 38, 42–43, 44,
        46–48, 56
    to Honduras, 54–55, 56
    and human rights, 34–35, 135
    to Lebanon, 105
"alibis for inaction," 135–36
allies, US, support from, 42–44, 120–21
    See also MNF (multinational force)
    in Lebanon
Almond, Edward, 49
American interests, protecting, 17
American-Israel Public Affairs Commit-
    tee (AIPAC), 189*n*60
"American Leadership is Back" (Reagan
    speech), 129
"The American Military and the Lessons
    of Vietnam" (Petraeus), 30–31
Angola, 28
anti-establishment movement, 23
anti-interventionist congressional actions,
    26–28
Arab Deterrent Force, 184*n*28
Arab-Israeli War of 1948–1949, 66
Arab-Israeli War of 1967, 61–62
Arab radicalism and Nixon Doctrine, 63
Arafat, Yasser, 71, 82–83
Arens, Moshe, 200*n*42, 203*n*81

arms control, 16, 18, 141, 157–58*n*76,
    205–6*n*97
Arms Export Control Act, US, 28, 46, 47
Arnson, Cynthia, 26
Assad, Hafez al, 99, 112
assassinations of leaders and "crisis of
    confidence," 4
attentive public (*vs.* mass public), 22, 23

Baker, Howard H., Jr., 72, 120
Baker, James, III, 53
Barnes, Michael D., 44
Batista, Fulgencio, 161*n*1
Begin, Menachem, 67, 93, 94, 105–6,
    203*n*81
Beirut, Lebanon
    Israeli attacks on, 66–69, 85–86,
        93–94
    media imagery from, 75–76
    PLO in, 62, 66–72
    restoration of authority in, 78–79, 80
    See also LAF (Lebanese Armed
    Forces); Lebanon; MNF (multi-
    national force) in Lebanon
Beirut International Airport, suicide
    bombing, 112, 125
Betts, Richard, 29–31, 30–31
Big Pine operations, 178*n*92
Bishop, Maurice, 114, 116
"Black Tuesday," 62
Boland Amendment, 127
bomb attacks, terrorist, 101–2, 112,
    134
British. *See* Great Britain
budget policy, 9–11
Bush, George H. W., 10

Cairo Agreement, 66
Camp David accord, 200n42
Caribbean Basin, 36–41, 114–25
    See also Cuba
Carter, Jimmy
    Carter Doctrine, 65, 75, 156–57n75
    Central American policy, 34–36
    "malaise" speech, 3–5
    Middle East policy, 64
    at Reagan's inauguration, 1, 3
    on Soviet troops in Cuba, 14–15
Carter Doctrine, 65, 75, 156–57n75
Casey, William "Bill," 37–38, 55–59,
    127–28
Casey Doctrine, 55–59
Castro, Fidel, 41, 42, 52–53, 161n1
Catto, Henry E., Jr., 182–83n91
ceasefire agreements, 67–68, 71, 112
Central America
    Carter's policies, 34–36
    Reagan's policies, 36–41
Charles, Eugenia, 116, *117*
Christian militia in Israeli aggressions, 67
Christopher, Warren, 35
Chtaura Agreement, 67
CIA, 27, 56, 127–28
civil-military relations, overviews, 19–20,
    113–14, 136, xiii–xiv
Clark, Dick, 28
Clark, William, 116, 128
Clark Amendment of 1976, 26, 28, 47
Clausewitz, Carl von, 28, 132
Cold War and Reagan's security plat-
    form, 12
Cold War internationalism, 24
colonialism, legacy of, 63
Columbia University, 45
Commission on the Beirut International
    Airport Terrorist Act of 23 October
    1983 (DoD), 125
Committee on the Present Danger
    (CPD), 16

"Common Sense and the Common
    Danger," 16
communism
    accommodation policies, US, 12
    and age of consensus perceptions,
        21–23
    in Central America, 35–36,
        42–43, 57
    spread of in 1970s, 35–37
    See also Cuba; Marxist insurgen-
        cies; Soviet Union
"Communist Interference in El Salva-
    dor," 42
confidence rebuilding, Reagan's platform
    on, 8
congressional-executive relations
    and aid to El Salvador, 45–48
    deferential, post-Cold War, 21–23
    and Grenada crisis, 119–20
    oversight, increase in, 25–27
    restrictions on executive action,
        26–28, 105, 120, 127, 135–36
        (*See also* War Powers Resolution)
containment policy, 21–23
Conte, Silvio O., *45*
corruption in government, influence
    of, 26
Council of Inter-American Security,
    165n24
counterterrorism program, 125–26,
    133–34
covert strategies, 14, 27, 56, 58
Cranston, Alan, 120
"crisis of confidence/spirit" in Ameri-
    cans, 3–4, 141
Cuba
    containment resolutions, 23
    and Haig Doctrine, 48–55
    as Soviet proxy, 164n18
    Soviet troops in, 13–15
    and support of Grenada insurgency,
        114, 123

and support of Marxist insurgencies, 34, 35, 36, 38–39
Cummings, Milton, 7
currencies of power, 131

Dam, Kenneth W., 116
Deaver, Michael, 2, 53
defense spending, need for increase in, 16–17, 22
degree of force issues, 30, 51–52
diplomatic mediation, 131
Dobrynin, Anatoly F., 49
Dodd, Christopher J., 72
domestic political realities
    overview, 19–20
    and use of force in Central America, 57–59
    and use of force in Middle East, 62–63
    and US involvement in Lebanon, 72–76, 84–85, 109
    and Weinberger Doctrine, 133
Dominica, 116
Druze factions, 103, 104, 106
Duarte, José Napoleon, 38, 46–47, 165–66n26
Duberstein, Kenneth, 119–20

Eagleburger, Lawrence, 43–44, 71
East Beirut, marines in, 98–99
economy/economic policy, 9–11
Egypt, 182–83n91, 182n20, 200n42
Ehrman, John, 21
Eisenhower (ship), 107
Eisenhower, Dwight D., 23, 62
election results, demographic analysis, 6, 137
El Salvador, insurgency in, 36–38, 38–41, 41–48
employment policy and supply-side economics, 10
"era of national renewal," 1, 3

"establishment," foreign policy, 21–22
"The Ethics of Power" (Shultz speech), 129
Europe, US relations in, 43–44, 120–21

failure of leadership, Reagan's platform on, 5, 13, 141
flexible response, 51, 52
"focused" *vs.* "unfocused" approach, 134
force as last resort, 28, 32, 124, 131, 133, 140, xii
force *vs.* power, 132, xi, xiv
Ford, Gerald, 28
foreign aid and human rights, 34–35
Foreign Assistance Act, 27, 172–73n58, 179n99
foreign oil dependency, 4
foreign policy overviews, 11–18, 17–18, 20–23, 25–27
    See also individual doctrines
Formosa, US actions in, 23
Forrest, Nathan Bedford, 50
France
    and Grenada crisis, 121
    in Lebanon, 80, 85–86, 99, 111, 199n31
Fulbright, J. William, 26, 134

Gaddis, John Lewis, 22
Gemayel, Amin, 91, 95–96, 99–100, 105
Gemayel, Bashir, 66, 85, 93–94, 95
Ghorbal, Ashraf, 192–93n91
Glenn, John, 46
"Golden Handshake," 32
Goldwater, Barry, 12
gradualist approach, 131–32
graphic imagery and public opinion, 75–76
gray-area threats, 114, 130–31, xiii
Great Britain, 61–62, 99, 121
"Green Line," 81
Grenada crisis, 114–25, 138
Guam Doctrine, 63

Gulf of Tonkin Resolution, 26–27
Gutman, Roy, 58
Gwertzman, Bernard, 39–40

Habib, Philip C., 67, 68–69, 71, 80–83,
    89, 100
Haddad, Saad, 184n29
Haig, Alexander
    on Cuba, 38–39, 40, 51
    on decisiveness in Korean War,
        49–50
    on El Salvador, 37, 40
    Haig Doctrine, 48–55
    on incrementalism, 50–52
    on limited war strategy, 51–52
    on proxies in Vietnam, 48
    resignation of, 71
    on security-assistance response, 47
Haig Doctrine, 48–55
"higher realism," 142, xiv
hiring freeze, federal, 9–10
Honduras, 54–55, 56
Hoover, Herbert, 6
hostage crisis in Tehran, 1, 2, 15, 16–17,
    38, 61, 118
hostile-fire-area designation, 46
Hughes, Harold, 27
Hughes-Ryan Amendment of 1974, 26,
    27, 179n99
human rights issues, 12, 34–35, 38,
    46–47, 135
Huntington, Samuel P., 19–20, 29

ideological split, post-Cold War, 23–25
inauguration of Reagan, 1–3, 6
Inchon, landing at, 49–50
incrementalism, 50–52, 131–32
inflation and "crisis of confidence," 4
"intellectual elite," 11
intelligence operations, US, 14, 27, 56, 58
Interagency Group on Human Rights
    and Foreign Assistance, 35

Intermediate Nuclear Forces (INF)
    Treaty, 157–58n76
interventionism, 35–41
Iran
    hostage crisis, 1, 2, 15, 16–17, 38,
        61, 118
    Nixon's "twin pillar" policy, 61–66
    revolution in, 61, 64–65, 182n16
Israel
    attacks on Lebanon, 66–69, 85–86,
        93–94
    US domestic opinion of, 74–75
    withdrawal from Shuf Mountains,
        103–4
    Yom Kippur War and oil embargo,
        63–64
Israeli Defense Forces (IDF), 85
Italy, 91, 99, 121, 199n31

Johnson, Lyndon B., 26–27
joint resolution strategies, 23, 26–27
Joint Special Operations Command
    (JSOC), 133
Jordan, 66
Jumblatt, Walid, 104

Kagan, Robert, 58
Kahan Commission, 196n3
Kennedy, John F., 4, 23
Kennedy, Robert, 4
Key, V. O., 7
Khomeini, Ayatollah Ruhollah, 61
King, Martin Luther, Jr., 4
Kirkpatrick, Jeane, 36, 152n50
Kissinger, Henry, 63, 175n79, 181n13, xiv
Korean War, 23, 31

LAF (Lebanese Armed Forces)
    rebuilding of, 77, 95, 100, 109
    success of, 112
    training of by US, 99
leadership, failure of, 5, 13, 141

leadership by US, global, 129–30
Lebanese Army Modernization Program, 100
Lebanon
    domestic reaction to Reagan's plans, 72–76
    historical context, 61–66
    MNF deployment and evacuation of PLO, 79–83
    and NSDD-64, 92–101
    and NSDD-92, 102–3
    Pentagon concerns over policy, 76–79
    post-massacre reaction of US, 86–87
    reconciliation government, need for, 89–90, 98–100, 104, 108–9
    Shuf Mountains dispute, 103–5, 103–6
    and Shultz Doctrine, 90–92
    Suq al-Gharb, defense of, 110–12
    US embassy bombing, 101
    US objective in, 87–90
    US perspective on, 66–72, 84–87
    US strategy, overview, 60–61
    US withdrawal from, 127
legitimate and decisive use of force.
        See use of force, legitimate and decisive
Lehrer, Jim, 40
Levin, Carl, 72
Libya, 134
Likud coalition, 67
limited war, strategies for, 51–52, 132
Long Commission, 125

MacArthur, Douglas, 49–50
MacNeil, Robert, 40
Marine Battalion Landing Team Headquarters, Beirut, 125
Marines, US, as diplomatic tool, 106–7
Marxist insurgencies
    El Salvador, 36–38, 38–41, 41–48

Grenada, 114–25, 138
Nicaragua, 33–36, 56, 127
massacre of Palestinian refugees in Lebanon, 85–86
mass public (*vs.* attentive public), 23, 25
McCarthy, Joseph R., 22
McFarland, K. T., 138–39
McFarlane Robert "Bud"
    and Cuban containment, 52
    on diplomacy in Lebanon, 89, 110
    and Grenada crisis, *115, 117*
    on large-force option, 88
    on MNS first deployment, 86
    on MNS redeployment to Lebanon, 92
    on Reagan's "honeymoon" period, 173n64
McNamara, Robert, 132
media, influence of, 75–76, 122–23
Meese, Edwin, III, 9, 11, 53, 148–49n26
Meet the Press, 78
Melanson, Richard, 20, 123
Middle East, historical context, 61–66
military aid. *See* aid, military/financial
military policy
    conditional use of force in Lebanon, 76–79
    and force as last resort, 28, 32, 124, 131, 133, 140, xii
    and need for stronger capacity, 15–16
    objectives, importance of defining, 28, 31, 118–19, 133, xii
    and power as tool of statecraft, 28–29, 106–7, 113, 134
    victory and concept of completion, 28–29, 30, 31, 118–19, xii
    See also use of force, legitimate and decisive
mission creep, 133

MNF (multinational force) in Lebanon
    conditional participation in first
        deployment, 76–79
    decision to redeploy, 85–87
    expansion of (1982), 96–97
    first deployment and evacuation of
        PLO, 79–83
    objectives of first deployment,
        69–70
    objectives of redeployment, 87–90,
        90–92
moral responsibility and foreign policy, 21
Moreno, Dario, 58
Morocco, 99
Moynihan, Daniel Patrick, 120
multinational force, Caribbean, 116–17
multinational force, Lebanon. *See* MNF
    (multinational force) in Lebanon
Muslim factions in Lebanon, 103

National Bipartisan Commission on
    Central America, 175*n*79
National Security Council Report 68
    (NSC-68), 22
"National Security Decision Directive
    on Cuba and Central America"
    (NSDD-17), 48, 55
national-security planning group meet-
    ings (NSPGs), 104
national security policy, 11–18
national will, 132–33, xiv
naval support, 107, 109, 110
neo-isolationism, 24
"Never Again" club, 31
New Jersey (ship), 109, 111, 112
New Jewel Movement, 114
The New York Times, 42, 44, 71, 123
Nicaragua, 33–36, 56, 127
Nixon, Richard, 61–66
noninterventionism, 34–35
NSDD (national-security decision direc-
    tive), 93

NSDD-17 "National Security Decision
    Directive on Cuba and Central
    America," 48, 55
NSDD-64 "Next Steps in Lebanon,"
    92–101
NSDD-77 "Management of Public
    Diplomacy Relative to National
    Security," 128–29
NSDD-92 "Accelerating the Withdrawal
    of Foreign Forces from Lebanon,"
    102
NSDD-103 "Strategy for Lebanon," 109–11
NSDD-110A "Response to Caribbean
    Governments' Request to Restore
    Democracy on Grenada," 117–18
nuclear weapons, 13, 15–16, 21, 120–21,
    141

objectives, military, importance of defin-
    ing, 28, 31, 118–19, 133, xii
Office of Military Cooperation (Beirut), 99
offshore support, 107, 110
Ohio State University, 45
oil embargo, 63–64, 75
O'Neill, Thomas P. "Tip," 119–20
"Only the 'Fun' Wars" (Safire), 138
On War (Clausewitz), 132
Organization of Eastern Caribbean
    States (OECS), 116
"other currencies of power," 131

Pahlavi, Mohammad Reza, 61, 64–65
Palestinian Liberation Organization
    (PLO), 62, 66–72, 79–83
    See also MNF (multinational force)
    in Lebanon
Palestinian refugees in Lebanon, 66,
    81–83, 85–86
Panama, 35, 36
patterns of civil-military relations, 19–20
PD-18 (presidential directive 18), 64,
    182*n*16

peace agreements, 94–95, 102–3
"Peace for Galilee," 68
"peace through strength" strategy, 17–18
Percy, Charles H., 44, 45, 73, 188*n*55
Persian Gulf region, overview, 61–66
Petraeus, David, 30–31
Phalangist Party, 85, 93, 98–99, 103
PLO (Palestinian Liberation Organization), 62, 66–72, 79–83
   See also MNF (multinational force) in Lebanon
Poindexter, John, 139, 140
political capital, risks of, 53
political realities
   and Grenada crisis, 119–20
   mid-1960s and 1970s, 23–32
   post World War II, 20–23
   and use of force issues, 57–59, 127–28
   See also domestic political realities
polls
   on Central American policy, 44–45
   on Grenada crisis, 122, 123–24
   on participation in Lebanon, 74–75
   post-election, 7
post-Cold War internationalism, 24
Powell, Colin, 139
power and diplomacy, balance of, 129–36
   See also Weinberger Doctrine
"Power and Diplomacy in the 1980s" (Shultz speech), 129
power *vs.* force, 132, xi, xiv
"pragmatists" *vs.* "absolutists," 160*n*35
presence patrols, 98–99
"presence" *vs.* "aggressive self-defense," 108, 109
prices, 9
protests by Americans, 45
proxy forces
   Cuba as, 164*n*18, xii–xiii
   Iranian, 61
   by Israel, 103

Marxist, 15
   by Syrians, 104
   by US, 32, 56, 58, 59, 62–63
   in Vietnam, 48–49
Public Affairs Committee, 129
public diplomacy, 128–30
   See also Weinberger Doctrine
public information task force, 55
public opinion/support
   and causality in foreign policy, 25
   and Grenada crisis, 119, 122–24
   and Reagan's Central American objectives, 41–43, 41–48, 44–48, 53–54, 127–28
   of use of force, 28–31, 31–32, 133, xii
   of US involvement in Lebanon, 74–75

rapid-deployment force (RDF), 64–65
Rapid Deployment Joint Task Force, 65
Reagan, Ronald
   "American Leadership is Back" speech, 129
   and Amin Gemayel, 96
   campaign speeches, 9, 11, 13
   on communism in Central America, 36
   economy/economic policy, 9–11
   election of, 6, 137
   foreign policy overview, 11–18, 17–18, 20–23, 25–27
   (*See also individual doctrines*)
   and Grenada crisis, 114–16, *117*
   on his platform, 7
   inaugural address, 3
   on Lebanon crisis, 87–88, 92, 110, 111
   Middle East peace initiative 1982, 94–95
   platform overview, 8–9
   policy overview, 140–41, xii–xiii

"Reaganomics," 10–11
"Reagan Revolution," 10–11
reassessment, importance of, 133, xii
reconciliation government in Lebanon,
    89–90, 98–100, 104, 108–9
refugees, Palestinian, 66, 81–83, 85–86
Regan, Donald T., 149–50n29
"rendezvous with destiny," 13, 140
reserve forces, use of, 31–32
"revenge" approach, 134
revisionism, 23–24
Roberts, Craig, 10
Romero, Carlos Humberto, 165–66n26
Roosevelt, Franklin D., 36
runway construction in Grenada, 114–15
Ryan, Leo, 27

sacrifice, Carter's urging for, 4
Sadat, Anwar al, 182n20
Safire, William, 138
Salem, Saeb, 192n91
Sandinista National Liberation Front, 33,
    38, 56
"Santa Fe Document," 165n24
Saudi Arabia, 61–66, 75
Schlesinger, James, 31–32
Schmidt, Helmut, 44
Schneider, William, 24, 25
Schoenhals, Kai, 123
Schweitzer, Robert L., 54–55
Sharon, Ariel, 100, 193n3
show-of-force operations, 56, 58, 110–12,
    124
Shuf Mountains conflict, 103–5, 111–12
Shultz, George
    on congressional restrictions,
        135–36
    on first MNF deployment to Leba-
        non, 81–83
    and Grenada crisis, 115, 117, 118,
        123, 124
    on marines as diplomatic tool,
        106–7
    on multinational forces, 69–70
    on need for counterterrorism pro-
        gram, 126
    on NSDD-64, 97
    and NSDD-92, 102–3
    "Power and Diplomacy in the
        1980s" speech, 129
    on public opinion and Central
        American, 128
    on Reagan's Middle East peace
        initiative, 94–95
    on resolve and commitment, 106
    on second MNF deployment to
        Lebanon, 88–90
    tests of legitimate power, 136
    "The Ethics of Power" speech, 129
    on use of force and diplomacy,
        131–32
"Shultz, Weinberger Nondifferences"
    (Fulbright and Tillman), 134
Shultz Doctrine, 90–92
Sick, Gary, 181n9, 181n13
Six Day War, 61–62
Soldier and the State (Huntington),
    19–20
Somoza Debayle, Anastasio, 33–34,
    35–36
Soviet Union
    and age of consensus perceptions,
        21–23
    and Cuba, 13–15, 49, 164n18
    and Grenada, 114, 116
    and Lebanon, 205–6n97
    in Middle East, 65, 182n20
    military buildup of, 15–16
    and Reagan's security platform, 12
    support of communism in Central
        America, 38
stability, electorate's desire for, 7

START (Strategic Arms Reduction Treaty), 205–6n97
Stockman, David, 151n39
Stoessel, Walter, 71
Strategic Arms Limitation Treaty II (SALT II), 13–14
strategic outpost concept of Lebanon, 93–94
Suez Canal, 62
suicide bombers, 112
supply-side economics, 10
Suq al-Gharb, 110–12
surrogates in Middle East, US, 62–63, 64, 65
Syria, 66–69, 88, 99–100, 103–4, 110–12

Taft, William Howard, 6
taxes, cutting, 9
Tehran, US embassy attack, 15
Tehran hostages, 1, 2
Tenth Amendment, 10
terrorism, 101–2, 112, 125–26, 133–34
Thatcher, Margaret, 208n23
The Tragedy of American Diplomacy (Williams), 24
This Week, 92
threat perception and age of consensus, 22
Tillman, Seth, 134
Tower, John, 26
training of foreign military, 43, 99
Trilateral Security Arrangements Commission, 103, 126
"troika" of Reagan, 53
Truman, Harry S., 22, 23, 62
"truth squads," 169–70n40
"twin pillar" policy, 61–66

unemployment, 9
Ungo, Guillermo, 165–66n26
UN Interim Force in Lebanon (UNIFIL), 67, 69

University of Michigan, 45
UN Resolution 242, 69
UN Security Council on Grenada crisis, 121
use of force, legitimate and decisive
    conditional, 76–79
    and diplomacy, 28–32, 124, 130–37
    need for in Central America/Caribbean, 36–41
    and political realities, 57–59, 127–28
    power *vs.* force, 132, xi, xiv
    and public opinion/support, 28–31, 31–32, 133, xii
    and Vietnam War, 31, 138
    See also domestic political realities
"The Uses of Military Power" (Weinberger speech), 129, 138–39, xi–xii
    See also Weinberger Doctrine

Vance, Cyrus, 16
Vessey, John W.
    and Grenada crisis, 118, *121*
    on participation in MNF, 70, 71, 86
    on rebuilding government in Lebanon, 76–78, 81, 91
    and US Syrian strategy, 108–9, 111, 112
victory and concept of completion, 28–29, 30, 31, 118–19, xii
Vietnam syndrome, 12–13, 17, 97, xi
Vietnam War
    and congressional oversight, 26–27
    and "crisis of confidence," 4, 12
    lack of objectives in, 118–19
    proxy forces in, 48–49
    and revisionism of 1960s and 1970s, 24
    and use of force issues, 31, 138
"vital center ideology," 21, 23

vital national interest and military power, 84–85, 88, 129–30, 133, xii
　　See also use of force, legitimate and decisive
"voodoo economics," 10

"war as last resort," 131
warmongering, civilian, 29, 32
War Powers Resolution, 26–27, 46, 47, 73–74, 106
The Washington Post, 74, 75
Watergate, 4, 26
Weinberger, Caspar "Cap"
　　conditional concerns for Lebanon policy, 76–79
　　on congressional restrictions, 135
　　on Cuban involvement in Caribbean Basin, 39
　　and Grenada crisis, 118–19, 124
　　on Haig Doctrine, 52–53, 53–54
　　on Lebanon situation, 68–69, 93
　　and MNF mission in Lebanon, 81–83

on public support, importance of, 54
on Reagan's inauguration, 3
on second MNF deployment to Lebanon, 89–90
"The Uses of Military Power" speech, 129, 138–39
on use of force and diplomacy, 130, 131–32
Weinberger Doctrine, 113, 132–34, 137–40, 176–77n88, xi–xiv
Weiss, Ted, 120
White, John C., 17
will, strength of, 132–33, xiv
Williams, William Appleman, 24
Wilson, Harold, 62
Wilson, Woodrow, 143n7
Wirthlin, Robert, 44
world peace, US role in, 11–12
World War II, 20–23, 22–23

Yom Kippur War, 63

Zablocki, Clement, Jr., 46, 72, 73